Surrounded
by Liars

Also by Thomas Erikson

Surrounded by Idiots

Surrounded by Psychopaths

Surrounded by Bad Bosses

Surrounded by Setbacks

Surrounded by Narcissists

Surrounded by Energy Vampires

. . . .

Surrounded by Liars

How to Stop Half-Truths, Deception, and Gaslighting from Ruining Your Life

Thomas Erikson

ST. MARTIN'S
ESSENTIALS
NEW YORK

Published in the United States by St. Martin's Essentials,
an imprint of St. Martin's Publishing Group

www.stmartins.com

The Library of Congress Cataloging-in-Publication Data is available upon request.

ISBN 978-1-250-33918-8 (trade paperback)
ISBN 978-1-250-36732-7 (hardcover)
ISBN 978-1-250-33917-1 (ebook)

Our books may be purchased in bulk for promotional, educational, or business use. Please contact your local bookseller or the Macmillan Corporate and Premium Sales Department at 1-800-221-7945, extension 5442, or by email at MacmillanSpecialMarkets@macmillan.com.

First published in Sweden by Book Mark in 2024.

First U.S. Edition: 2024

10 9 8 7 6 5 4 3 2 1

Contents

Why You Want to Read a Book About Liars

L et me reveal something to you that you've probably long suspected: Consultants don't always know what they're doing—far from it!

For many years, I worked as a management consultant. The job wasn't always easy to define, and attempts to describe it would often sound incredibly concrete and exasperatingly airy-fairy all at once. It spanned the range from carrying binders, to meeting with company management at Volvo Cars. One thing that always brought me great enjoyment, however, was a specific kind of workshop that I organized for people of all kinds.

In the 1990s, talk about core values was very much in vogue. Everything seemed to be connected to that. Everybody had to work on their core values. The statement, *"If we don't know our core values, we can't succeed at anything,"* applied even to those who didn't have a clue if they had any values. Or, perhaps, they didn't even understand what core values actually were.

But my industry kept promoting the idea. Time to define some core values! Let's go!

One exercise went something like this: You would gather a group of people within an organization. It could be a management team, or a group of salespeople, or any category of people you had some reason to bring together in the same room. I began by explaining what a core value was, and why the participants would no longer have any hope of achieving anything if they didn't have at least five or six of them.

Every member of the group wrote down their own suggestions, and then we negotiated our way to a set of shared core values. It might not come as a surprise that these discussions were often lively, especially in rooms with thirty or so people in them.

Now, don't get me wrong here. The exercise itself is valuable and very rewarding. That wasn't the issue. The problems began, rather, in the next session, when the time came for the group to define each value one by one. You see, there's not much value in just producing a bunch of platitudes. I want to keep this brief, but I hope you'll still allow me to give you a short example.

Ninety percent of the time that I've led this exercise (and we're talking hundreds of times), the word "honesty" is suggested as an important core value.

Honesty!, says the group. *Yes. We want that!* Everyone nods enthusiastically.

Good, I tell them. *Honesty sounds great. Now, define what it means, and—specifically—how a person should behave to demonstrate that they are being 100 percent honest.*

Their enthusiasm crumbles more or less immediately.

At first, it seems simple. *Tell the truth.* But then, somebody realizes that this can be quite tricky. Telling the truth, that is. The truth can be a heavy burden to carry. It can hurt people's feelings. Cause offense.

What's the solution? The group discusses this. Eventually, someone figures it out: Tell the truth, as long as it doesn't risk hurting anybody's feelings.

The *truth,* though? *What* truth? *Whose* truth? How much of it?

If a customer questions some of our practices—which are mainly for our own benefit anyway—we can't very well explain what management really thinks of our customers, can we? That's not information we'll share voluntarily, by any means.

This is getting complicated. Also, has everyone actually *earned* the truth from us? Some customers obviously lie to us because they want some kind of advantage. We don't have to be honest with *them,* of course. Those devious types deserve whatever's coming to them, really.

A lengthy debate soon ensues, resulting in a series of un-resolved dilemmas.

You get the picture. After some increasingly loud discussions, the group decides to strike honesty from their list of potential core values. They can't even agree what the blasted word means.

Honesty hasn't managed to make it to the end of this exercise once in all my times running it.

Why am I telling you this? Because I want to be upfront about one thing right from the start: As I give you my views on truth and lies in this book, it would be remarkable if you were to agree with all of them. For one thing, your own core values are likely to get in the way. For another thing, your definition of a lie is likely to be different from the one I propose.

Some of you will probably end up throwing this book across the room in disgust because I'm going to make you take a hard look in the mirror and try to answer these questions: Why do *you* lie? Do you have any idea how your lies impact the people around you?

Other readers will discover things about themselves. And— even more fun!—about others.

The reason why you need this book, however, is that it will give you all you need to spot a liar—whether it's a close friend or a coworker, your cousin, or your manager. I will also teach you some tactics you can deploy to identify a lie. And this is important, because you don't want to be deceived, do you?

The tools I'll be telling you about will be of use to you in all your interactions with other people. And—important— many people will be using these tools in their own interactions with you.

Let's be honest here—nobody's perfect.

The strangest thing about lies, I think, is that we all seem to accept them. The extent of this may vary, but I'm quite sure I've never met anybody who wants to hear nothing but the truth at all times. The truth is often painful, and the only other option than the truth is, basically, a lie. Right? Besides, we all lie, so nobody can honestly swear that they never resort to this tool.

I spent a long time hesitating over whether to write this book—it was actually on my list of upcoming projects for several years—and the difficulties were evident from the very beginning. My publisher told me that I would have to define what a lie is from the start, or I'd have a hard time making any useful points.

I suppose that's fair, really.

But it didn't take long before I found myself bogged down in issues ranging from white lies to half-truths. Or embellished truths. Or *my* truths. Or alternative facts. Statistics. Fake news and political correctness, which don't tolerate being questioned, or data manipulated to promote specific viewpoints. It's all a great big mess. Social media, other media. Whom can we really trust?

But I couldn't resist. This book was demanding to be written. I wanted to explore the subject once and for all. I will be opening the door to a world of manipulation, untrustworthiness, deception, and lies. But we will also encounter the truths we need to navigate the complex landscapes that each and every one of us find ourselves in today.

In this book I'll be teaching you how to detect a lie, how to expose a liar, and how to confront them with the truth.

But—I'll also be showing you how to stick to the truth yourself, to the best of your ability. Because, as we just saw, honesty is no simple matter. Although we all agree that it's important, we also know the countless problems that lurk ahead. And we all compromise the truth, practically at the first opportunity.

I mean this.

For once, I'll be speaking the literal truth when I say we're surrounded by . . . *liars*.

Because everybody lies.

Even you.

Even me.

However, perhaps we could do it a little less, and dare to

be a little more honest . . . ? Assuming we knew how. And why. So let's head off on this adventure with our fingers firmly crossed behind our backs.

A disclaimer is in order here: You're not going to agree with all of this. Some of the things I bring up may even upset you. If that happens, know that it was never my intention, although I must admit that I'd much rather have you react that way than just set the book aside and think, *So what?*

Welcome to this refreshing journey into the fascinating world of lies and deception.

1

A Reflection on Lies

I am sorry if you don't like my honesty,
But to be fair—
I don't like your lies.
—Unknown

Many take pleasure in lying just a bit. It's a way of adding some spice to everyday life, and getting away with it can be a thrill. Big lie, small lie, nobody caught me, ha-ha, I win. Managing to convince somebody to believe in an untruth can be particularly tempting, especially if you spend a great deal of your time in moral gray areas.

In today's fast-paced society, the thrill of not telling the truth has become greater than ever. After all, you get more or less instant feedback. Pathological lying, manipulation, and fraud have undeniably become common elements of human interactions. Regardless of whether it's a matter of fabricating upsetting news to gain attention, distorting and intentionally misinterpreting statistics to support one's own convictions, or repeatedly resorting to white lies to avoid embarrassment, the line between truth and deceit is becoming increasingly unclear.

DOES EVERYBODY LIE?

No. There is no irrefutable, statistical evidence that shows that *everybody* lies. Claiming otherwise would be a filthy lie. But it's still a reasonable assumption, based on my own experiences of human beings. I honestly don't think you'd disagree. And we know it's true, really. Everybody does a little lying here and there. It keeps things nice and simple.

I'm fine, thanks.

That dress really suits you.

I love you, too.

I'm on my way.

Oh! I didn't see you!

No, I don't mind.

I'd definitely say that it's reasonable to claim that we all lie a little from time to time.

However harsh this truth might sound, lying is actually fairly instinctive, and very common. If you're thinking, *No, I don't lie!,* I'd advise you to read through the examples above another time. And then, accept the truth.

Our reasons for lying will vary from person to person, of course, and from situation to situation. We might lie to defend ourselves, avoid a conflict, impress somebody, keep a secret, or win social approval by presenting ourselves in a flattering light.

Most often, we lie to protect people's feelings, and to keep them secure and happy. To some extent, these white lies and tiny omissions can even be justified. They might even benefit our relationships—that's what psychological research suggests, anyway.

If we presume, then, that anything that's less than 100 percent true must be a lie, the matter is settled. Sometimes we're asked questions about our inner feelings, and simply *can't* respond truthfully. Some things are too painful to admit, so we hope we'll get away with fudging the truth.

Two Sides of the Same Coin

However, things are rarely that simple.

Imagine a father lying to his eight-year-old daughter. That sounds like a dreadful thing to do. But suppose she has lost her favorite toy, and he saw it being crushed under the wheel of a car. He doesn't want to break her heart, so he tells her that it went to the toy hospital, and that it will be back once it's well/mended.

All quite innocent, really. The dad is lying to protect his daughter from pain. It's actually a compassionate lie. Even though his intentions are good, it's important to strike the right balance between protecting her feelings and letting her process what has happened and learn to manage some degree of pain. Life can be painful, after all. And challenges are inevitably going to pop up.

The little girl will soon be asking about her toy. Perhaps she'll want to visit it at the toy hospital—that's what people do, isn't it?

This will leave her dad with two options: He can either tell the truth and admit that he made the whole thing up—not fun, perhaps, but honest, at least. Or he can fabricate new lies to counteract the consequences of his initial lie.

Soon, he'll be caught up in a web of fraud and deceit that will be hard to escape, however good his initial intentions may have been.

Or, how about this example:

When I was in middle school, a classmate of mine told her best friend that his drawing had been selected for the school exhibition. In fact, it had not. While she did want to see him happy, she was also keen to divert his attention while she tried to get her own artwork selected for the same exhibition. The idea was that if his work had already been selected, he wouldn't work as hard on it, and this would in turn improve her own chances.

That particular lie rested on a mixture of good and selfish intentions. She wanted to make her friend happy, but most of all, she wanted to benefit herself. Lies like this can bring temporary rewards, but they also risk harming trust in the long run.

And that's the problem, I guess. Lies are double-edged swords. Sometimes they are told to protect people and grant them temporary sanctuary from the brutality of the truth. Other times, though, they are told for personal gain, out of jealousy, or to manipulate.

Most lies aren't malicious in intent, of course, but all lies bring consequences sooner or later.

Fake News and the Infamous Troll Farms

Once, the public trusted what they read in the newspapers, but that was a long time ago. These days, nothing is a given, and there are probably many among us who would prefer to see everything with their own two eyes to get a better grasp of events. For instance, take the case of fake news. This is supposedly factual reporting that is actually inaccurate, or that has been deceptively presented in order to confuse the recipient, making it impossible for them to tell what's true and what isn't. This is one of the reasons why so many people no longer watch the news on television. Their sense is that they have no idea how truthful the reporting really is.

The fact that most of the reports, day in and day out, are about dreadful events—the kind that attract clicks and readers or viewers—makes many people feel that news reports only depress them. When I think about this, it makes me very angry.

My thesis is that the people who make the algorithms that control our actions in social media have great insight into how people function, but seem to completely lack insight into how social media impacts us. Or they simply don't care about the consequences, as long as they make a profit.

Be that as it may, the advent of digital platforms has exposed us to a daily deluge of news and information. Unfortunately, many less-than-honest individuals and institutions have realized the power of fabricating and disseminating narratives to deceive and manipulate public opinion.

Some often find themselves competing for the latest, juiciest details of a story, and never stop to consider how dubious they actually seem. This prevalence of fake news actively incentivizes the distribution of untruths, which further increases the reach of alternative narratives designed to favor some agenda or other.

Fake news also exploits people's innate curiosity. It plays

on our emotions and values to generate clicks and engagement. Fake reports on the deaths of prominent celebrities or
the scandalous misdeeds of politicians give rise to extensive
controversy. We needn't name names here. Whatever your
political convictions may be, you can safely presume that the
party you support also twists the truth from time to time.

These particular examples might seem reasonably innocent.
However, there are also "troll farms," which do nothing but
produce propaganda disguised as news, and fill it with controversial claims about this, that, and the other. In Saint Pe-
tersburg, Russia, the Internet Research Agency, a troll farm,
works full time to promote the interests of Russian president Vladimir Putin and smear the United States and Ukraine.
Among other things, their campaigns are thought to have contributed to the public perceptions that allowed Donald Trump
to win the US presidential election of 2016. True or false?
Opinions differ.

Science Is Always Truthful?

Oh boy! In a world that runs on data, statistics and scientific
results serve as the basis for all kinds of convincing arguments and opinions intended to form public opinion and gar-
ner broad public support. A common argument used against
different ideas is that they *aren't based on science*. When
people decide not to believe something, they will tend to
disbelieve even the evidence of their own eyes unless it's
backed up and confirmed by at least half a million scientific
studies.

The curious thing is that people who look to science when
forming their opinions in one field are perfectly prepared to

disregard scientific evidence when it comes to other opinions they happen to hold. How is this possible? We'll be taking a look at different aspects of how emotions and opinions influence human beings who have IQs greater than their shoe sizes later on in this book. You see, we aren't rational beings.

But what about statistics? They're always accurate, aren't they? Numbers never lie and all that? Well, to some extent. Two plus two is still four. But liars use numbers too. Statistics are sometimes presented in highly deceptive ways, and this makes it increasingly hard to trust "facts."

Anybody who favors a certain position or opinion might be tempted to distort or selectively represent statistics in ways that shine a positive light on their own beliefs. This kind of manipulation tends to happen when somebody feels that their ideology matters more than the factual truth. They want to present the facts a certain way, however obvious it might be to everybody else that it doesn't make sense. So they fudge the numbers and selectively look for evidence that supports their fictional truth.

Suppose, for example, that statistics showed that people of a specific ethnicity were seriously overrepresented when it comes to certain kinds of criminal behavior. This kind of information could be related in different ways, to serve different interests. Somebody who wants better funding for integration projects and job market initiatives might use this statistic to promote those ideas. However, it's far from unthinkable that the same data could be used by somebody who would rather address the situation by emphasizing ethnic differences. What should the media do then? Refrain from reporting on it?

The temptation not to tell the truth, however, tends not to have such far-reaching consequences. Small, seemingly harmless lies (often referred to as "white lies") can find their way into our daily interactions too. White lies mostly stem from a fear of confrontation or a desire not to cause discomfort. They can also become a bad habit, something we resort to whenever the truth is uncomfortable. Although the intentions here will tend to be good, the consequence of this behavior is that we grow accustomed to dishonesty, and this hinders genuine understanding in the long run.

I'll return to all these varieties of lies later on and expand on this discussion. There's plenty more to say.

ON THE PERSONAL LEVEL

To steer clear of all the pitfalls related to lying, we need to recalibrate both our social values and our individual senses of responsibility. The path to honesty and sincerity probably begins with self-awareness and critical thinking.

We would probably all do well to question ourselves a little more often. As habitual consumers of excessive amounts of information, we need to give ourselves the time and resources to critically evaluate data and news that are presented to us. We need to take the time to fact-check and evaluate sources, avoid hasty and emotionally dictated conclusions, and see fake news for what it is.

Now, you might be thinking to yourself that that's impossible. Who has time for all that?

Well, that's my point. The sources of all the nonsense that washes over us are very aware of this, too. So they simply pour more of it out, fully confident that some of it is bound to actually stick.

At this point, we'd do well to remember what Joseph Goeb-bels, Hitler's Reich minister of propaganda, said: *Repeat a lie often enough and it becomes the truth.*

"You Don't Love Me Anymore"

Here's an example we might take a closer look at: A man's wife asks him why he doesn't love her anymore. Uh-oh. But why is she asking him this? And what should he say? The obvious answer is that of course he loves his wife. The reason for her question is that she feels he hasn't been giving her enough attention lately. And that might be true, for whatever reason. He might have been ruminating on his own problems too much. So she tells him that she doesn't think he loves her anymore.

This could very well be a lie. She might realize that he actually does love her but feels a need for some affection. And worst of all, he insists that he loves her more than ever, even though at that very moment he's feeling deeply annoyed that she's questioning him. This kind of behavior is precisely what makes him feel less affectionate toward his wife. He might even be lying. Perhaps he's just tired of her.

The wife repeats her thesis: *You don't love me anymore.*

She does this despite knowing that he's been going through a long busy spell, and that this is probably why he's forgotten all about flowers and affection. How should I know?

Again, her husband repeats that she is his number one priority, lying again. He's been spending a great deal of time at work. So now, he lists various reasons for his behavior, all designed to suit this particular moment.

Soon the two are embroiled in an emotional battle of attrition that neither of them can hope to win.

The simple solution, of course, would be for the woman to say that she doesn't *feel* loved when her husband spends so much time at work. And he could have replied by saying something about how he understood this, and how he was going to try to act in ways that showed her how important she is to him in the future. *How about a date on Friday?*

Wouldn't that be a lot easier? Ten seconds later, they'd both feel very relieved. (I hope you're taking notes.)

More Reasons to Lie

I'm sure all of us, at some point, have had a question from our boss and chosen to lie right to their face.

The report is almost finished, I'll have it on your desk on Wednesday.

Nobody answered when I called.

Sorry I'm late, the traffic was horrendous today.

My son has mumps, so I can't come to the conference.

Now, naturally, there are lies that are fully well-intentioned. Our parents teach us to thank our hosts for dinner and say how much we loved it, even if it tasted like roadkill. We're expected to remark on what a lovely home our Aunt Agatha has, even when Aunt Agatha's wallpaper is the kind that gives you nightmares. Morally, and ethically, being kind and polite is sometimes more important than being truthful.

We tell people we care about that *you'll do fine,* even when we seriously doubt how fine they will actually do.

So yes, certainly. Lies of certain kinds fulfill some kind of social function, and sometimes save relationships from be-coming difficult.

IS HONESTY REALLY THE BEST POLICY?

Well . . . as I mentioned earlier, honesty is of vital impor-tance in establishing trust and forming healthy relationships. There's no doubt that many people in history have claimed that nobody can live entirely without deceit, and this leads us to the claim that everybody lies in some way, or in some degree.

However, perhaps we ought not fully condemn all state-ments that deviate from the truth. There is a wide spectrum here, ranging from casual exaggerations to more serious de-ception involving fabrications and outright lies. Although most of us are perfectly able to make the odd, harmless em-bellishment in the interest of keeping relationships harmoni-ous or protecting someone's feelings, this doesn't mean that everybody lies to an equal extent in all situations. I've read many studies that suggest people actually tend to lie quite rarely in general, and usually reserve deceit for strategic pur-poses.

Honesty requires good intentions, while deceitful be-havior tends to be caused by a variety of factors. In some cases, lies can be instinctive reactions, motivated by a fear of seeming judgmental or suffering negative consequences. We simply have to accept the fact that not everybody lies with malicious intent. At least, that is, you and I don't. Ha, ha.

Human relationships are built on trust, and this makes

dishonest behavior quite harmful in general. An individual's sincerity and reliability can only be appreciated through long-term interactions, and lying tends to gradually weaken our trust. It impacts the social dynamic. And that only makes sense, really. Who wants to spend time around a liar?

Our Culture Influences the Ways We Lie . . .

Geography and upbringing can have a great influence on how people from a certain country feel about lying and truthfulness. For instance, cultures that emphasize respect, like those of East Asian nations, are keenly focused on values like virtue and ethics. Consequently, they emphasize the need for honesty and stress the importance of cultivating and promoting trust. Conversely, cultures like those of Western societies that place an emphasis on situational needs, that is, prioritizing doing what's best for yourself in each particular situation, display a greater frequency of lying.

The question of who speaks the truth in criminal circles is an interesting one. A collection of gangsters that includes a fair number of psychopaths and sociopaths who make a living lying and deceiving others—what kind of culture do they breed? Lies and deception are so deeply integrated into that world that I find it hard to believe that anybody who lives in it could ever trust anybody else. It's difficult for a law-abiding citizen to picture what it's like to have that point of view.

There are also plenty of examples of cultures in history where truth tellers have been rather unappreciated. Criticizing the government, for example, is fine in my part of the world, but less accepted in a dictatorship.

During the communist rule in former East Germany, so-ciety was governed by fear for decades. Close to one citizen in three was supposedly an informer for the state in some capacity or other, and as a result, everybody lied about abso-lutely everything absolutely all the time. Nobody dared take responsibility for anything, as this could involve the serious risk that the wrong people might find out how you felt about some issue or other.

Some cultures are also, undoubtedly, more corrupt than others, and corruption doesn't provide a good foundation for truthfulness beyond one's own front door.

Even here in little Sweden, which is a reasonably well-functioning society, we experience difficulties caused by lying. Now, our problems might certainly seem rather quaint from an international point of view. Here, traditionally, boasting about your own success has always been frowned upon.

If you happen to be more successful than the people around you find acceptable, you'd do well to expect somebody to try to knock you down a peg or two. If you make a lot of money, many will simply assume you've taken it from others, rather than earning it over years of hard work, at considerable risk. This attitude is reflected in the Law of Jante (whose creator was Danish-Norwegian), which essentially requires us to keep quiet about our personal achievements to make sure we won't annoy people too much.

What follows is rule 7 from the Law of Jante:

You're not to think you are good at anything.

What is the effect of this depressing attitude?

How did you land that well-paid position? Who do you know there?

What's the answer to that?

Ah, I just got lucky.

Under no circumstances should you admit that you've worked your arse off for nine years. It's quite strange, to put it mildly. But whatever else it is, it *is* a lie.

. . . And Sometimes It's Okay to Lie

What conclusion can we draw from all this? Perhaps this one: Even though it can actually be claimed that dishonesty exists literally everywhere, we tend to overlook the specific causes of this dishonesty. Because of this, it would perhaps be a little unfair of me to simply claim that *everybody lies* without taking into account the multifaceted and genuinely complex dynamics that determine human behavior. All people are capable of honesty, and the truest measure of character is how frequently a person decides to genuinely embrace and prioritize honesty. I find it all to be rather clear: I have a lot more respect for somebody who has the ability to lie their way out of a situation— but refrains from doing so—than I have for somebody who is simply incapable of lying. Consider that.

USEFUL KNOWLEDGE—THE FOUR COLORS

Differences in human behavior and personality traits are, as always, incredibly interesting and fascinating. So let's investigate whether there might be any connections between specific behavior patterns and lies. As you may be aware, I have written several books that discuss the DISC model and the four colors. If you've already read those books and consider yourself an expert on this theory, you might not need to read the following section. However, I'd like to suggest you give yourself a quick refresher anyway, just to make sure you'll feel at home when I refer to the colors later on in this book.

Let's go!

A Clever Approach to Discussing Human Behavior

You may have heard of the method in which human behavior is categorized using four different colors: red for dominance, yellow for inspiration, green for stability, and blue for conscientiousness. These are the basic ideas of the DISC theory, which is used all over the world.

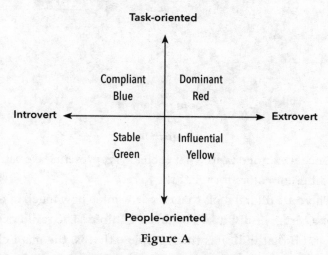

Figure A

As you can see here (Figure A), each quadrant covers two dimensions: task versus people orientation, and extroversion versus introversion. The colors are simply memory aids. Think of them as a learning tool. It's easier to remember that a behavior is Red-Yellow than it would be to remember that it is high in *D* over *I* with low *C*. The letter *D* stands for dominance, *I* for inspiration, *S* for stability, and *C* for conscientiousness.

Each color combines two dimensions at once, which means that a color is actually a combination of two measures. It simply depends on which axis you're on. Look at the figure below (Figure B). Here, you can see who is more task-oriented or more person-oriented. You can also see who is extroverted and active, and who is introverted and more passive.

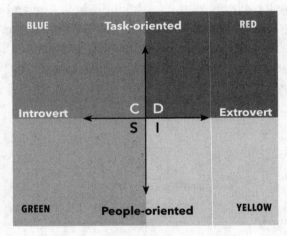

Figure B

Once we understand what each axis represents, we can see the different colors for what they are.

There are digital tools that can determine how much of each color a certain individual's behavior exhibits. The result of this is a graph that indicates their profile—that is, the main characteristics of their behavior as defined in terms of the DISC model. Even if somebody were to have a certain color dominate their *behavioral profile*, there would still be a number of interpretations left to make depending on the how much of each of the other colors is present.

I'm often asked if there are really only four kinds of people. The answer is very simple: of course not. As we can see in the figure above, while Red is always Red, it can still mean lots of different things. An individual who is in the top right corner would be very Red—perhaps exclusively Red. This means, then, that this individual would behave a certain way. We'll be able to understand what makes them tick almost immediately. On the other hand, somebody who is in the bottom left corner of the Red quadrant would appear different in certain ways. The position you're at *on each axis* will jointly determine your *behavioral profile*. This is, then, only a matter of how to describe the various basic ingredients.

As you're no doubt noticing, I'm going to some effort to highlight the phrase *behavioral profile*. It's important to remember that this model isn't a personality test. It is a self-assessment tool that describes behaviors.

Behaviors are the things that the people around an individual see and hear them do. Personality is always on a far deeper level than behavior. In order to define somebody's personality, you'd have to supplement the DISC analysis with other methods. The model doesn't in any way consider an individual's drive, motivations, interests, intelligence, abilities, or skills. It also doesn't address gender, sibling position, hypersensitivity, or diagnoses like ADHD or ASD (autism spectrum disorder).

I'm not making any claims as to whether the DISC theory is the best model ever; I'm content to focus exclusively on giving you a good description of how this particular model works. When used correctly, I am convinced that it is very useful for anybody who wants to understand human behavior and gain self-awareness.

The reason why I originally chose to write about the DISC theory in my first book, *Surrounded by Idiots,* is that the model is in use worldwide. It is practiced on all continents and has been translated into more than fifty languages. According to Selinus University, about thirty million DISC analyses had been performed worldwide by 2013. How many have been done now, more than ten years later? I don't know, but I'm willing to guess that it's a lot.

In Figure C, I list a variety of different characteristics that can usually be associated with each color. However, this list is only a guideline. The fact that *thinks on their feet* is listed under Yellow should not be taken to mean that an individual who displays more of the other colors is unable to improvise. It simply means that thinking on their feet is particularly characteristic of people with Yellow behavior. They tend to do it a lot of the time.

There is also an overlap between some of the colors. Red and Yellow possess more active qualities, while Green and Blue tend to have more passive qualities. This doesn't in any way mean that any color is better than any other—just that they are different.

Looking at the Green column reveals a number of characteristics that I think very few people would say they identified completely with. Somebody who displays nothing but these kinds of behaviors would be considered a full introvert with an exclusive people orientation. This is a more detailed description of Green behavior, but exhibiting all these characteristics should only be expected of somebody who ends up in the extreme bottom left of Figure B. The farther to the right we go in that quadrant, the fewer Green characteristics would be obvious to others, and instead, a variety of Yellow charac-

RED: DOMINANT	YELLOW: INFLUENTIAL	GREEN: STABLE	BLUE: COMPLIANT
Driven	Talkative	Patient	Nurturing
Ambitious	Enthusiastic	Relaxed	Orderly
Strong-willed	Persuasive	Controlled	Distant
Determined	Creative	Reliable	Polite
Forward-moving	Optimistic	Calm and collected	Conventional
Problem-solver	Sociable	Loyal	Hesitant
Innovator	Quick thinker	Modest	Objective
Decisive	Expressive	Understanding	Structured
Inventive	Charming	Fastidious	Analytical
Impatient	Vivacious	Steady	Perfectionist
Controlling	Self-centered	Careful	Slow-paced
Convincing	Sensitive	Discrete	Reflective
Performance-oriented	Adaptive	Supportive	Methodical
Forceful	Inspiring	Good listener	Facts-oriented
Results-oriented	Attention-seeking	Helpful	Quality-oriented
Takes initiative	Encouraging	Honors commitments	Scrutinizes
Keeps a high pace	Communicative	Durable	Stickler for the rules
Time-conscious	Flexible	Cautious	Logical
Intense	Open-minded	Considerate	Questioning
Imposing	Relationship-oriented	Kind	Meticulous

Figure C

teristics would present *alongside* a set of the Green ones. If you end up in the opposite corner of Figure B, that is, the top right corner of the Red quadrant, that would make you an extroverted individual who is highly task- and object-oriented. While people like this do exist, they aren't too common. Most Red types will end up in some other part of the Red quadrant of the chart.

In statistical terms, only about 5 percent of the population would display just one single color in a DISC analysis. This is the reason why so few people identify themselves as being, say, exclusively Yellow or exclusively Blue. They exist, but they're quite rare.

It's a sensible premise that people are too complex to be fully described by a few sentences on a sheet of paper—but we shouldn't ignore the things we can actually learn. It's true that we can probably never understand another individual 100 percent, but it's also true that we can document quite a lot . . . we just need to maintain awareness of the fact that we won't be giving a full description of them.

Here are some things I need to point out about DISC theory:

- Not all aspects of an individual's behavior can be explained in terms of DISC.
- There are many other models that can be used to describe human behavior.
- The colors aren't the only pieces of the puzzle we need to chart various patterns of behavior.
- The DISC model is based on psychological studies, is used all over the world, and is available in about fifty different languages.
- Statistically, about 80 percent of people display some combination of two dominant colors in their

behavior. About 5 percent display a single
dominant color. The rest display some combination
of three colors. The author of this book is one of
these, and this fact can sometimes cause no end of
problems.

- Fully Green behavior, or Green combined with
  another color, is the most common. The least
  common is fully Red behavior or Red combined
  with another color.
- There are certain gender-specific differences in
  behavior.

There are always exceptions to the examples I give in this
book. If you want to explore this model in greater depth, I'd
like to refer you to *Surrounded by Idiots,* which is dedicated
to these subjects.

When it comes to lies, of course, it can be very useful to
know what to expect from the people you encounter. This
simple color system offers a convenient way of avoiding the
worst pitfalls. As you read this book and do your own reflec-
tions on lying, consider your own colors, as well as the colors
of the people around you. Perhaps they're not even lying—
maybe you're simply misunderstanding them. Or maybe they're
misunderstanding you.

WHEN WAS THE LAST TIME YOU LIED?

Well, when *was* the last time you lied? There's no way I could
know this. Perhaps you lied this morning when you told your

neighbor you wouldn't at all mind picking their children up from day care. You'll do it, certainly—you did promise, after all. In that sense, you're reliable. But given the fact that you usually find getting your own little darlings home late in the afternoon to be quite a handful, just the thought of having to try to herd another pair of mischievous rascals into the car is giving you a bit of a tummy ache. They're not even yours! They'll be tired, and grotty, and as they are someone else's children, you won't even be able to raise your voice to them.

Who were you trying to deceive, really? Surely you didn't *want* to have to do this?

Relax! I get it. We all help one another out. But a more truthful answer might have been this: *I'll bring your kids home, too, even though it'll give me a migraine and gastritis and frankly be quite a pain. Having four exhausted little hooligans in my car isn't really what I need late on a Thursday, particularly considering what happened last time. The four of them practically tore our home apart. I sincerely hope you'll be returning this favor. Preferably tomorrow.*

Now there's a full truth! But sure, you'll help them *out*!

Again, when *was* the last time you lied?

Did you answer honestly when your partner asked if you'd like to go visit the Johnsons this weekend?

Did you answer honestly when your boss asked why you were late to the meeting yesterday?

Did you answer honestly when the police officer asked you if you knew how fast you were driving?

Did you answer honestly when your son asked why you couldn't play football with him?

Did you answer honestly when somebody asked how you've been doing?

You're the only person who knows the answer to these questions.

When was the last time *I* lied? Just now, actually.

Naturally, I'm no better than anybody else. I embellish the truth when it seems necessary to me to do so. And just like everybody else, I rationalize it to myself somehow.

Somebody I had to engage with for work was being a jerk. He made promises he didn't deliver on. Instead of calling him an idiot, I said that I felt that I sensed some challenges in our relationship. Really, he deserved a proper scolding, but that wouldn't have looked too great.

Or a few days ago, when I was on a popular American podcast answering questions, I was asked, Am I, a behavior expert, able to meet new people without immediately analyzing them? I gave them the answer I know people like to hear: *I can't help it, human behavior is just so fascinating!* And while that last part is true, of course I can't sit around performing detailed analyses of everybody I meet—it would drive me insane.

Or how about this:

At ten o'clock at night, my beloved wife asks me if I want to watch a movie. I'm chronically exhausted in the evenings, but she's a proper night owl. She's also a writer, and she happens to work very well in front of the TV. However, she doesn't like being up all night by herself in a dark house. So I tend to tell her that I'd love to watch a movie, just to keep her company, even though I'm practically half asleep already. It's not lost on her that I'm sound asleep on the couch thirty minutes later, but I'm physically present, at least. Perhaps this isn't one of the more serious lies you'll ever hear about, but it's still undeniably an untruth.

What does all this prove, then? That we lie to the people we love, too—but hopefully for the greater good!

Well, it's as I said: Lying is a complicated subject.

YOU CAN APPLY ALL THIS TO THE PEOPLE AROUND YOU, TOO

So far, we can tell that we're all different, both in terms of personality and in terms of culture. What do these insights mean in the context of the broader subject of lying? Perhaps this shouldn't be overstated, but I'm sure you can agree that we all view lies and truth in all kinds of sensible and senseless ways. And we're far from consistent in our chosen approaches.

INFAMOUS LIARS

The Devil

Readers are advised to remember that the devil is a liar.
—C. S. LEWIS

While we're discussing the difficulties involved in determining the intent of a specific lie, I'd like to introduce the greatest liar in history: the Devil, often referred to as Satan, Lucifer, or Beelzebub. In religious contexts, his role is often supposed to be that of sowing confusion and division among humans. Since we don't always feel like taking responsibility for our own actions, it can be convenient to have the Devil to blame. He's a figure who appears in many religious and cultural narratives, and often appears in moral tales about the importance of refusing his temptations. He's generally considered to be the embodiment of evil and betrayal, and somebody we're constantly told to avoid. But why exactly does the Devil have this reputation?

The Devil, often presented as the Prince of Darkness, is genuinely considered a truly malicious liar by many religious traditions. In the Christian tradition, he makes his first appearance in Genesis where, portrayed as a cunning snake, the Devil tempts Eve in the Garden of Eden.

The snake cunningly casts doubt over God's taboo against eating the fruit from the tree of knowledge of good and evil. Through devious manipulations, the snake/Devil brings Eve to question God's command, and promises her that eating the fruit of the forbidden tree will make her wise.

This account establishes the Devil's reputation as the father of lies. By tricking Eve—and then Adam—into disobeying God's instructions, the snake reveals its true nature. From this point on, the Devil is consistently associated with falsehoods and deception throughout the biblical narrative.

In Islamic traditions, Iblis (often equated with the Devil) is cast out from heaven because of his arrogance and pride. Remember that Christians believe the Devil to be Lucifer, a fallen archangel who was cast out from heaven. When Allah created Adam, all the angels were instructed to bow before him. They all did, except for Iblis. His deception? He lies to himself. He justified his disobedience by claiming that he was superior, made from fire, while Adam was actually made of clay, which seems far less impressive. His self-deception led to his downfall, and the story is fundamentally about the dangers of arrogance.

Although Hinduism has no immediate counterpart to the Devil, the Buddhist traditions have the character Mara. Mara tried to trick and distract Siddhartha Gautama, who later became Buddha, from achieving enlightenment. By promising him beautiful women, threatening him with unconquerable armies, and finally, generously offering him kingdoms and power, Mara tried to get Siddhartha to stray from his meditative path. However, he didn't fall for these devious tricks. (We'll have to assume he wouldn't have become Buddha if he had fallen for them.) Siddhartha's overcoming of Mara's wicked temptations became a decisive moment on his path to becoming Buddha. Mara can be said to be the closest that Hindu belief comes to a figure like the Devil. A mere trickster.

But we can find similar stories in literature. In Dante's *Divine Comedy*, and in *Inferno* in particular, we are given a rich portrayal of hell and its inhabitants. It was Dante who invented the nine circles of hell. Neither the Bible nor the Quran mention anything about hell having any number of circles. But according to Dante, Lucifer, a three-faced demon, gnaws on the greatest traitors in history for all eternity, at the very center of hell. Dante portrays the Devil as not only the punisher of those banished to hell, but also as the ultimate liar. His ice-cold realm strikes a stark contrast to the fires of hell that are often depicted, an intentional inversion meant to symbolize the contradictory aspects of the Devil's personality—the very essence of betrayal and lying.

Goethe wrote the story of Faust, a colorful narrative about the Devil's deceptive nature. Dr. Faust, dissatisfied with his life, makes a pact with the Devil, represented in the story as Mephistopheles. The Devil promises him unlimited knowledge and worldly pleasures. However, Faust soon realizes that these gifts are granted him at the expense of his own soul. Here, the Devil's deceit lies in obscuring the fine print—demonstrating his ability to manipulate human desire to bring people to behave in ways that are ultimately self-harming.

In various religions, myths, and cultures, the Devil (or his counterpart) is often presented as a master of lies. These stories communicate lessons of morality and illustrate the dangers of falling victim to lies and fraud.

However, it's important to note that all these stories are actually about human behavior. Regardless of whether the stories are about Adam and Eve, Faust, or Siddhartha, the choice between succumbing to or resisting the Devil's lies is always ultimately made by humans.

And that's surely the point of these moral tales, don't you think? Even thousands of years ago, the sages knew that people lie. And then, as today, they wished we could do it a little less often, because it caused a whole load of problems.

2

What Is Truth?

We swallow greedily any lie that flatters us,
But we sip only little by little at a truth we find bitter.
—DENIS DIDEROT

In order to understand what a lie really is, we will have to explore the concept of truth first. In essence, truth is a kind of representation of reality; a correct reflection of our knowledge, convictions, insights, and observations. It remains consistent, no matter how uncomfortable or unpleasant it may be.

I've given a lot of thought to the question of what is actually true while writing this book, and at first, I made a list of things I felt were definitely true. Things I didn't imagine anybody would question. But then, after some research, I found that almost anything is subject to question by people with sinister motives.

The truth, particularly in the context of philosophical discussions, can be a matter of interpretation. I can see how thought experiments concerning the things we see with our own eyes and how we interpret them can be exciting.

If a tree falls in the forest but nobody hears it, did it make a sound? That's a classic philosophical thought experiment designed to raise questions about the nature of reality and objectivity. Similar questions were asked by ancient philosophers, and these things can be fun to think about when you're not busy doing other stuff.

Truths are taken to be objective, as they remain consistent and unquestioned regardless of anybody's personal convictions or emotions. But are there really any undisputed truths?

ABSOLUTE TRUTHS

Mathematical truths might seem to be a good example of absolute truths. The principles of mathematics provide some of the most widely accepted truths. For example, the statement that two plus two equals four is true regardless of cultural, religious, personal, or situational considerations. Basic arithmetic, geometric theorems, and other mathematical theorems and equations are consistent across time and space. This ought to mean that mathematics is a solid example of absolute truth then, right?

Slow down, now. Nowadays, some—adherents of postmodernism in particular—claim that this isn't necessarily the case. Two plus two could just as well be five. I've not been able to determine exactly how this assumption can be reconciled with the foundations of mathematics, but I'm genuinely curious to see what their arguments are.

Certain **laws of physics** seem to enjoy universal acceptance. For example, this is true of the principle of conservation of energy, the first law of thermodynamics, which states that energy cannot be created or destroyed, merely converted from one form to another. There are some basic laws of physics that we simply have to take into consideration, and they are difficult to question. If we ask a random selection of people which direction up is, I'd be genuinely surprised if any significant number of them pointed to their feet.

Historical facts. Peace belongs to the victor, and we all know who history is written by. But while interpretations of historical events may differ, be subjective, and occasionally be deceptive, there are some historical facts that are genuinely beyond question. For example, the claim that the Second World War began in 1939 can be reasonably claimed to be a universally recognized truth. These fixed points in history, which are confirmed by a sufficient number of independent sources, are uncontested truths.

Personally, I am absolutely convinced that the Holocaust, Hitler's systematic mass extermination of Jews that was based on his inconceivable antisemitic views, is a historical fact. Nonetheless, there are people—perhaps not a large number, but a surprising number nonetheless—who claim that the Holocaust never even happened. Unbelievable.

Biology. In third grade I was taught that there are two sexes, and that this assumption is based on the configuration of our chromosomes. I learned that all mammalian species on the planet can be divided into male and female individuals. We were taught that females are the ones who become pregnant and give birth to offspring, and that this truth is based on the fact that having a uterus is a precondition for becoming pregnant.

These days, some people think that sex has nothing to do with biology, and that it is all a matter of identity, that is, one's own sense of which category one belongs to. You can call yourself what you like, basically.

Ancient truths. For a long time, human beings believed the earth was flat. Sailors were fearful of traveling too far from port because they had no knowledge of what lay beyond the horizon. In those days, the notion of falling off the edge of the world was a serious concern, and who knew what might really be out there? However, in time, people found the courage to explore, and discovered new worlds.

They believed that the sun orbited the earth, rather than the other way around. They believed that bleeding somebody to let evil illnesses out was a good idea, that prayers could cure cancer, or that doctors who had just performed an autopsy didn't need to wash their hands before going to deliver a baby. They believed that traveling any faster than twenty miles per hour would cause instant death. There is a whole host of such more or less unfortunate ideas, which can be difficult for a modern human to fathom.

Today, we know the truth about all those things I mentioned above. However, those beliefs were largely based on ignorance, poor science, or desire for power. It wasn't so much the lies that held humanity back as common human ignorance and the healthy dose of pride that went with it.

Religion. People who are born in a specific part of the world will often believe in a specific god. While the identity of a particular god may have been determined by nothing but geographical location, the existence of that particular deity was nonetheless an absolute truth to the people in the area. However, if God does exist, shouldn't God be the same everywhere? Maybe it all boils down to a question of interpretation. Where we happen to live, God is called

_____ (fill in the blank with the name used where you live). As the world has grown smaller because we have become able to travel all over it, this issue has become somewhat less clear-cut. Nowadays, most gods are present all over the place.

Science. Many of the great scientists in history have had their theories questioned—this is true of Darwin, Copernicus, and Einstein. Galileo was even jailed for expressing a truth no one wanted to hear at the time. He had the gall to claim what many had already begun to suspect—that the sun was actually at the center of our solar system. They simply didn't want to listen to him because he was challenging a notion that had been considered sacred until that point—that Earth and by extension the human race were the center of the universe.

However, reality proved to be different. Claiming that the sun orbits Earth simply because that's what you've been told in church, however, isn't necessarily a case of lying. It could just mean that you've been misinformed.

Although many truths are presently held as objective and universal by most of us, it's important to keep in mind that human knowledge is constantly evolving. What we might hold to be an incontestable truth might be refined or supplemented by further discoveries or future scientific progress.

The Earth Is Flat

While we're on the subject of serious misconceptions, let's take a closer look at one of the ones I just mentioned. I almost feel fraudulent to be wasting your time with this, but it can actually be quite entertaining to examine the idea of a flat planet in terms of lying and fraud. In a world where we have better access than ever to scientific knowledge, it's frankly bemusing to discover that there really is a movement—a growing one, even, although I can't imagine why or how—that sincerely claims that the earth is . . . well . . . flat.

These individuals aren't at all impressed by centuries of scientific evidence.

I've always thought that people who make these kinds of claims simply suffered from some psychiatric disorder or other. But in fact, this is not at all the case. There is a multitude of reasons why people spend their time trying to convince the general public that the earth is flat. Join me, and see if you feel the same way I do about this seemingly deranged theory.

In a digital age, where content is king, controversial and peculiar opinions can be a quick path to attention and acknowledgment. Anybody who publicly promotes the flat-Earth theory will tend to gain followers in social media platforms and have their posts widely shared, both by their fellow believers and by people who find the whole idea idiotic. This attention can be converted into financial gain through advertising, sales of various goods and services, or even invitations to give public talks about one's peculiar beliefs.

When I googled this theory, I smiled at the things I found. There is, as far as I can tell, a rather lucra-tive market for "flat-Earth products" (Are those a thing?) and various events where people meet to share their experiences. I'm full of questions as to who these people really are, but that's just me, I guess. (Imagine the small talk: How are things on your end? Is your garden still flat?) For some, this is all a business, and their main incentive is the profits they make.

For others, belief in a flat Earth provides a vague sense of identity and belonging to a specific (although controversial) group in society. Convincing others to join the holy cause cements one's own belief system, further strengthening one's ties to the community.

The flat-Earth theory, as far as I can tell, is also connected to other conspiracy theories that ultimately revolve around distrust of authorities, whether they be the government, the scientific community, or mainstream media. All of these authority figures—who must be resisted in every possible way, of course—promote the notion that the earth is round, and you can't possibly trust anything they say. Promoting the thesis that the earth is flat, then, is ultimately a way of convincing one's fellow humans to constantly distrust and question authorities. The flat Earth itself is really a bizarre symbol for something else.

Speaking of power, I suspect that the very act of getting others to believe the most insane ideas can make people feel powerful. Making others believe the earth is flat, despite the overwhelming evidence to the contrary, might make some people feel somehow superior. Just look at the Church of Scientology. Surely the fact that L. Ron Hubbard, who founded the church, is on record as having stated—long before he had even thought of the church itself—that founding a religion would be a good way to get rich is cause enough for caution?

Manipulation and control: Spreading disinformation and doubts about generally accepted facts (like the fact that the earth is round) can be a way to manipulate and control others. Those who are convinced of the value of questioning established knowledge may well be susceptible to other kinds of manipulation. If you start out by bringing them to believe that Earth is flat, you might be able to convince them to embrace other, more sinister, ideas.

Let's say the earth really was flat. What would that matter? It wouldn't make much of a difference in practice. Gravity wouldn't suddenly work differently if the UN declared that we live on a flat Earth. However, if I can convince you that Earth is flat, I might also be able to convince you that I met Jesus when I visited some country or other last week.

Or that climate change is all a hoax. Or that Bill Gates has secretly bought all the farmland in the US and is going to raise the price of wheat once all other kinds of food have been made illegal.

Who knows what I might have you believing next?

GOOD INTENTIONS

Now, speaking the truth has probably always been considered a virtue, an ideal to which we should all aspire. The philosophers of ancient Greece held *aletheia*, the truth, in extremely high regard. For them, it wasn't just important to speak of the world in precise terms, it was also a way of revealing the true nature of things. In this sense, telling the truth wasn't just a moral duty, it was an essential part of what it meant to be human. What can we learn from this? Is lying somehow inhuman? My own armchair reflection would suggest the exact opposite. Just as erring is human, so is lying.

Also, this doesn't just apply to the ancient Greeks. Great thinkers in all times, all over the world, have singled the truth out as an especially idealized notion, sometimes to the point of accepting every consequence of this principled stance. Some have been imprisoned, others tortured and executed.

Even Socrates himself came to a horrible end because of his forthrightness. He was undoubtedly guilty of the crimes he was accused of. He renounced the city's gods, and he encouraged people, particularly his young followers, to challenge authority figures. He was sentenced to death by poison, and he emptied the cup voluntarily. That's how strong his faith in the truth was. I'd like to see a present-day opinion leader, influencer, or politician (or anybody at all, really) who would be prepared to do the same thing for their beliefs.

In a relativistic world where the truth is often a matter of perspective or opinion, it's easy to lose your focus. It can often be tempting to tell small lies, twisting reality in ways that favor you or omitting facts that don't seem very interesting in the moment. But every time you do this, in a way, you're undermining the foundation of your relationship with the person to whom you are speaking.

What Do We Stand to Gain from Telling the Truth?

When we tell the truth, we show respect for ourselves and for others. We recognize our own fallibility and the limitations of our knowledge. We realize that others are just as entitled to the truth as we are, and we honor their autonomy by providing them with the facts they need to make informed decisions. In other words, we don't keep anything from them.

Truth telling is also a form of self-expression. When we tell the truth, we reveal something about ourselves—our thoughts, our feelings, our values. It's a way of asserting our existence and our place in the world. It's also a way of connecting with others, of forming relationships based on trust and understanding. How are you supposed to get to know somebody else on a deeper level if they never tell you how they feel about X, Y, or Z?

I would even claim that honesty is a vital path to personal growth. It's only when we accept the truth about ourselves, however painful, that we are able to change and grow. If you never come to see your own faults and shortcomings, you'll never be able to do anything about them. If you do what you've always done, you'll get the same results you've always had. You'll never make any progress.

We can confront our fears, our weaknesses, and our mistakes

and claim ownership of them. In this way, honesty can be a source of healing, a way to make peace with ourselves and others.

Of course, it isn't always easy to tell the truth. It can require courage, self-awareness, risk-taking, and a great deal of personal integrity. It can involve facing criticism or addressing uncomfortable emotions. But the sacrifice is well worth it!

Philosopher Friedrich Nietzsche is often attributed with the notion that the truth may be bitter, but it is always invigorating.

The times when I have learned the most about people are probably when I've told the whole, untarnished truth, without cushioning any part of it.

I am writing this during a week when I've been coaching a very successful Swedish influencer. This client arrived late to one of our meetings. Now, I didn't make a thing of this, but it came up in our conversation anyway. The message I was given was, *I'm a bit of a time optimist, and that's why I'm always late.*

My counter to this was, *Do you think you would have arrived on time if it had been Barack Obama who was sitting here waiting for you?*

Their answer? *Oh, yes!*

So I remarked, *What that seems to mean then is that you can stick to a time when something's important enough.*

Silence for almost half a minute.

And then, the important insights. It was very invigorating.

In a conversation you can always tiptoe around these kinds of things, but I find it refreshing to tell the truth, even if it means I might upset people sometimes. It's a risk I'm willing to take—perhaps not always, but most of the time.

One Hundred Percent Truthfulness

This invites the question of whether we really need to always be telling the truth.

Well . . . how often is *always*?

And besides, *whose* truth are we talking about here?

Are there situations where it makes sense to lie or withhold the truth? Some philosophers actually claim that there are exceptions to the rule of universal truthfulness.

For example, the philosopher Immanuel Kant (one of my favorites in this context, as you will see in this book) argued that we have a duty to tell the truth even if it leads to harmful consequences. It doesn't matter what kind of misery it might cause. The truth must be told at any cost. He even claimed that by lying, a man would forfeit his dignity as a man. It's heavy stuff.

On the other hand, utilitarians like John Stuart Mill would claim that the consequences of our actions are what matter the most, and that there can be situations where lying produces the best outcomes.

Although there are some situations in which it's hard to draw the line between right and wrong, it's also important to consider the long-term impact our actions might have. Even minor lies can erode trust and harm relationships. Over time, they can create webs of deception that can be difficult to untangle.

So what should we say about all this? Telling the truth is a fundamental aspect of human existence. It's a way of showing respect for others and for ourselves, expressing our individuality, and connecting with the world around us. It's important to our personal growth, and it helps us form relationships based on trust and understanding. Although it can be hard to tell what the right approach is in some situations, striving for truth and integrity is generally worthwhile. While the truth can be painful, it's also liberating.

However, as I mentioned, it can sometimes feel difficult. For example, I've lost count of how many times an author has handed me their book and asked me to read it, and then, the next time I meet them, I have to navigate my way around the fact that I either haven't found the time to read their book, or I *have* read it but didn't enjoy it much. Either way, I'm expected to have an opinion to give, and preferably a positive one.

I've tried not to use diversionary tactics, like *You must have worked hard on this book*, or *Where did you get the idea for it?* My hope was that I wouldn't have to say anything about the actual content. Nowadays, I try to be more honest (*I didn't like the main character very much*), but it's hard to do that when you know how much work goes into writing a whole book. It's easy to hurt an aspiring writer's feelings. I'm speaking from experience here. We protect our material like a mother protects her child, and sometimes we can be terribly sensitive about criticism.

NEWS COVERAGE AND POLITICAL BIAS

This section might ruffle some feathers. How easy is it, really, to communicate the truth when you're required to do it in a way that's interesting, commercial, and profitable—all at once? I'd imagine it's not particularly easy.

In Sweden, a recurring topic of discussion is the political leanings of Swedish journalists. You might be wondering why this would matter? Well, political beliefs can influence people's perspectives on things, just like religious beliefs can. It's really not that strange. I'm not talking about the *truth* here; I'm talking about how people choose to *report* on the truth.

There have been two studies made of this. Both of them show similar results. For instance, the study by Norwegian liberal think tank Civita, published in 2020, compared the political opinions of Norwegian and Swedish journalists with those of the respective nations' populations at large.

Their survey showed that around 70 percent of the Swedish journalists who responded would have voted for either the Left Party, the Social Democratic Party, or the Green Party if there had been an election to the Riksdag on the day they were asked. In the population at large, however, only about 40 percent would have voted for the Left bloc parties.

Naturally, the results of this survey have been questioned— anything else would have been remarkable. The sample size isn't particularly large. Asking a few hundred journalists simply isn't enough to allow for reliable conclusions.

In the survey, however, sympathies for the Left Party and the Green Party are particularly overrepresented among journalists in comparison with the general public. This applies both in Norway and in Sweden.

Why is this the case? I have no idea. I'm not sufficiently knowledgeable about media studies and politics to feel confident about drawing any conclusions from this. Those who don't like the findings of these surveys might even feel that I shouldn't have mentioned them here. However, as far as I can tell, the data I've presented here are accurate. Of course, we can't rule out the possibility that those responsible for the survey exhibit some kind of bias. We run the risk here of ending up in some strange meta-level discussion that would only make people unsure about what to believe. At the least, this shows that there is cause to be cautious and critical of one's sources.

In 2017, a team of Norwegian media researchers published a study titled "Perceptions of Journalistic Bias: Party Preferences, Media Trust and Attitudes Towards Immigration." In this work, they showed that public perceptions of how influenced journalists are by their own opinions tended to correlate strongly with people's sympathies for different political parties. The newspaper in which I found the Civita study, as it happens, is a conservative publication. Does this impact the way the story was reported? That's entirely possible—but it would only confirm the hypothesis that newspapers often fail to be neutral. If the principle holds at one end of the spectrum, you can expect it to hold at the other end, too.

Unfortunately, there aren't any other studies for us to look at. It would actually be very exciting to find a different study that lent support to the opposite thesis, but I can't find one. Either way, we can establish that journalists are human just like the rest of us. How does this impact news reporting in Swedish media? How are the stories selected, how are the headlines set, and how do the journalists choose to interpret their stories? Which opposing parties are invited to TV debates on heated topics, and why? We can only speculate on this—and like I said, you're going to have to draw your own conclusions. I think the problem really is that not enough of us give much deliberate thought to the ways that journalists, whether consciously or not, might be inserting bias into their stories.

When I reflect on my own behavior, the conclusion is inevitable: Sometimes I only mention the aspects of reality that I wish to acknowledge. I think it's just human nature.

In any case, you should be critical of information that's presented to you, wherever you come across it. Don't accept anything you read or hear without careful consideration. Question the facts you're presented with, consider other points of view, and try to find other sources of information.

Be mindful of your own preconceived notions. We all have our prejudices, and it's important to be aware of them and challenge them. For example, you might spend a minute reflecting on how you reacted to what you just read.

In conclusion, bias in news coverage is a serious issue that can significantly impact our society and our democracy. It's important as a news consumer to remain conscious of the possibility of bias in the media and to cultivate a skeptical mindset when consuming news. Ultimately, it's up to us to seek the truth and demand more from the media.

As you navigate these waters, cross-reference any stories you're told with reputable sources, be skeptical of sensational headlines, and think twice before pressing the share button.

Alternative Facts

It gets worse, however. The term "alternative facts" gained public attention after a specific event that occurred shortly after the inauguration of Donald Trump to the US presidency in 2017.

The phrase was coined by presidential adviser Kellyanne

Conway during a press event after being asked a question about a statement previously made by White House press secretary Sean Spicer. Spicer had claimed that the crowd at Trump's inauguration was the largest ever to watch a president be sworn in to the office. This claim was easily refuted by photographs taken during the event.

When Conway was confronted with this obvious falsehood, she defended it by claiming that Spicer was giving *alternative facts*. They had a truth all their own, basically.

Naturally, this soon became the target of ridicule from journalists, pundits, comedians, and the general public. It became symbolic of what critics perceived as the Trump administration's less-than-rigid adherence to truth and their attitude toward the media. It also appeared in more general conversations on truth, the reliability of public information, and the role of the media in the modern era.

Even though it's not at all unusual for different sources or individuals to present differing interpretations or points of view in regard to a specific event, the term "alternative facts" seemed to many to be a very blatant attempt to legitimize a sheer fabrication in the service of a certain agenda.

NUMBERS DON'T LIE, DO THEY?

Statistics, when used with integrity, can inform, educate, and emphasize important messages. However, with the addition of a dash of deception, they can be made as persuasive as a snake oil salesman in a market.

Of course, statistics can just as well be used to provide valuable insights as to deceive or oversimplify highly complex issues. By methods like cherry-picking the data, misrepresenting the implications of the data, or failing to account for confounding variables, statistics can be manipulated to support almost any claim.

Throughout history, the delicate art of "statistical lying" has been honed and refined by countless individuals and organizations. The allure of this devious craft lies in its subtlety. On the surface, the data presented seems genuine and reliable. It looks and sounds completely credible. However, in-depth examination can reveal the scam. Assuming you're reading this book in 2024, you might be thinking that people must have been pretty stupid in the past. But consider that in the present day, we're falling for lies that are just as well-substantiated as the ones our ancestors fell for. We just don't know which ones. Yet.

Tobacco Industry Trickery

During the first half of the twentieth century, amid growing concerns about the health risks of smoking, tobacco companies found themselves facing a looming crisis. If the public were to get the idea that smoking might be causing death, it seemed plausible that sales might suffer as a result. A fairly reasonable presumption, really. To counteract these undesirable developments, the tobacco giants turned to "scientific" studies to prove that smoking was actually completely harmless.

Cigarette advertisements from the 1940s and 1950s made claims like, *More doctors smoke Camels than any other cigarette.* Today, we might imagine that this meant that there was a single doctor foolish enough to recommend smoking, and that they happened to smoke Camels. In fact, the claim was based on a nationwide survey. But what was the survey actually about? The question asked wasn't which brand was the healthiest, it was just which brand doctors *smoked the most*. The selection criteria for participating doctors and the methodology used were at best unclear, at worst downright fraudulent. No documentation exists to give an account of how the survey was actually carried out. Nobody knows.

What about the results? The public was led to believe that if doctors favored a certain brand of cigarettes, that brand must be less harmful. Of course, the actual health data, which were published years later, revealed a bleaker reality. Smoking was unequivocally linked to lung cancer, heart disease, and a myriad of other disastrous afflictions. It turned out that not even doctors were immune to the harmful effects of the tar in cigarette smoke. But by then, many had already been fooled by those mysterious statistics about doctors and their smoking habits.

Cigarettes caused coughing and throat irritations. That much was known. But the tobacco companies marketed their products as *better than the competitors*. It wasn't as though *all* cigarettes would give you problems—it was just the *other ones*.

As the dangers of smoking have become known to us in the Western world, various lobbying organizations employed by tobacco companies have reportedly switched over to promoting the use of other tobacco products. Not to mention the ongoing attempts to encourage more people to smoke in countries where smoking has not yet become stigmatized. The lobbyists seem to believe that more people ought to smoke in those nations. Obviously, I'd like to know more about the reports they're presenting there when it comes to the risks of smoking.

Two Examples of Lying with Statistics

THE DEPRESSION: GRAPHICAL TRICKERY

Background: The Great Depression (1929–1939) was a time of economic disaster. As the stock market crashed and unemployment rose, accurate reporting of economic data became paramount. However, to prevent a panic, statistics were sometimes presented in what we might call "creative" ways.

One of the most notorious examples of this involves a graph used to present the number of unemployed Americans from 1929 to 1933. By manipulating the y-axis, the graph was made to appear as though the rate of unemployment had been steadily dropping. But when the figures were plotted on a graph with a consistent, regular scale, a very different reality was revealed: Unemployment had skyrocketed from less than 5 percent in 1929 to over 25 percent in 1933. This little trick involving the y-axis led many to believe that the economy was recovering when it was actually plunging deeper and deeper into the abyss.

THE MISLEADING LINKING OF MMR VACCINES AND AUTISM

Perhaps this kind of fudging of numbers is a thing of the past? Surely we know better today? Unfortunately, we don't. A more contemporary example is given by an article published in 1999 in the renowned medical journal

The Lancet. The study suggested that there was a causal link between the MMR vaccine, which is given to prevent measles, mumps, and rubella, and autism. This paper had far-reaching consequences—it caused a dramatic reduction in vaccinations and, subsequently, the reappearance of these serious diseases, which could have been prevented by the vaccine.

So how did this happen? The sample used for the study was just twelve children, even fewer participants than in the study on journalists. However, this didn't stop journalists all over the world from publishing the results. A sample that small is in no way representative, anyone could tell you that. This is particularly true when you're looking to make serious claims about a life-saving vaccine. Later evaluations of the study would also reveal that the data collection and interpretation were deeply flawed. For example, there were inconsistencies in the timelines between MMR vaccination and onset of autism symptoms among participants. In the article, these factors were generalized in order to suggest a causal relation. Someone wanted this story to be true for some reason—it's that simple.

The consequences of this fraud were enormous. It took years of extensive research performed by teams from all over the world to debunk the claims. Suddenly, all those claims had to be disproved. The new studies included hundreds of thousands of children, and found no causal link between the MMR vaccine and autism. But the damage had already been done. Fear had taken root in millions of parents. I'm sure you know of people who are skeptical of vaccinations in general? Specialist doctors I have spoken to have told me that the whole idea originated in this particular misleading study.

These examples serve as grim reminders that while numbers themselves may be neutral, they can be presented in ways that give rise to narratives ranging from the mildly misleading to the downright dangerous. As consumers of information, the onus is on us to approach data critically, and question the sources, methodology, and intent of any study. It's just as the old saying tells us: *Trust, but verify.*

THE VALUE OF SILENCE

The proverb *speech is silver, silence is golden* is rooted in the fact that although words can be valuable (like silver), there are times when saying absolutely nothing can be even more valuable (like gold). This idea seems more relevant than ever today, given how noisy modern society has become.

You're probably familiar with the expression that you have to *cut through the noise*. It means that in order to be heard in a noisy society, whether it be at work, in the media, or in some other context, you have to stand out. And sometimes you simply have to raise your voice a little. The problem today, of course, is that it's no longer a case of "noise." These days, we're dealing with an increasingly deafening roar, which hardly anything can penetrate.

How did it come to this, then? Can silence really do the

same work for us as fudging the facts a little? Is silence even an option worth considering?

Let's take a closer look at what this ancient saying means in the present-day context. And, also, whether choosing this path is viable at all.

In the digital age, we live under a 24/7 bombardment of information, opinions, and background noise coming to us from social media, news channels, and countless communication tools. There is virtually no silence anywhere. In an environment like that, the ability to step back, keep silent, and process information becomes a vital edge. Silence allows us to filter the noise out and keep the substance. It offers us a rest from all the noise. We all need silence of some kind, in some quantity.

The continuous flood of messages, notifications, and other things demanding our attention can be mentally draining. Scheduling moments of silence, whether through meditation, digital detox, or simply being quiet, can help maintain your mental well-being. Zen monks' pursuit of undisturbed environments probably rests on a solid strategy. It's simply not possible to connect with yourself on a deeper level if you're surrounded by deafening noise all the time.

In a society that often encourages us to speak up when we're unhappy and express our opinions as soon as we've formed them, silence gives us the space we need to listen actively. Doing that allows us to better understand other people's points of view, empathize with others, and form deeper relationships. In rhetoric, it's often said that silence is an undervalued tool.

Some Telling Examples

Apart from writing books, I also give several lectures every year. Sometimes I walk onto the stage before a lecture as slowly as I possibly can. When I do this, I always see people in the audience using their mobile phones. They are so preoccupied that they can't find the time to look at what's happening in front of them, even when it's something they've paid to see. Sometimes I feel mischievous. And when I'm in that mood, I might decide to start the lecture by simply standing at the front of the stage, without saying a word.

The people in the audience crane their necks, wondering what's going on. Eventually, even those most severely addicted to their phones react and turn the screens off. *What's about to happen?*

The longest I've ever stood like that, in silence, in front of thousands of people is just over a minute. I can attest that it feels like two hours. Everyone's staring, everyone wonders what's up. Someone laughs nervously at the sheer unusual nature of the silence. However, it's also a remarkable experience. All those people in a room together—and no one is talking! You should try it sometime.

Anyway, one thing I can promise you is that I have everyone's attention by the time I finally start speaking.

This trick also works in everyday life. Instant communication tools like mobile phones and various apps encourage us to respond quickly, often without reflection. Who can take the time to think when they are subjected to constant flashing and beeping? But by embracing silence, we can actually refrain from making impulsive comments or taking actions that might later prove ill-advised.

Do you like to share everything in your personal life? Everything? No, I didn't think so. In an age when sharing personal information on public platforms has become an increasingly accepted norm, choosing silence can be a way to maintain your privacy and protect your personal space. A personal touch can often be appreciated, but do we really need to be sharing things all the time? I don't think we do. Perhaps some secrets ought to be kept. In fact, your fellow human beings can become embarrassed if they're force-fed more than they really want to know about their neighbors. Or their relatives. Or even their partners. What remains to be discovered once all the secrets are out of the bag?

Silence can also facilitate more thought-provoking conversations. When every conversation, especially online, risks turning into a debate, an argument, or even an outright quarrel, the choice of silence can help you avoid unnecessary confrontations. Choosing when to engage allows us to contribute more meaningfully to interpersonal discussions. Now, this isn't to say we should be overly afraid of conflict, but when it comes to unnecessary ones based on misunderstandings, I really can't see the point of getting involved.

Sometimes words fall short of capturing the essence of an experience, a feeling, or a moment. Silence can allow us to fully immerse ourselves in an experience, whether it be appreciating nature, enjoying art, or investing in our relationships with our loved ones.

A good friend of mine was traveling somewhere on the planet, probably in the Pacific Ocean—I can't remember exactly. When he was out on a boating trip with the family, the skipper spotted some whales jumping. My friend immediately picked up his video camera to capture the moment. Quite a common reaction, I suppose. But the skipper pushed his arm down and said, *Drop that stuff. Look at the whales instead. Live the moment!*

Consider the implications of this attitude.

While communication is undeniably crucial to our modern, online society, so is the art of silence. Making room for moments of silence in our lives has nothing to do with neglecting communication. Rather, it's a matter of choosing the right times to speak, and valuing the profound power of silence.

Does Silence Have a Color?

Of course, it's interesting to think about which personality types happen to be better or worse at keeping quiet. If, for the sake of simplicity, we stick to the DISC model that I described in the previous chapter, we will discover some interesting patterns.

To begin with, I can tell you about the people who can't stand silence: Yellow people have an extremely difficult time with silence. Now, this is a bit of a generalization, but these individuals are good at expressing themselves. Their main strength is communicating with words. Many of them dislike silence as it makes them feel insecure. Many will even feel nervous if there's too much silence.

I'm not suggesting here that a Yellow person, who is extroverted and relationship-oriented, would find it unbearable to sit alone in a room reading a book, for example. That wouldn't be a problem, of course. But they *are* relationship-oriented.

As soon as other people enter the room, the urge to talk will often be very strong for Yellow people. The same goes for anybody whose profile combines Yellow features with other colors. Being Yellow usually means being good at expressing yourself, and enjoying being the center of attention. These are difficult to achieve while keeping silent. At least, that's what a Yellow person would say.

Green people have similar tendencies. They are relationship-oriented, like Yellows, but they are also introverted. This means that they spend more time inside their own head than outside it. They are also good listeners. They actually hear what the rest of us are saying. They also have no need to be the center of attention, particularly if their Green is combined with Blue. They're perfectly happy to stand off to one side, watching what everyone else is doing. In the company of friends, however, where they feel safe and secure, even Greens will often get quite involved in conversations. In that situation, they might even find silence difficult. As I mentioned earlier, there are an incredible number of people who simply can't sit in a room with other people without saying anything. Humans are rather social beings, and it simply doesn't feel natural to us.

What about Reds? Well, they're extroverts, but they're task-oriented. In short, this means that they like action. They find it difficult to sit still, but they don't necessarily need to have other people around to keep them going. Being extroverted isn't the same as being sociable—that's actually a common misconception. Being sociable is a Yellow trait, and socializing in a natural way requires a strong focus on other people.

But that's not what Reds are like. Remember what I wrote in *Surrounded by Idiots*. Red people feel more like they're surrounded by idiots than other people do. They simply can't tolerate foolishness. So what does this mean? It means that Reds can be quiet among other people without any greater issues. They simply switch their ears off and go about their business.

However, if they hear something they strongly dislike, bad news that's going to affect them personally, they won't remain silent. They will loudly and clearly declare what they think about what they just heard. Even if doing so happens to be highly inappropriate. Red people often react very quickly, and in some cases, they have little or no impulse control. The line between thought and action disappears.

Okay, then, who are the people who are able to remain silent in most situations? The ones who thrive on silence, who have no need to express themselves even if they should hear something they know is false or that they disagree with?

You guessed it. Blues.

Like the Reds, they are task-oriented, meaning they're less concerned with other people than Yellows and Greens. On top of this, they're introverts. They're perfectly comfortable in their own heads, and they can solve difficult problems even in a crowd of loud, noisy people. Just like Reds, they just switch off and keep focus on their thoughts.

Blues are able to sit and listen to lengthy discussions about difficult and important issues and never say a word, even if they know what the answer is all along. *Why is that?*, you ask. Well, nobody asked them. Before you tell me that this makes no sense, let me remind you that for the Blue person, it's all perfectly logical. They already knows the answer and is happy enough with that. They often feel no need to communicate their solutions to the rest of the world.

If I had a few pennies for every time this has happened to me, I'd be a rich man. (I've even asked them: *If you knew the answer, why didn't you say anything?* They look so innocent when they answer: *You could have asked.*)

What can I say? People are all different.

Lying and Silence by Personality Type

The relationship between lying and silence is essentially this: Instead of telling a lie—be it a white, innocent one or a deceitful, wicked one—I could always choose to be silent. This makes it useful to know what my tolerance for silence is.

My own profile consists of high Red and Blue bars, equal amounts of each in fact, and a rather high degree of Yellow mixed in. No Green to speak of. Sorry. My own reflection is that with increasing age, I have found it easier and easier to just keep my mouth shut. Maybe this is because I've finally come to realize that my opinion on some issue or other is far from always being what people actually want. Now, my ego is perfectly capable of refraining from adding my own words to a discussion that's already been resolved. This is more of a theory than anything else, but it makes sense.

The connection to lying is interesting here. Let me give some examples of when silence is a viable alternative to saying something that may not be entirely true.

Situations When I Should Have Kept Quiet

A friend of mine has radically changed her hairstyle. Deep down I'm a little horrified, because I thought she looked great before she had her hair cut off. The specific hairstyle in question doesn't matter here, this is just an example. When she asks me what I think, what I really want to do is scream at her: *What were you thinking?*

But that would hurt her feelings.

So instead, I ask her to turn her head around so I can see her from different angles. My strategy is not to have to say a word about the actual haircut. Instead, I nod and smile. I leave it to her to interpret this however she wants. If she asks me more directly, I might have to say something. Then I'd say that she's brave to have made such a drastic change, and that I admire her for that.

Or how about this: My neighbor is proudly showing off his new car and wants to know what I think. Having been quite knowledgeable about cars since my youth, I know that there are a variety of reasons why this purchase was not a good one.

I might say: *Dan, that car has performed very poorly in every test I've read. What were you thinking?*

While that would be true, it might also make me look like a miserable old grump. And I don't want that. This is where I have to consider the option of opting for deception.

My natural impulse might be to say: *I love the color!*

That would be a standard diversionary tactic. It would skirt the issue and shift focus to something else than the car's quality and handling. It could work, too, if I happened to like the color. But I don't, unfortunately. In fact, I think modern cars tend to be fugly (that's a technical term). So saying that would be an outright lie.

Instead, I walk over to my neighbor's driveway, smile, and make a few laps around the car. I don't say anything, though. He smiles broadly, interpreting my silence as approval. Everyone's happy.

I might ask a question about the color or the accessories. But I'm not really commenting on the car as such. Everyone's happy. That is, until the fourth time he has to call for a tow truck.

Another example: My wife likes animals. She wants to buy a horse.

But horses are big animals. We don't have the space, and, most important, we have nowhere near the time keeping horses requires. Just thinking about it makes me anxious. The very idea is an absolute dead end.

What would be my honest reaction here? I would immediately start listing factual counterarguments. I could point out how far from the nearest stables we live, or that she simply doesn't have the time to take care of a horse. I could tell her that getting an animal is a serious undertaking, and that it's only cruel to do that if you aren't in a position to give it the conditions and care it needs.

All this would bring on a loud conflict. Why is that? Well, my wife is all Red. She has only one bar—Red. Nothing else. She would eat me alive in an argument about horses.

However, rather than pointing out the obvious, I could lie. I could say that it would be amazing if we could bring home a horse. (Which it wouldn't be, as I'm allergic to anything that has fur and it would cause me a lot of suffering.) I could tell her that I'd be happy to take care of her horse for her when she is out traveling. (That would also be a lie, though. I have no desire at all to do that. Not everyone is passionate about animals, and besides, I travel a lot more than she does.)

Of course, I could also point out that we could almost certainly find some young girl or boy in the neighborhood who would be willing to make some extra money taking care of the animal. (Feel free to think of me as a miser now, I don't mind, but I simply have no desire to spend my money on something like that.)

I don't want to start an argument and bicker with my wife. I also don't want to deceive her into thinking that I'm fine with the idea of having a horse just to spare myself an argument. I refuse to lie to my wife.

So what do I do?

I keep quiet. I nod, listen, and take in her explanations for why she wants a horse. How she'd love to get back into riding now that we live in the countryside. (We practically live in the woods.) I don't agree, but I also don't argue. I just listen. And I hope to dear God that she won't ask me outright what I think of the idea. With a bit of luck, she'll never get that far. Hopefully, hearing her own arguments for getting a horse will put her off the idea. (If she should ask a direct question, however, I'd tell her the truth: It's an exceptionally bad idea. And I'd have to deal with the conflict. Because I can't lie to my wife. I just can't.)

So Was It Right of Me to Keep Quiet?

In both the case of my neighbor's unfortunate car purchase and my wife's nonexistent horse, I can simply keep my mouth

shut and let them do the talking in the hope they won't notice that I'm very obviously not giving them any positive
feedback.

Now, you may be thinking: Withholding your true thoughts
from people you care about—isn't that also lying, in a way?

And yes, you have a point.

I recognize that this isn't all black and white. That's precisely why the whole subject of lying is so incredibly complicated. Sometimes there's just no way out.

Nevertheless, I'd still recommend trying silence as an
alternative to telling white lies.

Every time you say something that's not truthful—*I really
like your new haircut. I've heard that's a really good car. I'd
love to get a horse*—it will add a problem to your life. Now,
you're going to have to keep a log of all these little innocent
lies somewhere in your mind. If you've claimed that Dan's
car purchase was a good move but happen to discuss it with
other people he knows and say what you really think of his
chosen brand, well, that will let him know that you can't be
trusted.

How can he trust anything you say after that?

And that's not even the worst part. The most serious problem is the fact that you know you lied. You'll have reinforced
the self-image that you're somebody who chooses dishonesty
over truth. This isn't going to do wonders for your character
development.

Everything has an impact. If you fudge things a little here,
this will increase the chance that you'll fudge things a little
there. Telling small lies can lead to telling bigger lies. Before
you know it, you'll be up to your neck in it.

The danger here is turning yourself into something you

don't want to be. And the question, I suppose, is whether it's really worth it.

THE TRUTH, TACT, AND COMPLEXITY OF ABSOLUTE HONESTY

Okay, so you know more about truthfulness now. But there's one thing I wonder if you've considered. Do you realize that this is all actually even more complicated? It's easy to say that we disapprove of liars. But what is the opposite of a liar? Well, someone who always tells the truth, of course. Somebody who honestly and sincerely tells it like it is, regardless of the consequences this may have for them or for others. Somebody who delivers the truth even when it's painful as hell.

And what do we think of people like that (assuming they exist, that is)? Do we appreciate somebody who never avoids adding the truth to a conversation, and who always gets everything they say and do right? Somebody who's never exposed as having told even a tiny white lie? You know, that type who's always righteous and principled and always declares the truth, the whole truth, and above all nothing but the truth?

If your skin is already crawling at that thought, I can tell you that you're probably not alone.

For centuries, philosophers and whole cultures the world over have revered the virtue of honesty, granting it the same exalted status as other qualities like integrity, bravery, and kindness. Those are all nice, absolutely. But to examine how much people actually value honesty, it's necessary to consider the real-world consequences that absolute truth tends to bring. Do we really want relentless and unfiltered honesty from everyone around us? Are we sure about that?

What Do We Think of People Who *Never* Lie?

While honesty is undeniably valuable, totally unfiltered truths can have rather profound psychological implications. People all possess complex sets of emotions, varying degrees of self-esteem, and differing capacities for receiving bad news. Because of this, everyone isn't always prepared to hear the truth.

Here's a classic question that most couples have struggled with. (What the right answer is remains shrouded in mystery.) Are you ready? Here it comes:

Does this make me look fat?

Ugh, there simply isn't a worse question to have to answer. We really hate it. What can you say to that?

Yes, it makes you look very fat, actually. Maybe not as fat as the one you wore yesterday made you look, though.

Phew!

According to the research of psychologist Elliot Aronson, cognitive dissonance, or inconsistent thoughts, beliefs, and attitudes, can induce stress and discomfort. Absolute honesty, especially when it contradicts one's self-image, can emphasize this cognitive dissonance.

For example, telling someone that they're no good at something they've spent years doing can cause deep anxiety and self-doubt, which can ultimately make them abandon their great passion in life.

No, you don't sing that well, really.

Ouch.

Humans are social beings. Anthropologist Robin Dunbar theorized that the complexity of our social relationships has played a significant role in the development of our large brains. Some argue that it has to do with the fact that we started to eat meat, but let's presume that social relationships played a part. Social harmony often requires tact, diplomacy, and, occasionally, a willingness to spare people the full burden of hearing the truth. It simply keeps things more peaceful.

For example, consider a scenario where a friend asks for your opinion on an outfit that they're clearly enthusiastic about. You hesitate, because it looks kind of ridiculous. Bluntly telling them that their outfit is unflattering without thinking it through first might cause unnecessary hurt feelings on their part, and will undoubtedly disrupt the harmony of your friendship.

The philosopher Friedrich Nietzsche is credited with saying that there are no facts, only interpretations. This statement actually underlines the subjective nature of truth. In many situations, the truth is simply someone's opinion. When someone claims to be expressing an absolute truth, they may in fact just be affirming their own subjective view of a particular situation.

Here's an example: In discourse on art or music, a person's honest opinion about whether a particular piece is good or bad is completely subjective, but these opinions are still often presented as universal truths. For instance, this is what happens when I ask the kids at home what on earth they're listening to. (I might have thought somebody was setting off bombs upstairs.) They claim that all they're doing is enjoying a piece of good music, but of course, it's plain as day to me that they're actually wrong about that.

Continuous exposure to pure, unfiltered truths, particularly negative ones, can have detrimental effects on our mental health, and persistent, negative interactions can exacerbate depressive symptoms.

Another example: If an individual in a workplace constantly receives truthful negative feedback without being given any positive reinforcement to balance it out, this can lead to burnout and depression.

Although lies are generally frowned upon, there are some scenarios where they can be considered morally defensible. This is called altruistic deception. Not telling the absolute truth can sometimes protect someone's feelings, mental health, and even physical well-being.

For example, doctors giving patients a placebo are engaging in altruistic deception, as they believe that the symptoms might be relieved by the placebo effect. It works, too. There's no shortage of studies that demonstrate the positive effects of placebos. The human brain is truly incredible. For comparison, it's worth pointing out that placebos don't work at all on another type of patient: dogs. Consider that.

Honesty, particularly when delivered without empathy, can feel cold and harsh. Empathy—the ability to understand and share the feelings of others—is essential for softening the impact of the truth. Empathy can prevent aggressive behavior when someone is confronted with hurtful truths.

If a person is struggling with a personal challenge of any kind, then, blunt, factual messages that don't take their feelings into account can actually do more harm than good.

WHERE DO YOU DRAW THE LINE?

What about you? Where do *you* draw the line between silence, lies, and truth? Let's take a test and see how you respond to these ten questions. I need hardly mention that
there's no point in lying here because only you will know the
truth about your answers anyway. The following is a simple
self-assessment test, and there's no need for you to post your
results on Facebook.

1. **Your friend buys a new dress and asks your
opinion. You find it unflattering. What do you do?**
   A. Tell them it looks good to avoid hurting their
      feelings (lie).
   B. Tell them you're not sure, and quickly change the
      subject (silence).
   C. Express your true thoughts carefully, and pro-
      pose an alternative (truth).

2. **You notice that a colleague of yours has made a
minor mistake in a report, which can easily be cor-
rected. You . . .**
   A. Say nothing because their mistake might make
      you look better (lie by omission).
   B. Keep quiet because it's not your responsibility
      (silence).
   C. Immediately ask your colleague to correct the error
      (truth).

3. **Your partner has made dinner and is excited for
you to try it, but you don't enjoy its taste. You . . .**
   A. Tell them it's delicious and eat it anyway (lie).

B. Praise the effort, but don't comment on the flavor (silence).

C. Thank them, and propose that you cook it together next time so you can adjust the recipe (truth).

4. You arrive late to a meeting because you overslept. What do you do when you enter the meeting?

A. Apologize and say traffic was terrible (lie).

B. Just apologize for being late without giving a reason (silence).

C. Confess to oversleeping and apologize (truth).

5. A child asks you if Santa Claus is real. You . . .

A. Say yes to keep the magic alive (lie).

B. Deflect attention from the question by asking what the child thinks (silence).

C. Explain the idea of giving to others without actually touching on the existence of Santa (partial truth).

6. At work, you find someone's unlocked mobile phone, which contains sensitive information. You . . .

A. Tell your colleagues that you've found something without revealing what it is (partial lie).

B. Keep it to yourself, and wait to see if they ask if anybody's seen it (silence).

C. Announce exactly what you found and where you found it (truth).

7. Your best friend's partner flirts with you. It makes you uncomfortable. What do you do?

A. Laugh it off as a joke if it ever comes up (lie).

B. Avoid the person in question and say nothing to your friend (silence).

C. Tell your friend what happened immediately (truth).

8. You accidentally see the price tag on a gift you received. It's much less than you expected and you're deeply disappointed. You . . .

A. Express your gratitude without mentioning the price (lie).

B. Make a joke about how they shouldn't have spent so much money on you (truth).

C. Never bring the price up because it's the thought that counts (silence).

9. A colleague asks your opinion on a sensitive issue that you'd prefer not to have to discuss at work. What do you do?

A. Maintain a neutral opinion to avoid controversy (lie).

B. Politely refuse to comment (silence).

C. Share your honest opinion despite the sensitivity of the topic (truth).

10. You're asked about your past experience during a job interview, and you lack an important credential. What do you do?

A. Exaggerate your experience slightly to improve your chances (lie).

B. Focus on your strengths and the things you can bring to the role (silence about weaknesses).

C. Be honest about your experience but express your eagerness to learn (truth).

This is how to interpret the results:

If you chose mostly As, you tend to prioritize the
   feelings of others or your own benefit over strict
   honesty.
Choosing mostly Bs indicates a preference for avoiding potential conflicts or discomfort, sometimes at
   the expense of full transparency.
If you chose mostly Cs, you value honesty and are
   willing to accept the consequences of truthfulness.

The next step is to reflect on your answers and consider
what each choice says about your values and your attitude
toward communication and ethics.

What's right and what's wrong? That's the challenge: knowing the difference.

LEARNING TO RELATE TO THE TRUTH

What conclusions can we draw from all this? Something
along these lines: The relationship between human beings
and the truth is anything but simple. While honesty remains
a celebrated virtue that we teach our children (they start lying between the ages of two and four, an important step in
their social and cognitive development), the implications of
relentless truth telling are complex. It's probably important
to strike a balance between truthfulness and compassion,
and to appreciate the nuances of human interaction and the
subjective nature of what people often hold as "truth." Ulti-

mately, it's not so much about avoiding the truth as it is about delivering it with tact, empathy, and understanding.

One of my favorite lines of all time comes from a film with Sandra Bullock and Hugh Grant. The film is *Two Weeks Notice,* and the character Sandra Bullock plays in it is prim, straightforward, and honest.

Hugh Grant's character doesn't like that at all, and tells her: *No one wants to live with a saint. Saints are boring.*

There is actually something to this, of course.

Truth, as we have seen, is a complicated thing that can't be easily defined. Approaching truth carefully and feeding it with good intentions makes it easier to handle. However, when we turn our backs on it and resort to using its great enemy, lying, it has a way of punishing us in the end by making a sudden and unexpected appearance. On those occasions, it can really sting.

Although the truth is supposed to set us free, as the old saying goes, it can be incredibly difficult to accept. This is particularly true when people throw the truth about us in our faces.

INFAMOUS LIARS

Anna Anderson

If one is to be called a liar,
one may as well make an effort to deserve the name.
—A. A. MILNE

We discussed silence in the previous chapter. Now, I'd like to tell you about somebody who was uniquely skilled at taking this to its absolute extreme.

In 1920, a suicidal woman was pulled out of a canal in Berlin. She refused to reveal her identity and was taken into care. After two years, she suddenly announced that she was Anastasia Romanov, the daughter of the murdered tsar of Russia.

Many people found her beautiful and believed her to be the real Anastasia. She even had scars that she claimed had been left by the knives of the Bolsheviks who killed her family. She told a story about how a soldier had found her alive and helped her escape to the West.

Over the next few years her following grew, and she became acquainted with one Gleb Botkin. He was the son of the Romanovs' family doctor who had been executed along with his patients during the Russian Revolution. Many of the Romanovs' relatives and acquaintances interviewed the woman, and they were impressed by her resemblance to Anastasia and her knowledge of the family. However, others were skeptical, mainly because she was unable to account for important details and crucial events in the life of the real Anastasia.

The biological uncle of the real Anastasia eventually hired a private detective to determine the identity of the woman who was claiming to be Anastasia. He eventually discovered that she was really Franziska Schanzkowska, a Polish-German factory worker who had disappeared in 1920. She had been injured in a factory explosion in 1916, which explained the scars on her body.

This is where the scam could have ended—especially if people had given the whole story a bit more thought. Sometimes, though, I think people choose to be fooled just to enjoy the excitement of being part of a fascinating life story. And don't you agree that it would be more appealing if this woman really were the daughter of the tsar rather than an ordinary factory worker? The truth was a lot less romantic, in this case. The impostor would probably have agreed, because her plans didn't end there.

In 1928 she suddenly appeared in New York, where she informed journalists at a press conference that she was visiting the United States to have her jaw restored. She claimed that it had been broken by a Bolshevik soldier after her escape from the execution of the family of the Russian tsar. Now, remember that there was no internet in those days, and most people didn't have a telephone. TVs were far from common in people's homes, and the radio stations of the world had more problems to report on after the protracted First World War.

However, she was treated like a celebrity and began to attend high-class parties and stay at expensive hotels. The woman, who became known as Anna Anderson, continued her struggle to have her fictitious identity recognized, losing several major court cases as a consequence. In 1968, she married a history professor (ironic, much?) and became a permanent resident of the United States. She didn't pass away until 1984.

Eventually, DNA technology was invented, and a sample that had been preserved after a minor operation she had undergone was compared with DNA samples from a living relative of the Romanov family—the duke of Edinburgh. It was also tested for matches with the recently discovered bones of Alexei, the son of Tsar Nicholas who had been murdered along with the rest of his family.

I think you can guess what the outcome was. There was no match. The final nail in the coffin for the romantic fairy tale of Anna Anderson was the fact that her DNA did match that of the grandson of Franziska Schanzkowska's sister, Karl

Maucher. It was finally proven, once and for all, that Anna Anderson was the missing factory worker, not the last surviving member of the Russian tsarist family.

This was the end of a beautiful, although somewhat depressing, tale. Why would anyone do such a thing? Did Anna Anderson believe that she was the missing Anastasia? Was she simply crazy? Or had she just hatched an idea that might become her livelihood?

Who knows? My own theory is that she was a highly motivated fraudster, who also possessed a number of narcissistic, or even psychopathic, traits. She was a parasite in human form who had figured out a way to make a living without having to work. She also had an instinctive appreciation for the principle that if you're going to tell a lie, you might as well make it a big one.

This story also proves something: It is actually possible to tell very big lies and get away with it. At least for a while.

3

What Is a Lie and What Is *Not* a Lie?

A bald spot is like a lie.
The bigger it gets,
the harder it is to cover it up.
—UNKNOWN

Chapter 2 was all about the truth. Now, let's move on to this question: What is a lie? Agreeing on what a lie actually is may not be the easiest thing in the world, but it might be possible. If we google the term, we'll be presented with lots of different variations.

The shortest definition of a lie I found is this: A lie is lying. Well, why not?

THE ANATOMY OF A LIE

Very simply, a real lie can be thought of as the opposite of the truth. If it's the middle of the day and someone tries to tell you that it's dark as midnight, that would definitely be a lie. Unfortunately, things are rarely that black and white.

I've given a lot of thought to where the line between possible untruths and outright lies ought to be drawn. Here's how I would like to formulate it:

A lie is an *intentionally* false statement or deceptive act, deliberately stated or performed with the aim of manipulating or deceiving others. It's when I know that I'm about to say something that I'm fully aware is less than truthful.

I might tell my wife that I have no idea why her new sports bag isn't in the wardrobe. That would be an ugly lie, supposing I had borrowed it without asking her, and then managed to leave it on the roof of my car twenty miles from our home. On the other hand, who knows where it actually blew off?

Conversely, suppose she's running around looking for it and my actual suspicion is that she herself left it on the roof of the car and lost it that way—and I tell her I don't know where it is. Quite different situations, right?

Either way, the bag would still be lost forever.

The anatomy of a lie also includes several key components.

The intention to mislead or hide the truth is only the first part. This intention, of course, is the very motivation for the lie, which is formed out of self-interest to avoid punishment or criticism or to gain an advantage over somebody. The motive for the lie is its very driving force.

The second part of a lie usually involves a fabrication of information or a distortion of actual facts. This can involve exaggeration, omission, or even outright invention of new facts. Liars deliberately modify or manipulate the truth to fit their desired narrative and to help them achieve their devious aims.

For example, I might say that I've never seen that scratch on the car door before. I might add that I thought I saw the neighbor parked rather close last week, as the scratch is on the passenger side. Or I might simply add that I saw a strange moped down in the garage, and that I saw the driver scratch the whole side of the car with a screwdriver. There are various ways I might cover up the fact that I'm a bad driver.

Another aspect of a lie is the verbal or nonverbal communication that goes into it. Lies can be conveyed through words, gestures, facial expressions, and actions. Verbal lies, of course, include false claims, misleading information, or claims that completely contradict reality.

Many liars will exaggerate their gestures and expressions to show their surprise at hearing that nobody has called the important customer back. They were so sure the task had been assigned to somebody else. They roll their eyes at this incompetence—knowing full well, of course, that they were the ones who dropped the ball.

Nonverbal cues, however, like avoiding eye contact or showing nervousness, can also accompany lies and offer subtle indications of possible deception.

Many people struggle with making eye contact, but people who don't normally have an issue with it might start looking at their shoes more than usual.

Furthermore, a lie is characterized by a deliberate disregard for or violation of someone's trust. By lying, the liar undermines the trust of the recipient. It's a transgression against the social contract that dictates that everyone act honestly and truthfully and never lie for personal gain.

Finally, a successful lie will naturally depend on winning the trust of the deceived party. The liar tries to convince the recipient that their fraudulent story is true. They might achieve this by skillful fabrication, manipulation of emotions, or exploitation of other people's prejudices.

Now, are all lies equally serious? My personal answer would be no. Some lies are very serious, while others should be treated as more or less harmless.

In Cold Blood

In human interactions, where words and actions are in a state of constant interplay, lying emerges as a complex and intriguing behavior. While white lies and innocent exaggerations are widely accepted in ordinary interactions because they are ultimately well-intentioned, real lies are something else entirely.

A real lie is a deliberate attempt to present a version of events or facts that the liar knows to be untrue. It is a deliberate deviation from the truth, often designed to deceive or manipulate another party.

A core component of the concept of real lies is intent. It's not enough to simply be misinformed, the underlying motive is an essential part. This is similar to the legal distinction between premeditated murder (intentional) and manslaughter (unintentional). The victim's fate is the same in both cases, but the reason for the act is different.

Someone might unknowingly pass on false information. This doesn't really qualify as a lie because there's no intention to mislead. A real lie has a purpose, and there needs to be a conscious choice to mislead. Someone chooses to lie in order to achieve something.

Of course, different motives can bring different individuals to lie. Some do it for personal benefit whether this be securing a job, earning someone's trust, or gaining some tangible reward. Others lie to evade consequences such as punishment or embarrassment. Then we have the lies that are told to protect someone's feelings or keep the peace. Whatever the specific reason, the essence of these lies remains the same: a deliberate deviation from the truth that is made to pursue a clear intention. We'll be returning to this in the chapter titled "The Real Reasons We Lie."

WHITE LIES

I don't think it would be too bold to claim that most people would be far more prepared to forgive a white lie than a "real" lie.

The word "lie" is very old. The concept of "white lies," however, is more recent.

The *Oxford English Dictionary* traces the origins of the expression to the fourteenth century. "White" is traditionally associated with goodness or purity, while "black" signifies evil or darkness.

By the way, the use of "white" here has nothing to do with ethnicity. Another example of this is black magic and white magic.

But what *is* a white lie? I carried out a very limited survey among my acquaintances to find out. Most people agree that white lies are lies that don't really matter (which is actually a curious idea, as there seems to be no point in lying in the first place if it doesn't matter).

How did you like the dinner? Oh, it was good.

Rather than admit that the steak was tough, the sauce was

sticky, the potatoes were cold, and the wine was undrink-able, we say that everything was as it should be. Very few people would be offended by a simple lie like that. It's mostly told to avoid embarrassing the chef (if you're at a friend's house) or to avoid making a scene (if you're in a restaurant).

And I'd have to agree. What harm can it do? I've said it myself hundreds of times. *The food was fine.* How do I deal with it afterward? I don't go back. Most people I've spoken to are understanding of this kind of behavior.

Or suppose I decline an invitation to a party on the grounds that I'm not feeling well, but actually have a different reason not to go.

This brings us to an interesting question: What is the reason to decline that I'm hiding that makes the whole thing a white lie rather than something considerably more deceptive?

Declining Peter's Party Invitation

Let's examine this through a series of different scenarios. First, let's suppose I receive a dinner invitation that doesn't particularly excite me.

Peter calls to invite me to a party. I actually like Peter, he's a nice bloke, and he's funny and pretty entertaining. However, I tell him that I can't go because I'm not feeling well. I have no idea how it is that I already know how I'm going to be feeling on Friday.

Now, imagine some different reasons for my saying this:

I'm actually not feeling very well at the moment, and I'm afraid I won't be able to recover by Friday. So my answer contains a degree of speculation regarding my future health.

Is this an adequate reason to disappoint Peter? Maybe it is, maybe it isn't.

I actually feel healthy as ever, but I'm exhausted after an intense few weeks of work.

If I had known Peter better, I might have been comfortable with telling him the truth: I simply don't have the energy to spend a whole evening in polite company. Staying up late with a bunch of people I don't know that well would only make me even more exhausted. Perhaps Peter would counter this objection with a refreshing appeal to the idea that a party is probably just what I need. And do you know what? He could very well be right about that. But I don't want to go.

How about this one:

I don't know Peter well enough to want to visit his house and meet his other friends. This one is tricky. The only way to get to know someone, obviously, is spending more time with them. But being the way I am, I decide that it's better to blame my health.

In fact, I suspect that Peter may have invited me just to be polite and is secretly hoping that I will decline.

This is just speculation, or even pure imagination on my part.

Maybe I don't like Peter's wife. In my eyes, she's a ghastly woman who's full of prejudice against just about everything. No, thank you.

Obviously, saying that is out of the question. Far better, then, to claim to be feeling a bit under the weather.

I don't enjoy parties. However, admitting to that is like saying you don't like going on holiday. People will give you quizzical looks, and the whole thing will be an embarrassment.

I could go on: lack of time, sick children, general logistics issues, because Peter has the poor taste to live where he lives, or just about anything you could think of. And I'd guess most people reading this can relate to all these reasons. It's a string of white lies, pure and simple.

But how about this (real-life) reason why I lied about not wanting to go to his party:

I had already been invited to another party at Steven's house. I'm going to be attending that party instead.

Now, suppose Peter and Steven are bitter enemies for some reason or other. They can't stand each other, and would never accept being neglected in favor of the other. I know about this already, of course, and will now have to keep it a secret that I went to Steven's party. For months, or even years.

Is what I've produced in this case a little, white, innocent lie—a harmless fudging of the truth committed so as not to upset my good friend Peter—or have I lied straight to his face?

What do you think?

Entangled in White Lies

If Peter had been a casual acquaintance, none of this would have mattered much. But in this case, we know each other quite well, and I don't want to hurt him. Is that reason enough to lead someone down the garden path? This is where the real problem enters the picture: When we're endangering a valuable relationship, things get a lot more complicated.

Telling a friend that they look terrific in a horribly ill-fitting outfit is something we've all done. It's a white lie.

But what if someone finally tells them the truth? *My God, don't you look a mess?* And suppose our friend realizes that this is the truth? If that happens, I might very well be confronted with having lied, and I would be in danger of losing face—and perhaps even a friend.

In those situations, it's far easier to just go along when a colleague at work expresses a volatile opinion just to preserve the harmony of the group. I wouldn't run much risk by withholding my real opinions.

You look great in green. *(Not even Kermit the Frog looks good in green.)*

I like Labradors, too. *(As long as they don't come anywhere near me because I'm actually terrified of dogs.)*

Yes, I agree, Thailand *has* gone downhill these last few years. *(I've actually never been there, but I'll be damned if I'm going to admit that.)*

It's fine that you scratched my car, it's an old banger, anyway. *(I almost lost my mind when I saw the scratch, but since you start crying whenever I criticize anything you've done, I'll pretend it doesn't matter. Who could handle all that drama every week?)*

The list could fill this whole book:

Yes, she's such a great actress! *(Who's that?)*

I apologize for being late for work, the traffic was horrendous today! *(I could barely bring myself to get to work today. Again.)*

That was delicious! *(Dear God, please don't offer me another serving!)*

Unfortunately, I just ate—I would have loved to join you. *(I'd rather starve than have to listen to you chattering for a whole lunch hour.)*

I like your new hairdo! Where did you get it done? *(I want to make sure I don't ever go there by mistake.)*

Of course I remember you! How long has it been? *(Who IS this?)*

Wow, I've always wanted a brass mortar! Thanks *so* much! *(Everyone knows that stone mortars are better—what were you thinking?)*

I'm terribly sorry for not replying to your message—my phone never notified me. *(Actually, it did, but I didn't feel like spending my Saturday night in a nonsensical text message exchange with you.)*

Well, the *X* party's proposal sounds good to me. *(The party's leader sounds like a total psychopath, but what do I know?)*

The biggest challenge of telling a white lie is having to maintain and manage all of its potential consequences. Once a white lie has been told, it can commit you to telling a whole web of additional lies just to sustain the deception, and this can all get difficult to keep track of. If the truth ends up never being revealed, a white lie can cause feelings of guilt or add strain to relationships, since the discovery of deception can damage the trust you've built.

Further, white lies can cement misconceptions, which can cause significant challenges in future communications with the person in question.

For instance, there is the time when I was staring at a bush in my garden a few years ago, considering whether I should prune it or not. My neighbor comes up to me and asks what I'm doing, and I tell him that I'm thinking about *how* to prune it. This is a very helpful neighbor, so he says he doesn't know how to do it, either, but that he knows of a great gardener who might be able to do it. Do I want him to check with his contact?

Seeing as he only wanted to help, I replied that it would be very kind of him, and that I'd be happy to receive some advice.

The first problem this caused was that I could no longer prune the bush then and there, as I had originally intended, because I had just claimed that I didn't know how to do it. If I had gone at it immediately, the whole thing would have seemed very strange.

Fortunately, I had some other gardening chores to attend to.

But that wasn't the end of my problems. Since a white lie can often be very innocent and meaningless, this in turn means that people often fail to remember telling it.

So the neighbor gets back to me a week later to tell me that he has discussed the matter with his esteemed contact, the popular and busy gardener. So now I get a whole account of how that rather dull shrub should best be handled.

But having forgotten what I said just a week before, in my surprise I blurt out, *I know that, of course.* My neighbor is offended and I can't understand why. That is, until I get back inside the house and remember our previous conversation.

This story is quite innocent, of course, but it still highlights the dangers of telling white lies. Even little innocent fibs like that can cause a lot of complicated problems with other people and affect how they perceive you.

What should I have told him the first time? That I'd manage fine trimming the damned bush all by myself, but thanks all the same for the offer.

LYING REQUIRES A CREDIBLE STRATEGY

When you decide to lie, this triggers a particular cognitive process: You need to be clear about the truth—*I took the money*—before you can construct a remotely plausible lie—*someone else took the money, probably Roger.*

This story must then be kept consistent in order for the lie to remain undetected. This takes effort, memory, and sometimes even additional lying as it becomes necessary in order to support the first one. Real lying isn't an accidental act, it is a fully conscious decision that requires energy.

But the beauty of it all is that this is the very reason why it's quite easy to spot a liar. Most people aren't able to carve out sufficiently credible strategies for their lies. And that, I suggest, is why we often get a funny feeling when somebody tells us a lie. Something about it doesn't add up. We don't always know what it is, but we can tell that something isn't right. The various parts of the lie simply don't fit together.

Becoming a good liar takes practice, but I would advise you to avoid that kind of practice. On the other hand, it makes sense to train yourself to detect signs of lying and deception in others. There's almost always a pattern to be found, but spotting it can take some time. We'll be getting back to this, too.

The Ethical Aspects

While the cognitive aspects of lying are fascinating, it is the ethical ones that tend to be the focus of discussions of the topic.

Every culture and every system of morals ostensibly holds truth to be a virtue. The notion that lying a little is perfectly fine has never been stated in any government decree, never been included in the values statement of an organization, and never been part of anyone's marriage vows.

Honesty is universally preferred, and lies are condemned in general. Evidence of these attitudes is everywhere, but it doesn't fairly reflect the genuine, underlying truth.

The reason for this universal condemnation is the potential damage that lies can cause. Real lies can destroy trust, break relationships, be punishable by law, and even bring far-reaching societal consequences.

One example of this is the repeated claims by US government officials that they had evidence of the existence of weapons of mass destruction in Iraq. In hindsight, they had to confess that what they had claimed was quite far from the truth. And that they may even have realized this at the time. The consequences of those lies were devastating for many people.

Nevertheless, it's important to recognize that lies exist along a spectrum of sorts. While white lies are often considered harmless or even necessary, real lies, given their intent and potential consequences, are held to be unethical.

Moreover, in our present-day digital age, the concept of lying has taken on new dimensions. Thanks to the anonymity offered by the internet, lies can be spread more easily and quickly than ever before. False information, outright fabrications, and misleading stories spread at the speed of the internet (I almost wrote *at the speed of light,* but even if that would have sounded cooler, it wouldn't have been entirely true), blurring the lines between reality and deception. Naturally, this only makes critical thinking and media literacy even more important, as the traditional concept of a lie has evolved in the light of recent technological advances. As a result, we're all forced to somehow try to keep a cool head.

WHAT *ISN'T* A LIE?

We have examined the truth. We have examined lies. But what is there in between the two? A lot, as it happens.

One specific kind of behavior in this area is something that we're all guilty of. I did it just this morning. When I was asked how I was doing, I replied, *I'm fine.*

For a variety of completely uninteresting reasons, I was actually far from fine, but this particular white lie is one that we've all resorted to when we wanted to get out of having to tell people about our miserable lives. Sometimes it can be a way to avoid having to share your misfortunes in the wrong situation. But other times, it's actually the opposite of that. Sometimes it's a cry for help, a lie told in the hope that the other person will ask more questions. Crossing the line and letting an outsider know that you're feeling bad about something isn't easy to do.

Withholding the Truth

There are other effective ways to lie, of course. For instance, we can withhold all or part of the truth. Teenagers tend to be very good at this, for example.

You weren't out all night, were you?, says the worried parent.

No, the teenager replies, *we went straight to Maja's place.*

The fact that they went straight there at five in the morning is more than Mum needs to know. And technically, it's night until six o'clock, isn't it? So no, I wasn't out *all* night.

If we approach this from an ethical and moral point of view, the lines between telling the truth, withholding information, and lying are often blurred. What's the deal, then? Are you lying if you don't tell the whole story? While the answer to this may seem simple, we're entering a complex landscape here where context, intentions, and consequences all play important roles.

Let's start with what we've already agreed on: A lie is a false statement given with the intention to deceive.

However, not telling the whole story, or withholding certain facts because it suits me, can't necessarily fit into that same definition. The gray area here depends largely on the motives for withholding information and how much potential there is for it to be misleading.

From an ethical point of view, truthfulness is upheld as a virtue because mutual trust is the foundation for functioning relationships. Sticking to the truth is crucial for building and maintaining that trust. If someone were to consistently withhold critical information, they could be perceived as untrustworthy, even if they have technically never told a lie. This can undoubtedly bring about the same sense of having been cheated.

The philosopher Immanuel Kant even proposed that lying by omission is unethical, as it manipulates the agency of a fellow human being. By withholding information, we tamper with other people's ability to make informed decisions. The consequences of this are exactly the same as those of telling a lie.

Reasons for Lying

There are, of course, times when withholding truth is done for malicious reasons. A truly hardened liar will stop at nothing when it comes to concealing the truth. Naturally, some people will give incomplete status reports in a professional context in the hopes of outmaneuvering competitors and securing a promotion for themselves.

Of course, an unfaithful wife won't simply tell you that she took a long lunch to meet her lover and that this is why she wasn't in the office when her husband came around. She might refrain from actually lying and just say she was out to lunch. Which, technically speaking, may well be true.

And, of course, it'll be hard going to bring the truth that a teenager's mates are selling drugs to light. But that section of the lying spectrum is obvious. Nobody expects criminals to tell the truth. I find it more interesting—and definitely more challenging—to make sense of the lies of people you would actually expect to be telling the truth.

But there's more to this. The context will also influence the intent and outcome of the lie. When there is a surprise birthday party planned, friends might omit details or give partial truths in order to keep the party a secret. The intention here isn't to mislead, it's to make someone happy. Like the time my sister, entirely against my will, organized a sing-along party for my fiftieth birthday. While I didn't appreciate that at all, I didn't cause a fuss about it because I knew she meant well. She's the greatest sister in all the world, actually. (And yes, she will read this book, and I love her very dearly.)

Moreover, in professional fields like medicine or law, doctors and lawyers will sometimes withhold information to prevent unnecessary stress or panic in the belief that this is ultimately in the best interest of their patients or clients. In cases like that, we might well regard their behavior as a benevolent kind of omission. But this still raises a different moral question: Who gets to decide which information it is justifiable to withhold?

If we're considering treating withholding information as somehow equivalent to lying, we'll need to evaluate the consequences. If leaving parts of the story out leads to an incorrect conclusion or causes harm, an omission may be the ethical equivalent of an outright lie. For example, somebody who's selling a secondhand car might not be lying as such when they fail to disclose all of their car's known defects, but the omission will nonetheless cause problems, and most people would say it can't be ethically justified.

You didn't ask if the brakes worked. You only have yourself to blame.

I've been the victim of this kind of lying myself, and now, I ask a lot of questions, enough of them to drive some people up the wall. Some take this as a matter of questioning their integrity, but I simply want to know this: What exactly is going on here?

Personal beliefs and upbringing also play a role. Some individuals may have been raised to believe that any deviation from the absolute truth, including omission, is a lie, while others may regard omission as a permissible strategy for avoiding conflict or harm.

We all have a friend like that. The kind of person who will happily point out every potential risk and problem in the interest of openness and honesty. This can often deflate people's motivation to carry on entirely. And this is where problems arise.

Our reaction will tend to be to find the person in question to be incredibly negative. But it could be that all they're doing is pointing out genuine challenges. If that's the case, this means that we don't actually want the whole story. We want to hold on to our delusion that everything will be fine. And maybe it will, I don't know. Maybe we've just been to a seminar on positive thinking.

As usual, the central issue here is the intention behind the withholding of facts. If information is omitted with the aim of misleading someone, this is tantamount to lying. On the other hand, if details are left out unintentionally or because they are determined to be irrelevant, we ought *not* call it a lie. The seller may have had no idea that the car's brakes weren't working properly. In that case, it wasn't even a lie. It was just plain old bad luck.

To successfully navigate this gray area, it's important to be introspective and evaluate your own motives for withholding information. Basically, you need to take a look in the mirror. After all, the crux of this issue is humanity's eternal quest for truth and trust, the two pillars that support the bridges of all human contact.

My Friend Christian—A Sad Example

A good friend of mine—let's call him Christian—would often take detours when he drove home from work. His wife began to notice that he kept arriving home later and later (this was before the age of mobile phones—I know, it sounds like ancient history, but there really was such a time), but she couldn't understand why.

When she asked him about it, he told her that there had been a lot of traffic and that he'd needed to take some detours. However, the wife was a resourceful woman so she decided to listen to the traffic reports. No traffic jams that day. So she confronted him again: Why are you taking detours when you drive home?

He explained to her that he was stressed and needed some alone time to think.

That's a perfectly good reason, but it wasn't the whole truth, of course. If his wife had asked him what it was he needed to think about, he would probably have lied. But she never asked, and he never said anything. Until, that is, it was already too late.

The thing that was stressing him out, that he needed to think about, was that he felt controlled by her. All of her questions and poking around in what he regarded as his private sphere had made him feel stifled.

Was this a major concern?

Well, that depends on how you view the way it all ended—in divorce. You see, her lack of interest in what was stressing him out and his inability to tell the whole truth would eventually lead to a rather messy breakup.

Things are often more complicated than they first appear. Perhaps he could have told her the whole truth, and perhaps that would have led to a fruitful conversation about their marriage or counseling—I don't know. Perhaps she would simply have left him sooner. I really don't know, and neither do either of them.

LYING WITH GOOD INTENTIONS

Of course, half-truths and deliberate omissions can have just as great an impact as outright lies, if not even greater. Withholding the truth brings us to a moral gray area where the boundary between lies and complicity is challenged and ethical dilemmas arise.

It's crucial to understand the underlying reasons why somebody chooses to withhold the truth. In some cases, they may believe that sharing worrying news might cause more harm than leaving someone in the dark. Rather than telling their child that the doll might not be repairable, the parent says it's going to be fine. This is actually a common problem. You refrain from telling the whole truth—even if everything else you said was genuinely true—because you don't want to upset a child. Or an adult, for that matter.

We'll investigate the noise from under the car, but it's probably nothing. But actually, the mechanic recognizes that the whole car is really a rusty wreck that's going to fall apart at any moment. To salvage some of the hard-pressed car owner's hope, they'll look a little closer to see if they can find any positives to report back.

Undoubtedly, though, the act of withholding significant truths can have huge implications for both the liar and those affected by their deception. People who have big secrets to keep can develop feelings of immense guilt, anxiety, and shame. This mental burden can quickly manifest itself in deteriorating mental health, depression, and other fragile emotional states.

Of course, this doesn't apply to people who exhibit narcissistic or psychopathic personality traits. This is a whole different issue (you can read more about it in chapter 8), but these individuals simply aren't affected the same way the rest of us are. They don't like being exposed as the notorious liars they really are, but deceiving everyone constantly doesn't give them the slightest problems sleeping at night. If you want to know more about these two personality disorders, I can recommend my previous books *Surrounded by Psychopaths* and *Surrounded by Narcissists*.

Moreover, this kind of lying undermines the trust that keeps relationships going. Of course, divulging part of the truth rather than all of it isn't exactly conducive to an atmosphere of mutual trust. The strain of keeping unpleasant truths secret can grow exponentially through a kind of domino effect, and eventually upset the balance of both our personal and our professional relationships. The person you're withholding the truth from will probably have a feeling that something's missing, but won't know what it is. This will only lead to uncertainty, and it definitely isn't a solid foundation for a functioning relationship.

A Dishonest Act of Mine

The behavior I just mentioned above is a form of lying I've been guilty of myself, as it happens. An acquaintance of mine had been struggling with his finances for some time. After a harrowing divorce, his bank account had taken some really hard knocks. I'm by no means a saint, but I promised early on that I would help him get through the situation—both by helping him honor his commitments and by helping him make a plan for how to deal with his rather difficult situation.

Being a former banker, I'm quite well-versed when it comes

to how banks and the tax authorities make judgments, and I soon recognized that he was going to face some immediate, and rather serious, problems. My good friend was about to lose everything he owned with the possible exception of the clothes on his back. His future looked anything but bright, to put it mildly.

I promised to help him in any way I could. My first impulse was to live as I teach, give him the truth, and make him fully aware of the peril he was in. Most of all, I wanted to get through to him and make it clear that if he didn't address his situation immediately, with vigor and determination, he and his two daughters would end up living on welfare for many years to come.

But when I saw his anguish over the situation he was in, essentially through no fault of his own, I just couldn't do it. Instead, I decided to give him all the hope I could, and let him believe that we would be able to resolve his situation quite successfully.

You realize, of course, that I'm simplifying this account a great deal. But that's not important. The point I want to make is this: If I had told him what was happening—that the clock was ticking, and that the debt collectors were closing in—he would have lost all hope. I was simply afraid that he was going to do something really stupid if he realized that he might not be able to get out of his precarious situation.

We worked away at it. He kept struggling to untangle himself from everything. I supported him in every way I could and kept repeating that everything was going to work out. I told him it might feel bleak, but that there was hope. In the end, we found some positives to latch on to. He's fundamentally a strong person, and once he got some momentum, I began to let more of the truth in and emphasized the importance of not giving up.

I thought he would be able to address issues he should already have resolved long ago, as long as he could just regain some motivation first. And sure enough, several years later, his situation is still not exactly perfect, but things are definitely looking up.

This whole affair has kept me up at night a number of times.

Did I do the right thing? Was keeping the truth from him really ethically and morally defensible? *You're on the brink of ruin, mate.* Would he have been even more motivated if I had told him the truth? Or would he just have crumbled under the pressure?

As I said, I'm definitely not a saint, and I've made some pretty serious misjudgments along the way. But I've always told myself that I did it for everyone's best. For my good friend, for his daughters, and even for myself. Of course, my doubts have been somewhat alleviated by the fact that he's been able to get back on his feet, partly thanks to my efforts. So I feel good about it.

But no, I wasn't honest with him. And that still torments me to some extent. One day, he'll realize how close he came to losing everything he spent more than twenty years working for, and that I, supposedly his best friend, didn't level with him about it. So yes, things can get sticky in this particular gray area.

STUDYING THE MOTIVE

The most common motive for withholding the truth is probably the fear of the consequences that openly revealing certain information might bring. I would guess that many find temporary relief in hiding the truth from their loved ones, employers, or society at large in the hopes that they will be able to avoid unwanted consequences that might shatter the lives they know.

Anxiety and doubt tend to invade various aspects of life when reality fails to meet expectations, and these emotions can erode the trust you could normally achieve. So yes, good intentions can expose people to risks.

The psychological consequence of deliberately withholding the truth is cognitive dissonance, a tension that's caused by holding conflicting beliefs or values. In plain English: It's going to feel wrong.

Accepting and internalizing withheld truths can force dramatic shifts in perspective and result in evasive behavior. These adaptations can cause what is referred to as toxic behavior. This behavior is rooted in a perceived need for protection from what one takes to be betrayal, and expresses itself through retribution, pent-up frustration, or isolation.

INFAMOUS LIARS

Anna Delvey

While we're on the topic of withholding some or all of the truth, we might take a look at a more contemporary con artist.

Anna Delvey, whose real name is Anna Sorokin, is infamous for her skillful fraud. She posed as a wealthy New York socialite and lived a lavish lifestyle that she couldn't actually afford. Her achievements constitute a striking example of how deception and manipulation can captivate the media and the public alike.

Anna Sorokin, a Russian-born woman, arrived in New York City in 2014 with dreams of becoming a prominent art collector and entrepreneur. Posing as a wealthy German heiress named Anna Delvey, she employed a combination of charm, confidence, and fabrications to infiltrate the city's elite and most luxurious environments. Her extensive falsehoods all centered on the claim that she was an heiress. It was never revealed to whom she was an heiress or what she had supposedly inherited. She manipulated people with such a remarkable degree of control that I can only assume she must be a very special kind of person.

One of the most striking examples of Sorokin's deceptions was her attempt to convince a bank to grant her a loan of $22 million to finance a private art club. She submitted falsified financial documents and wove a web of lies in support of her claim that she had significant sums available for investment. However, the bank grew suspicious and denied her the loan. They questioned why she needed to borrow all that money if she was already so wealthy . . .

But the attempt itself is very impressive. Imagine trying to swindle someone into giving you $22 million. That certainly takes some gall.

Sorokin stayed in some of New York's most exclusive hotels. She visited fine dining restaurants and flaunted her alleged wealth by paying for extravagant meals. However, many of her credit card transactions were rejected due to insufficient funds. To maintain the illusion, she often convinced friends and acquaintances to cover her expenses by promising to reimburse them later. Of course, she never did. When I say *friends and acquaintances,* I might as well call them *resources.* This kind of person doesn't really have friends the way you and I do.

One of her more sensational lies involved an unpaid bill at the luxurious 11 Howard hotel. Having stayed there for several months without paying her bill, she managed to convince the hotel staff that her funds were temporarily tied up in a fund and that she would pay in full as soon as they were released. Once again, they chose to believe her, despite the loud alarm bells that were going off all around her.

She had left a trail of unpaid bills and creditors in her wake, and you might think that she'd want to lay low at this point to avoid drawing attention to herself.

Oh no. Instead, Sorokin decided to host a grand art gala, promising that famous artists and celebrities would be present. She rented a prestigious venue and began soliciting donations and favors from various individuals and companies. However, as the date approached, it became clear that many of her claims had been outright lies. The artists and performers she had supposedly recruited had never even heard of her, and the whole event fell apart like a house of cards.

In 2017, her scheme collapsed entirely, as this type of fraud tends to do eventually. Anna Sorokin was arrested and charged with multiple counts of grand theft and other offenses related to her fraudulent activities. During the trial, the young woman who had masterfully manipulated everyone around her for personal gain was finally exposed for the fraud she was.

In 2019, Sorokin was found guilty and sentenced to four to twelve years in prison. At the time of this writing, she has been released from prison but is on house arrest and will remain so for some time. Will she have learned anything from her mistakes? No. My analysis, after studying her activities in detail, is that she is a full-blown psychopath.

Her ability to coldly, unscrupulously, and persistently swindle so many people out of such huge amounts of money indicates distinct psychopathic traits. Being able to walk into a bank and ask for $22 million without the slightest trepidation requires an almost inhuman degree of cool. Or damage to the part of the brain that controls stress and nervousness (the amygdala, which is underdeveloped in psychopaths).

She'll be older, but she won't be any wiser. She's bound to launch new scams at the first opportunity because that's what psychopaths do. They don't change, and they can't be cured. They're always going to be predators, helping themselves to anything the rest of us have to offer.

Does that sound a bit sinister to you?

I can imagine that it might. And it *is* sinister.

PS: Anna Sorokin's life has also been turned into a Netflix drama—*Inventing Anna*—in case you'd like to know more about her.

4

The Real Reasons We Lie

Once you'll stop telling lies about me,
I'll stop telling the truth about you.

—Unknown

hy people lie might seem obvious at first glance, but if you give it some thought, you'll no doubt realize that it can be a valuable observation to make to gain a better understanding of liars: Why do they—really—lie?

The temptation not to tell the truth, or the temptation to lie, can stem from various psychological, social, and situational factors. Who can really claim to know the specifics of that? People's reasons for lying can probably vary just as much as the contents of their lies.

NINE REASONS TO LIE

Obvious as it may seem, this is important, not only because it can be an aid in studying the world around us—also because it can give us insight into ourselves and help us reflect on why we behave as we do. Although I make no claim to have covered all possibilities, the following sections give some common examples of how people tend to behave when they feel that sharing the truth would be too difficult. Perhaps you can come up with more reasons if you give the matter some thought?

You Lie to Protect Yourself

People may lie to avoid punishment, judgment, or negative consequences. Lying can be a way to protect themselves from potential harm or negative consequences.

We sometimes think we can evade these consequences by concealing the truth. Here is an example most of us will recognize: Imagine a living room in which a cherished antique vase is prominently displayed on a shelf. The children in the room have been repeatedly warned by their parents not to play near the vase because of its sentimental and monetary value.

One day, while the parents are away, the son decides to play with a ball indoors with one of his friends. Naturally, the ball goes flying in the wrong direction, knocking the vase from its place and making it a thing of the past. When the parents return home and discover the smashed vase, they immediately ask their son what happened. Panicking, he tells them that he saw the cat knock it over.

Fearing the consequences of his actions, the son shifts the blame to the family cat, an innocent party who can neither confirm nor deny his accusation.

Though this is a simple example, it still reflects our basic human tendency to seek to avoid negative outcomes or judgments, and can manifest itself in countless ways in different scenarios and stages of life. The story doesn't present the cat's account of events.

You Lie to Protect Your Relationships

In some cases, people can lie to protect or maintain relationships. They might believe that telling the truth could hurt or disappoint others, and therefore, they choose to lie to avoid conflict or maintain harmony.

It makes perfect sense in the short term, of course. However, honesty can also serve as a catalyst for emotional closeness: Choosing to be honest is to invite our loved ones to experience our true selves, and can foster a more genuine connection based on mutual understanding and acceptance. Lying, on the other hand, raises a barrier that can get in the way of authentic exchanges of thoughts, feelings, and experiences.

Here's an example of a lie told to protect an existing relationship.

What do you think? Is this behavior right or wrong?

Imagine two people who have been best friends since secondary school. We can call them Emma and Sophia. Emma has always had a good memory for important dates. This year, she decides to organize a surprise party for Sophia. She's excited about how much fun it's going to be.

A few days before her birthday, Sophia mentions that she'd like for them to spend it together. Maybe they could go out for dinner or go to the cinema? Emma replies, "Oh, I might be too busy with work that day to meet up. I'm terribly sorry. Maybe we could celebrate the day after?"

Sophia is disappointed, naturally.

Emma's lie, of course, is told so as not to ruin the surprise. She believes that temporarily deceiving Sophia will allow her to give her an even better experience when the surprise is ultimately revealed. This lie isn't intended to harm Sophia, but simply to preserve the impact of the planned surprise. Emma values their relationship and hopes that the party will reveal the strength of their bond. And, with any luck, Sophia will appreciate the surprise.

Full disclosure: If somebody had done that to me, I would have had to reconsider our relationship. You see, I don't at all enjoy celebrating my birthday.

In this example, the lie isn't intended to mislead, but rather to maintain the relationship and protect the surprise that Emma believes will strengthen their bond. Nonetheless, it remains a lie.

You Lie for Personal Gain

This is certainly not a shocker, but there's no denying that many people lie to further their own interests. Lying can even be viewed as a legitimate way to gain an advantage, whether it be a matter of achieving personal goals, acquiring a competitive edge, or securing financial gains. People can lie to boost their reputation, enhance their CV, or manipulate situations in ways that favor them.

In a competitive world in which gaining an edge over others is often viewed as a path to success, lying can be a tempting strategy. Here's an example of how it can happen.

John is competing with several other candidates for a lucrative position at a prestigious technology company. The role requires a range of skills, including knowledge of a special piece of software that John is not at all familiar with. However, he's acutely aware that appearing to possess this expertise would significantly improve his chances of securing the job.

During the interview, naturally, John is asked about his knowledge of various software tools, and answers confidently: *Yes, I've done extensive work with X software on several projects over the last few years.* He even comes up with a fictitious project in which he supposedly used this particular software to optimize certain processes, in the hope that this will further impress the interviewers.

John's lie is a strategic move, intended to make him appear to be the ideal candidate for the position. By claiming to have expertise he doesn't have, he hopes to gain an advantage over other candidates and improve his chances of being chosen for the job. But what exactly is he thinking? He's thinking that if he gets the job, he can quickly learn how to use that software, or maybe delegate any tasks that require that specific skill.

In this example, the lie is designed to give John a competitive advantage in a situation where perceived competence can bring tangible benefits, for example, securing the desired position. However, this type of deception also carries significant risks, including reputational damage or even losing the position if the lie is ever exposed.

I've experienced this kind of deceit myself, and when it dawns on everyone that John doesn't even know what *X* software actually is, he's not going to enjoy what follows.

You Lie to Avoid Embarrassment

Lying can also be a way of hiding embarrassing truths. Some people embellish the truth or fabricate stories in order to present themselves in a more favorable light or hide their mistakes, flaws, and insecurities.

Embarrassment is certainly a deeply human emotion, and in vulnerable moments the temptation to lie to escape it can be great. However, lying to avoid embarrassment will require us to remember the details of our fabrications, and this will probably only reinforce our anxiety and fear over the possibility of being exposed.

What might it look like? Something like this, perhaps:

Rebecka is at a social event of some kind when she sees an acquaintance she hasn't seen for years. She remembers having some nice conversations with him, but frustratingly, she can't remember his name (which is David by the way) . . .

David walks up to her, smiling warmly, and says, *Rebecka! It's been such a long time! How have you been?*

To avoid the embarrassment of having to admit that she has forgotten his name, Rebecka replies, *Yes, it's been ages! It's so good to see you again!* She had hoped he might introduce himself to her, but when he doesn't, she decides to try to cover up her temporary memory lapse. Maybe he can tell that she can't place him and asks if she remembers him. But of course she recognizes him! At least, that's what she claims.

Rebecka's lie is motivated by a natural desire to save face and avoid the discomfort and embarrassment of having to admit that she has forgotten the guy's name. Who hasn't been in that situation? Honestly confessing to being unable to remember someone's name could suggest to them that you didn't find your previous encounters meaningful, even if that's not the case. By pretending to remember, Rebecka hopes to keep their relationship positive and avoid all sorts of discomfort.

Lying is, essentially, a defense mechanism we use to protect ourselves from potentially embarrassing situations, and to ensure the smooth continuation of a social interaction. And perhaps this kind of lying is forgivable?

You Lie to Gain Acceptance

What others think of us has always been important, regardless of what some people say. We all care what others have to say about us when we're not present, and that's simply all there is to it. Some people can even lie to gain acceptance or approval from others. They might lie to fit in with a certain group, to impress someone, or to avoid rejection. Social exclusion is something many people fear, and exploiting this fear can be a way for others to exercise power.

In our quest for acceptance and approval, lying can seem to be an attractive shortcut to fitting in or gaining validation from whatever group we currently find ourselves in. However, acceptance gained by lying will feel false to us. When other people accept us based on lies, what exactly is it they're accepting? Something that might not even exist.

Here's an example of how this could look.

Maja is a first-year university student, eager to fit in and make new friends. Some popular students that Maja looks up to are always talking about going to music festivals and seeing the latest indie bands play. Maja, on the other hand, has always been a fan of classical music and has never been to a music festival in her life.

When the group discusses their most epic music festival experiences from last summer and asks Maja about her own favorite concert experience, she replies, *Last summer I went to* (inserts the name of a popular festival she's heard about). *The atmosphere and the bands were incredible!* By claiming to have attended a music festival, she believes she will be able to relate better to their experiences and be accepted into their circle more easily. Her lie serves as a bridge to shared experiences and common interests.

In this example, lying is an expression of the universal human need for acceptance and belonging, which is particularly strong in new or unfamiliar social settings. I've actually done this precise thing myself. I even did it quite recently, as it happens.

At a dinner party attended by a bunch of people I didn't really know very well, who I was keen to make a good impression on, I heard everyone at the table voice their agreement that eating GMO food was wrong. I nodded and hummed to display discreet agreement. Why did I do this? Well, I had no idea what GMO food even was. When I was asked what it was that made me stop eating GMO food, I was in a pickle. I wanted to ask what the different potential reasons might be, but instead, I mumbled something about ethical consequences. Yes, it was wrong of me, but I have no issues with recognizing that I am human. We all are.

You Lie to Preserve Your Integrity

Lying can also be a way to protect one's privacy or preserve personal boundaries. Some might resort to lying to prevent an invasion of their privacy or to protect sensitive information.

We all need to maintain certain boundaries around our emotional, physical, and psychological spaces. Lying is a violation of these boundaries because it distorts or hides our innermost thoughts, feelings, or actions.

Is there an example here? Of course!

Tom is an artist on the rise, gaining a name for himself with his contemporary paintings. He's worked hard for years and is always on the lookout for opportunities to showcase his art. Finally, a well-known and influential art gallery approaches him and offers to produce an exhibition of his works. However, the curator has a specific theme in mind for the exhibition and wants him to make artworks that conform to that particular theme. This particular theme doesn't align in the slightest with Tom's personal beliefs and values, but he fears that refusing this offer might cause him to lose other future opportunities.

Tom explains that he's hugely honored by the offer and that he has been working on a series of paintings that he feels would be a good fit with the requested theme. However, due to prior commitments for another exhibition, he won't be able to create new works specifically for this theme within the time frame proposed by the gallery.

Here, Tom's lie becomes a kind of buffer, making him able to decline the offer without directly challenging the curator's vision or thwarting potential future collaborations. In this scenario, lying becomes a tool for preserving his personal integrity and artistic authenticity, albeit it at the risk of missing an opportunity.

I've done this myself, too. I refuse to work for tobacco companies, arms manufacturers, and gambling companies. It wouldn't align with my values. However, I'm always careful not to offend anyone, so I tend to refer to my busy schedule when I turn these offers down. Of course, now that I've admitted to this in writing, we'll have to see how long I can maintain that particular deception.

You Lie to Gain Control and Power

Of course, lying can be used to exercise control or power over others. For example, by manipulating information people can influence the perceptions, beliefs, or actions of others, thereby gaining the upper hand or an advantage in certain situations. Politicians from all camps do this constantly. Religious leaders do it. People promoting all varieties of opinions do it. Climate activists do it. Climate skeptics do it. Everyone does it.

In reality, genuine control can't reliably be maintained by means of deceptive behavior, as lies tend to be exposed sooner or later. When this happens, any credibility and authority gained will be lost or undermined. Moreover, manipulating the truth can foster an atmosphere of insecurity and suspicion. By emphasizing honesty and transparency, we can base our relationships on trust and respect, and these are far more conducive to cooperation and influence.

So what might this look like in a family? It could look any way, really, but here's an example.

Sarah and Ted have been married for several years and have two children. Sarah has always been the more dominant partner in the relationship, and she often makes quite significant family decisions without consulting Ted. She justifies this behavior by saying that she knows what's best for everyone.

Ted has often felt resentful about his lack of input into important family matters. Recently, he found a great school for their oldest son. He's excited about his discovery and believes it would be a perfect fit for his son's interests and needs.

But when Ted presents this idea at dinner, Sarah announces, *I've been told by several parents that the school you mentioned has had a lot of issues with bullying and poor academic performance.*

Ted is surprised at this, but he does some research and finds no evidence whatsoever to support Sarah's claims. When he confronts her, she stands by them, but is unable to provide any specific sources. She's basically arguing for the right to decide this matter as well.

Sarah's bluff is aimed at maintaining control over the family's decisions. By discrediting Ted's choice without justification, she attempts to steer the decision in the direction she wants. Or perhaps it's really just a matter of maintaining her dominant role within the family. That could well be the case, too.

This everyday scenario reveals how lying, even in seemingly mundane situations, can be used manipulatively to establish control and dominance over others and override their points of view and wishes.

In most relationships, one person will take the role of the alpha. This person will usually be used to getting to make the decisions, however, of course it isn't always the case that they would resort to outright lies to outmaneuver the other person. I hardly need to tell you how much damage this behavior can cause relationships in the long run.

Lies and Deception in the World of the Reptilians

Now, you might have been thinking that the flat-Earth theory is the craziest idea you've ever heard. Well, it's nothing compared to the idea that the earth is secretly ruled by lizard people masquerading as humans.

The reptilian conspiracy theory, which is based on the idea that the world is secretly ruled by some kind of shape-shifting reptilian humanoids, is one of the most bizarre and enduring conspiracy theories in contemporary culture. Trying to determine how anybody could even come up with something so preposterous is enough to make your head spin. However, despite the bizarre nature of this idea, plenty of people nonetheless seriously believe in this theory and try to convince others of its truth. If we can understand the potential motives behind this deception, that might shed light on why someone would try to convince you, or others, that the world really is run by lizard people.

Buckle up, and buckle up tight! Things are about to get weird.

The whole idea of this reptile conspiracy is thought to have originated in a story by the creator of the character Conan the Barbarian, Robert E. Howard. This particular story was based on theosophical ideas about the lost worlds of Atlantis and Lemuria, and referred to dragon men (you'll have to imagine some kind of beings with human bodies and the heads of snakes) whose powerful civilization once existed on some kind of lemurian continent.

Anyway, these guys were apparently able to take on human form at will, and lived in underground passages from where they used their shape-shifting and mind-controlling abilities to infiltrate human society. And now, some people claim that this actually happened, and that they exist all over society today, particularly in its highest circles.

I told you it was bonkers. Howard was actually a qualified lawyer. Embracing and promoting an idea as unusual as the reptilian conspiracy theory can give some people a sense of identity and make them feel like they belong to a unique subculture. Convincing others to believe in the theory serves to both reinforce the individual's own belief system and strengthen the bonds within the community.

As is the case with the flat-Earth theory, belief in the reptilian conspiracy theory often correlates with a deep-seated distrust of authority figures and institutions. By convincing others that the world is run by reptilian overlords, the proponents of the theory can encourage the rest of us to question and distrust people in power more broadly, and thus confirm their own skepticism. Are these lies or simply mistaken beliefs? That's a good question.

In a world that can often feel chaotic and unpredictable, belief in conspiracy theories of different kinds can offer a sense of control and order. The reptilian conspiracy implies that a hidden force is orchestrating global events, and that's an amusing detail in this particular context.

Promoting such an unusual theory will, of course, inevitably attract attention and perhaps even notoriety, both online and in the real world. Online posts related to the conspiracy of lizard men who are hiding among us have been widely distributed on social media platforms, and the proponents of the theory will often gain a following of like-minded individuals as well as the idly curious and nonbelievers. I imagine that a lot of people find watching the freak show from the sidelines quite fascinating. Again, insanely, there is a market for various products and events related to the reptilian idea. Convincing others to believe in the reptilian conspiracy can bring financial rewards through advertising revenue, sales of merchandise, and speaking engagements. I don't know what I find crazier, the people who live their lives taking this to be true, or the rest of us who have failed to point out how bizarre the notion they've dedicated their lives to actually is.

But as usual, the point of spreading disinformation and casting doubt on the nature of reality is that it allows you to manipulate and control others. It's quite logical, really.

If I can make you accept this lie, I can probably convince you of anything I like.

Anything.

I.

Like.

You Lie for Fear of Consequences

People can also lie because they are afraid to face the consequences of their own actions. They messed something up again, and they simply can't handle coming clean about it. So why not tell a lie? Whether it's owning up to a mistake, admitting a fault, or facing the legal consequences of your actions, the fear of negative reactions can motivate some people to lie.

However, this fear of consequences can cause us to isolate ourselves from others, creating further barriers. Lying perpetuates this isolation by preventing normal communication and building walls of distrust between people.

You want an example? Let's get a little more specific this time. In a medium-sized city, a chemical company has been operating a plant for several decades. Over the years, due to lax regulations and flawed oversight, the plant has been improperly dumping its chemical waste. Unbeknownst to the residents of the city, these harmful chemicals have slowly seeped into the main water supply, and now constitute a serious health hazard for thousands of people. Unfortunately, things like this happen from time to time in all parts of the world.

There has been a recent increase in health issues like unexplained illnesses and birth defects among the city's residents, particularly the children. An investigative journalist suspects that the water supply might be the source of the problems.

As rumors of this journalist's findings begin to circulate, city officials and the plant's management hold an emergency meeting. Fearing the massive backlash, legal consequences, financial damages, and general panic that this kind of news might cause—not to mention all the personal accountability this would entail—they decide to make a joint statement:

> *After thorough testing, we can definitively state that our water supply remains clean and uncontaminated. The recent health issues we've seen are completely unrelated, and are being investigated as separate incidents.*

Covertly, they initiate efforts to clean up the water supply and fix the leak, in the hope that they can rectify the situation before it becomes more widely known. My God, I think there have even been films made about stories like this.

City officials and plant management are almost paralyzed by their fear of the potential consequences of admitting the truth. They have messed up, and big-time.

What they fear, of course, is loss of public trust, potential prosecution for negligence, massive lawsuits, financial ruin, and the general chaos that might ensue if the public were to learn that they have been consuming contaminated water for years. Their lie becomes a desperate attempt to maintain order and control at the expense of the very people they are supposed to be protecting and serving. Essentially honest—although careless—people end up deceiving an entire community for fear of the consequences they might face.

You Lie Out of Habit

Sometimes things just happen. For some people, lying becomes a habitual pattern of behavior. This can stem from past experiences, a lack of consequences in the past, or a belief that lying is the easiest or most effective way to navigate social interactions. Who can say how this actually works for each and every one of us? However, bad habits like this form quickly, but are hard to break.

Here's how a seemingly innocent untruth might look: Emily has always disliked having to burden others with her problems. From a very young age, her automatic reaction has always been to say she is fine whenever someone asks her how she is, whether or not she actually was fine at the time. Over the years, this has almost become a reflex of hers.

One day, Emily's colleague Anna notices that Emily is obviously upset—her eyes are red, and she appears to be on the verge of tears. Concerned, Anna walks over to her and asks her how she is. *What's going on?* Without pausing to think or process this question, Emily immediately replies: *I'm fine, thanks.*

Emily's lie isn't fueled by some immediate desire to deceive or manipulate. It's just a deeply ingrained habit. Over time, her automatic response has become so natural to her that it happens without any conscious thought on her part, even if it happens to contradict her actual feelings. This common lie serves as a protective barrier. It excludes anything that might hurt her or prevent her from delving into and sharing her feelings with others, even when it would be in her interest to do so.

This *fine, thanks* reflex is a good example of how some lies can be the result of long-standing habits, often developed as coping mechanisms, and can be told even in the absence of any clear or immediate reason for deception.

LYING FOR MONEY

Now, there are some areas of life where you will find very specific reasons why some people will deliberately bend the truth a little (or even a lot). For instance, simply throwing a bag of money into the mix tends to cause countless complex problems to arise. Some people lie most shamelessly in these contexts.

I spent fifteen years working in sales training. In short, my job was to train salespeople of all kinds to help them get better at promoting their product or service and sell more of it. I can confirm, for certain, that there is good reason not to offer all salespeople your trust willy-nilly.

I've encountered salespeople who would lie about the side effects of a drug or keep the inspection reports for a used car secret from the buyer, and I've dealt with real estate agents who would tell the owner of a house to paint over the mold in the basement right before the viewing and then act dumb about it to the best of their ability.

It's important to note that while there certainly are those who will go to any lengths to close a deal, they are few and far between. Most salespeople actually try to do the best job they can.

Personally, I love sales. Without sales, a huge portion of the trade in the world would come to a standstill. The task of a sales trainer, then, is to teach people how to make an effective argument, how to better identify a customer's needs, and how to respond to a customer's objections. Or, even ask a client who's struggling to make up their mind to just agree to the deal. Most salespeople are actually sincere, too.

But regardless of how honest they may or may not be, most salespeople are pretty mediocre. They tend to be completely harmless if you don't actually want a deal. So there's no need to worry. I've met salespeople who could never get me to sign a piece of paper, no matter what they happened to be selling. They don't understand the psychology of gaining someone's trust—first for themselves and then for the product they represent. Their approach basically boils down to this: *Buy this thing.* How they ever manage to earn a living is a mystery.

In any case, they need regular training to stay proficient, at least when it comes to the fundamentals. Now, I've received my fair share of reactions along the lines of *How can you stomach teaching people how to be even more manipulative?*

But as I see it, this reaction is a huge misunderstanding. Let's return to what we discussed earlier: intentions.

There's no way you could accuse a salesperson of having a hidden agenda. We already know their intentions. Everyone knows what a salesperson's job involves. Their job is to sell things and make money, for their employers and for themselves. We're all fully aware that this is the case.

Please, never make another complaint about car showroom sales staff being all in your business. They're just doing their jobs. When a car salesperson—I keep returning to that particular example because of the unfortunate and somewhat undeservedly bad reputation this particular profession struggles with—approaches you in a dealership, don't look at them as though they suggested that the two of you should team up and rob your great-grandmother of her life savings. If you're not ready to talk business yet, just tell them, *I need to walk around the room first and take a look at what you've got*. It's as simple as that. Very few salespeople can counter that line.

Now, don't think I'm suggesting that there are no problems at all here. In sales, the line between persuasion and fraud can sometimes get blurred. As customers, we don't get to see what goes on behind the scenes. Salespeople, pressured to hit their targets and maximize profits, will sometimes resort to lying or twisting the truth in order to close a deal. This raises important ethical questions regarding the nature of sales, the responsibilities of salespeople, and the consequences of lying in commercial contexts.

"Would You Buy a Used Car from This Man?"

Selling is fundamentally about persuasion. Because of this, salespeople use various techniques to convince their potential customers of the value of the product or service and persuade them to take immediate action. In and of itself, there isn't necessarily anything unethical about this as it's still just a matter of doing your job.

However, problems arise when the persuasive techniques used cross over into the domain of deception.

Lying in sales can take many forms—for example, you might make exaggerated claims about the benefits of a certain product. One salesperson I met said that "his" exercise bike burned more calories than any other brand. That's a pretty stupid argument. Of course, the deciding factor will always be how much I pedal.

Or, it might involve keeping the most obvious limitations of the product from you, like failing to mention that the proposed software is unable to communicate with other essential software without four million plug-ins, or making false promises of after-sales service or warranties. *We've got you covered every step of the way.* Until, that is, you turn up at the shop, angry as a wasp, and somebody reads you the fine print. It's enraging.

You might keep quiet about additional costs that you know will be incurred, but that your prospective customer remains blissfully unaware of. The car costs a mere, manageable $499 a month. But then, of course, there are some additional fees. You want the service agreement, right? Taxes. Insurance premiums. Before you know it, we're talking $657 a month. Whoopsy-daisy!

These tactics can certainly bring short-term gains, but they can also bring long-term negative consequences for the salespeople and the companies they represent. For example, when too many customers start to feel cheated by this approach, they will begin to tell the world about it on social media—which represents a new arena for the exercise of consumer power.

Lying during sales can be thought of as a means to achieve a specific end. If lies can help with closing a deal and achieving the desired outcome, they might be considered justifiable by many salespeople. Deceived customers, of course, are free to take their business elsewhere in future if the product should fail to fulfill their expectations. But a lot of this reasoning is surprisingly shortsighted. It's easy to get the idea that the world is full of potential gullible marks. If that's the case, what's the harm in making people disappointed?

Deontology is the doctrine that actions and principles of behavior are to be judged based on the inherent value of an action, regardless of the consequences. From a deontological point of view, lying to close a deal would be unethical because it violates the moral obligation to be honest and truthful.

Immanuel Kant—still a favorite of mine—argued that lying is always wrong because it undermines the basic principle of trust that is essential to all human interaction. According to his view, a salesperson would be morally obliged to provide accurate and complete information to their customers on just about any detail that might affect a sale, even if this would mean that the salesperson might lose a potential deal and end up struggling to pay their rent.

Ultimately, the question of the ethics of deception in sales is a complicated and multifaceted one. While the pressure of meeting the targets set by management and maximizing profits can be intense, it's important for salespeople to consider the ethical implications of their actions and always strive to maintain a sense of personal integrity, even when their situation gets challenging.

Not All Salespeople Are Scammers

In a world where consumer trust has become more important than ever, honesty and transparency in business are not just moral imperatives, but also good business practices. Companies that prioritize ethical behavior and dedicate themselves to gaining the trust of their customers are more likely to succeed in the long term. This means that it is in the interest of both salespeople and the businesses they work for to promote a culture of ethical sales practices and strive to adhere to the highest standards of honesty and integrity.

As I said before, I love sales. Selling is fun, it's challenging, and it can give you quite a buzz. I also believe that it's entirely possible to work in sales and make a bright future for yourself without ever resorting to dirty methods or dwelling in the ethical gray areas. The best salespeople close big, profitable deals because of their skill and passion, and their customers love them for it. They appreciate the value of good service and of giving their customers their undivided attention.

Since I've been using car salespeople as examples so much already, I might as well end with a great example of a salesman who operates on a level most of us will never even get to witness. This guy sells a fairly common brand of car, but it's not one of the most popular ones here in Sweden. He sells so many cars each week that he doesn't even have the time to deliver them. The guy simply never sits still. He's always busy meeting new customers.

However, having the car delivered and demonstrated to me and getting a moment with the salesperson is an important part of the process for me as a customer. Nobody likes to sign away tens of thousands of dollars and then be completely ignored. This guy has solved this problem by delivering ten cars at a time. Yep, you read that right. He gathers ten customers, ten families, into a semicircle, offers everyone a drink, and tells them about their new cars. He tosses the keys out to the buyers as they cheer and applaud him. He fills the delivery experience itself with positive energy. And his customers absolutely love him. You can imagine how much time this saves him.

Unfortunately, professionals like him also suffer a loss of trust when bad salespeople have to resort to unfair methods and cheating in order to compete. I think that's a shame.

UNDER A FALSE FLAG

Another area in which there can be reasons to bluff and make things up is, naturally, the internet and social media. Here, people lie to be seen and cut through the noise. Many people consider this fact alone an adequate reason to lie about all kinds of stuff.

One of the most obvious ways to fake it on social media, I would say, is to assume an identity that doesn't even exist. Within the vast digital realm of social media, where avatars and usernames can grant people a tempting cloak of anonymity, a curious phenomenon has come into existence: fake profiles.

At its core, this concerns the art (or, perhaps more fittingly, the *craft*) of adapting, exaggerating, or simply fabricating your online personality. It's a lot like applying a filter to a photograph, but instead of just smoothing over a spot or two, you're creating an imaginary person who doesn't actually exist in the real world.

Imagine walking into a party wearing a mask over your face, adopting a foreign accent, and claiming to be some distant relative of Queen Elizabeth of the United Kingdom. Laughable? In the real world, yeah, it would be. People would see right through that inept display and call you an idiot. And they would be right.

However, in the digital ballrooms of social media, these kinds of masquerades are not only possible to pull off but worryingly common. You don't really know the first thing about the people you're watching or interacting with. They could be a cousin of your cousin. How on earth would you know?

But why is it people try so many scams online? For some, it's an attempt to fit in with a community they want access to, or seeking acceptance that they feel might not be extended to their "real" selves.

For others, the attraction is simply the thrill of escapism, of living a virtual life unburdened by the mundane challenges of their real—perhaps rather dreary—lives. And then, we have a more malicious subset: the people who set out to deceive others for financial gain, personal advantage, or simply for the thrill of their bizarre games. Unfortunately, there's a lot of money to be made here, and Mammon isn't necessarily a god whose ten commandments include a stern requirement for honesty.

Can Alex Be Trusted?

I'd like to introduce you to Alex—or, as his X followers know him, Alexander the Tech Guru. Alex claims to be a top-level executive at a leading tech company, and posts his daily insights on current developments in the fields of AI, cybersecurity, and software development. The CV on his profile is impressive and includes degrees from top universities. To top it all off, he also has a glamorous profile picture. Alex looks like a Hollywood star. He has made a name for himself as an influencer, and lots of aspiring tech enthusiasts follow his every post.

However, a curious journalist decided to dig a little deeper after noticing a few inconsistencies in Alexander's posts.

It turned out that Alexander the Tech Guru is actually a seventeen-year-old high school student whose name actually is Alex. He's certainly passionate about tech, but he's not any kind of executive anywhere. His "insights" were mostly gleaned from tech blogs and magazines. And that glamorous profile picture of the elegant model showing off his day-old stubble and washboard abs? Stolen from the internet.

This discovery sent shockwaves through the X tech community. Many felt betrayed after being offered the advice and insights of someone they had believed was an industry expert. Now, Alex hadn't meant any harm. He had started his account as a fun project, a way to connect with the industry he hoped to join one day. But as his follower count grew, his excitement about maintaining this fabricated façade grew stronger. In the end, he found himself unable to give up his fraudulent ways. He was stuck in a web of lies he couldn't escape.

The story of Alex highlights how easy it can be to create and maintain misleading digital personas. In this day and age, when the internet and social media have given us access to everything in the world at the touch of a button on our smartphones, it has become more important than ever to scrutinize anything presented as fact with a healthy dose of skepticism. Since the internet allows us to put on so many incredibly trustworthy masks, it's important to remember that behind every Alexander the Tech Guru there could be a person or an institution that's looking to entertain itself at the expense of others. Remember that in the enormous universe of social media, not all that glitters is gold. It might not even be glitter—it could be something else entirely.

Bots—Not Real People

Now, the fun doesn't stop with inventing fictional characters to pretend to be. You can go much bigger than that. All you need is sufficient motivation and a flexible attitude regarding right and wrong.

Imagine that you're witnessing a majestic performance and that the audience's cheers and applause are deafening. Now, imagine discovering that half the audience is really an army of humanlike robots that have been programmed to applaud whenever signaled to do so. That would be exciting, right? But what a strange show it would be.

Welcome to the captivating world of social media, in which "bots" play a key role in the dissemination of lies.

Social media bots are pieces of software that are designed to mimic human behavior online. They can like posts, share content, comment, and even engage in seemingly genuine conversations. What's their purpose, you ask? Sometimes it's entirely benign, like automating repetitive tasks. However, they are often used for what we call *false amplification*.

False amplification is the artificial amplification and boosting of certain messages to make them seem more popular than they actually are. This can influence public opinion and artificially cause certain topics to gain almost incomprehensible levels of attention. The practice is intended to distort our perception of what is popular or accepted.

Let's take a look at a classic use of bots in this field.

Imagine this: A new song is released by an artist who aspires to succeed in the charts and gain money and fame. Overnight, the song garners a million likes and thousands of reposts, and your Instagram feed is flooded with rave reviews of it.

So many people are into this song! It must be a hit, you think to yourself. Only later do you learn that a significant portion of this sensational success was caused by our beloved imposter, the bot, who inflated the numbers and was used to create hordes of fake, devoted fans.

What concern is this to the average social media user? How does this really impact the likes of you and me? Surely we can just ignore that stuff, right? Well. Pop music is one thing. And books like the ones I write might not have too much potential to cause harm. Fashion tips are fine. Stupid top-ten lists of the best burger dressings, car brands, garden tools, skin lotions, wallpaper patterns—whatever you can imagine. The worst thing they could do to anyone is put a hole in their wallet. Unfortunately, though, it doesn't stop at that.

Imagine this same technology being applied to influence and reinforce political views. Large numbers of bots can be used to make outlandish views seem perfectly normal. When something is normal, that means that it has become the norm and the general perception is that lots of people accept it. By amplifying a particular message, the illusion can be created that the majority feels so and so about issue *X,* and ultimately, unsuspecting people might even come to agree with that opinion. Many of us are simply far too easily influenced. Soon, an idea that's absolutely bonkers will have been made commonplace, and people might not even react too strongly to it anymore.

Just think of the popular topics you find yourself bombarded with on a daily basis. Bots can artificially push a certain topic or person to the top of the agenda, divert the public's attention from more critical issues, and even spread false information.

Whether they're offered to people looking to buy followers or likes—or getting you and me to share some very weird content without giving it much thought—bots can play a huge and dramatic role. That influencer who has a million followers? A significant portion of them could just be bots, lending the influencer a false air of credibility. I've even heard of influencers whose followers were supposedly 95 percent fake. It's scary, isn't it?

The key here is to recognize that people can have reasons to behave fraudulently. It's not always easy to see what that reason might be. Personal benefit is an obvious candidate. But what benefit? With whose support? And at whose expense?

Being a writer and lecturer, I'm quite active on social media myself. This has become a natural part of every public figure's life, regardless of how we all might feel about it. I am not at all good at it, and the so-called engagement of my small band of followers is far from what it could be. That's definitely my own fault. I obviously haven't cracked the code.

However, I see others in my field getting a completely different level of engagement from their followers. Over the last six months, I've made a point of looking into this, and there's no doubt in my mind that a lot of the stuff you see from some very well-known people, both in Sweden and abroad, is almost entirely based on bots.

They're not hard to spot: Their comments are very simple, their pictures are often incredibly attractive, and their profiles are usually locked. They have very few followers of their own and very few posts. Nothing looks like it adds up. You can simply tell they're not real people. However, many people obviously deem them a suitable means to an end.

WHY DO YOU LIE?

Okay, that was an extensive list of reasons for dishonesty. If I had to give you some advice, it would be something I've been trying to practice for several years by now (I say *trying*, because like everyone else, I fail from time to time).

I *want* to tell the truth, but find myself hesitating. There are risks involved. I ask myself: If I decide to be honest—it could be about a minor matter like not wanting to visit the Jonssons on Friday or having made a pretty serious mistake at work that I need to clean up right away to save myself from being fired—what's the worst thing that could happen?

What's the worst thing that could happen if I tell the truth?

I prefer considering this over thinking about what might happen *if I lie*.

The truth is a worthy cause, and I try to stick to it as far as I can manage. This approach has cost me everything you could imagine in the past. Relationships. Money. Business partners. Friends. Sleep. Pain. Worry. Anxiety.

But on some fundamental level, I wonder if lying doesn't actually cost even more.

In the end, all you can do is look in the mirror and ask yourself this question:

What is the worst thing that could happen—if I tell the truth?

THIS IS WHY WE LIE

Sometimes I feel like a conservative old grump, longing for a world where you meet real people you can reach out and touch, if you know what I mean. But we are where we are. Nobody knows where things will go from here.

My own guess is that a pretty strong backlash is coming. Many of the younger people I spoke to while preparing this section told me they know that most of the stuff online is fake, and they've started to distance themselves from it all. They've started meeting up in real life instead, just like my friends and I did when we were young. Sitting in someone's living room, about a dozen people on a Friday night, listening to music and laughing. You could see that everyone there was who they said they were, and in a way, life was easier.

So What Have We Learned So Far?

That people lie for many different reasons. They lie for their own benefit, for money, to build a reputation, out of habit, to avoid consequences, or simply for fun. The reasons will vary from person to person, and there is no shortage of "truths" concerning who tends to lie.

When surveys are conducted—a number of them have been made, but I haven't found any completely Swedish ones—into which professional groups lie the most often, naturally, no statistical evidence could ever really prove anything at all. But the groups that are often *claimed* to lie a lot, or at least bend or twist the truth, are—unsurprisingly—

politicians, lobbyists, used car salespeople, and (alarmingly) journalists.

The only professional group mentioned above that I have any extensive personal experience of is, as I mentioned before, car salespeople. In my own experience, they don't lie any more than anybody else does, but then, I've only worked with people who deal in new cars. Perhaps there is a difference between new and used cars in this regard, and perhaps the real liars mainly work in the used car sector.

We've also taken a look at social media, and my only intention in pointing out the abuses that go on there is to give you a wake-up call. Because a war is raging for people's attention out there, and because it is a good example of an environment where full-blooded narcissists thrive, I simply want to encourage you to put your smartphone down for a moment and think.

I want you to overcome your possible naivety and realize that you can barely trust anything that's out there anymore. Abstaining from engaging with social media is probably a great way to preserve your mental health.

But hey. Don't take my word for it! I'm simply voicing my preferences here. Make sure to base the decisions you make on conclusions that are your own.

INFAMOUS LIARS

Caroline Calloway

We just discussed social media and the existence of fake profiles. Now, I'd like to tell you about one of the more blatant attempts ever made to grab people's attention. This doesn't concern an imaginary person, but a real person who tried to present herself as considerably more interesting than she really was. Caroline Calloway is a social media personality and influencer who became famous for her acclaimed stories and posts on Instagram. She's a captivating storyteller who has achieved huge reach and popularity, and her posts depict a seemingly idyllic life.

Note that I'm using the present tense here. Stick around until the end, and we'll see what you make of it all. One of the most significant aspects of Calloway's online presence is her ability to weave compelling stories. All the way back in 2014, she reached a wide audience, presumably because of the strikingly intimate details about her life she shares. These posts, in turn, laid the foundation for her flourishing career as an influencer.

In carefully devised posts and captions, she presents an image of herself as a liberal young woman with a passion for literature who sets out to explore the world. She regularly shows off her bohemian lifestyle, sipping matcha tea or sunbathing in a sea of flowers. Her posts instill a sense of awe and admiration in her followers. It's all so beautiful, so amazing.

However, as time goes by, Calloway's posts begin to raise questions. Something isn't quite right here. One thing she seems to desire more than anything else is to establish herself as a writer, and one of her more notable controversies is centered around her Creativity Workshop Tour of 2019. Conceived as a series of creative workshops in several cities around the United States, the event ends in chaos, provoking a widespread backlash and eventually morphing into something popularly dubbed Tourgate. (Yes, all scandals end in "-gate" since Watergate.)

Calloway's tour is characterized by a lack of planning and organization. The organized events were dubious at best, and the furious participants found themselves in disorganized venues where the promised supplies and/or experiences never appeared. Some of the participants who never receive what they signed up for describe the event as a scam. There is a lot of anger.

Calloway compounds the problems by consistently misrepresenting how the tour is going on Instagram. As with all her other activities, she hugely exaggerates the popularity, enthusiasm, and attendance at the events. On her Instagram account, everything looks wonderful. However, the reality of the events is nothing like what she presents.

In the midst of fierce criticism and stormy interactions with fans and participants, the public view of what happened during the tour becomes increasingly blurred—the line between reality and fiction dissolves almost completely. For those who aren't there in person, it becomes virtually impossible to determine what's really going on.

But this is far from the whole story. In recent years, Calloway has been accused of lying about the celebrities she claims to hang out with, her college credentials, and even fabricating her entire lifestyle. One example of this is her alleged connection to the legacy of Oscar Wilde himself (one wonders why she even attempted to pull off such a massive scam . . .).

Calloway's ghostwriter Natalie Beach (no, she didn't even write it all herself!) revealed the lengths to which she would go to manipulate her own story. Calloway callously exploited other people's private experiences and personal tragedies to create her own content. Her aim, of course, was to create sensational stories that would engage online audiences.

Besides the controversies and the blatant fudging of the truth, Calloway's penchant for sharing intimate details of her life on social media has also attracted attention. Many have criticized her and ultimately questioned whether what she is doing is genuine storytelling or calculated manipulation.

While Calloway's supporters empathize with her struggle—although I must confess, I've never quite understood what she's fighting for—and appreciate her vulnerability, her critics point to her controversial publicity stunts and her unwillingness to take responsibility for past actions or explain apparent inconsistencies.

An analysis of Caroline Calloway's online presence reveals a complex picture of an influencer who has faced serious backlash and been accused of fraud, fabrication, and questionable ethics. Caroline Calloway's reputation as an irresponsible liar has been largely caused by her lack of clarity on where the line between fact and fiction lies, and as a result of this, she isn't perceived as authentic in her encounters with her followers.

Here's my own analysis of Caroline Calloway: If it's really her who's doing all this stuff, and if the criticism that has been leveled at her is even 50 percent accurate, it seems clear to me that we're dealing with a full-blown narcissist. What do I base this on?

Well, for one thing, the fact that she just carries on as usual. If you check her profile on Instagram, for example, you'll find that she describes herself as:

Caroline Calloway, author. Underneath the name, you'll find: *No, not that one. The other writer. The one you love. Buy my long-awaited (and critically acclaimed!) first book HERE!* And then about twenty-five or thirty different emojis.

What she seems to be doing now, as far as I can tell, is forging a new career out of her past as a scammer. And yep, that's the title of her book.

5

The Consequences of Lying

*You may tell the greatest lies
and wear a brilliant disguise,
but you can't escape the eyes of the one
who sees right through you.*
—TOM ROBBINS

The ancient practice of lying is a complex phenomenon that continues to baffle psychologists, sociologists, and ordinary people. Being human, we've all indulged in a few lies here and there, but have you ever stopped to consider the real consequences of these seemingly innocent fabrications?

Think back to your childhood. Remember the time you snuck a cookie out of the jar and denied having done anything wrong, but the crumbs around your mouth gave you away? You lied because at that moment, it seemed more important to avoid potential punishment than to admit to your sugar heist.

As we get older, the reasons for lying become more complex. Teenagers tell lies to fit in, while adults tell falsehoods to navigate complex personal and professional landscapes. Sometimes it's a basic survival mechanism, while at other times it's brought on by vanity, insecurity, or a manipulative urge.

How is it that something everyone does can have such profound consequences?

NOBODY LOVES A LIAR

In the last chapter, we read about the fraud Caroline Calloway. Many of her most loyal fans seem to genuinely love her. At least, that is, if you believe the comments on her Instagram account. However, she'd have to be considered an exception: In many societies, one of the core moral precepts passed down from generation to generation emphasizes the importance of honesty. *Honesty is the best policy, the truth will set you free,* and countless other sayings all emphasize truth. Why is it, though, that lying is so out of favor? After all, as we have seen so far, it would be more or less hopeless to try to eliminate the phenomenon of lying entirely from our daily lives. Why don't we just accept that lying is a fact of life? Like we do with rain on Midsummer Eve?

Personal Cost

You don't have to be a philosopher from three thousand years ago to realize that the truth is probably easier to bear in the long run. Again, I don't want to sound too preachy, but my own memory just isn't good enough for me to have a bunch of lies to juggle all the time.

With increasing age, I'm also becoming less inclined to

care what everyone else thinks of me as a person. I'm not suggesting that I feel I have the right to behave poorly, but if someone is annoyed by something I state as truth and starts to like me a little less because of this, I can live with that. After all, you can't be loved by everyone.

The question I asked at the end of the last chapter concerned the worst thing that might happen if you tell the truth.

Now, imagine we ask the opposite question instead: *What is the worst thing that could happen if you lie?* How badly could things actually go?

Relationships Are Built on Trust

A loss of trust would probably be the most immediate and obvious consequence of fibbing. Whether this loss happens between friends, family members, or lovers, once trust has been broken, it can be difficult to regain it. For example, consider a scenario where one partner finds out that the other has lied about where they've been spending their evenings. How are they to feel certain that the next assertion this person makes is in any way truthful?

Trust can take an incredibly long time to build, but it can be torn down in an instant. It's also usually a matter of something you've done or not done.

I don't even have to be the victim of the lie to lose trust. If I hear John lying to Linda, all I'll be able to think is John going to lie to me, too?

Trust can be very simply described as a bonding agent for human relationships. It constitutes a belief in somebody's reliability. The famous psychologist Erik Erikson (no relation) said that trust is the very first moral guide that people develop. According to his theory of psychosocial development, the initial stage—trust versus distrust—determines whether a child will view the world as a safe place or a place full of uncertainty and evil. Thus, our entire framework for how we interpret the world is based on the concept of trust.

An example: Consider a simple game between two individuals. It involves throwing a ball and, according to Erikson, is based on trust: You have to trust that the other person will throw the ball in a sensible way that allows the game to continue. I also have to trust that the other person will catch it when I throw it. If one person deliberately throws the ball too hard or in the wrong direction, trust will be broken and the game can no longer continue as intended. The conclusion is easy to draw: *This person can't be trusted. What a jerk.*

THE TROUBLE LIES CAN CAUSE

How far-reaching the consequences of lies will be depends on how serious they are. They can change people's views of not only the liar, but also of other, unrelated individuals and situations.

Psychologist Albert Mehrabian's research on communication emphasizes the point that a lot of the exchanges between people are nonverbal. This means that the words we hear are only a small part of the messages we pick up on. In other words, when someone is lying, this fact will often reveal itself in some aspect of their body language. One thing comes out of their mouth, and another is expressed by other parts of their body. This can give the other party mixed signals, which can lead to misinterpretations and misunderstandings. Not to mention confusion.

Here's another example of confusion, and by extension distrust: Suppose somebody finds out that their partner lied about their whereabouts one night. After this, they may start to doubt other things their partner says, even concerning matters unrelated to the original lie.

Lying Causes Inner Tension

Lying isn't only harmful to the people who are deceived; it also takes a toll on the liar. One study I've read showed that dishonesty can produce shameful feelings in the liar, driving them to engage in what psychologists call cleansing acts.

For example: A student who cheats on an exam might feel an inexplicable need to clean their room afterward. This symbolic act is a way of cleansing themselves of their dishonesty. This is an interesting phenomenon that's apparently quite common.

The protagonist of the film *Knives Out*, starring Daniel Craig, is a character called Marta. While being interviewed by the police, she claims that the mere thought of lying makes her vomit. It's a fun effect in a film, certainly, but is it in any way based in reality?

Well, it's not implausible, actually.

Apparently, dishonesty makes the brain enter a state of heightened alert, and this stress will vary in intensity depending on the extent of the lie (many studies indicate this). Why, then, is the brain so preoccupied with honesty? What are the implications of this?

Well, being social animals, we're all concerned with maintaining our reputation. If we're not allowed to join the pack, this makes us outcasts. And we simply can't make it on our own. Consequently, we attempt to maintain an image of credibility and integrity in order to increase our chances of survival. It's really that simple.

Lying increases the pace of our breathing and our heart rates. We sweat, our mouths get dry, and our voices may become unsteady. Feel free to refer to the section on the classic lie detector test in chapter 9.

X-rays of the brain (known as CT or brain scans) have produced some insights. Symptoms of anxiety will frequently occur because lying activates the limbic system in the brain, the same system that initiates our so-called fight-or-flight response. If someone is being truthful, this area of the brain shows minimal activity. But if they are lying, it lights up like fireworks. An honest brain is relaxed, basically, and a dishonest one is in a frenzy.

I'm sure you'll agree that that's pretty interesting. Living a lie, then, can actually do harm to the brain. That's good to know.

Some studies suggest that significant anxiety can cause nausea, and this makes it reasonable to presume that such a condition might already be present in somebody who experiences constant anxiety. Now, I suppose it's possible that someone could actually vomit just from lying, but I haven't found any evidence of it ever happening. However, there is something called the gut-brain axis. This is the two-way communication channel that exists between these two body systems. This might offer an explanation for why we sometimes get butterflies in our stomachs when we're nervous.

Other studies suggest that the long-term effects are minimal because we seem to grow increasingly comfortable with lying the more we do it. In other words, we're able to quickly develop a concerning tolerance when it comes to lying.

Brain imaging experiments conducted at University College London reveal that the brain actually adapts to dishonest behavior. Participants showed reduced activity in their limbic system during prolonged dishonest behavior as they told more and more lies.

What can we conclude from this? Well, if you have children, it might be a good idea to confront any lies you discover—and be on the lookout for more, especially when they're in their teens—at the earliest opportunity, to keep your little rascals from growing too accustomed to compromising the truth.

Lying can weigh heavily on our conscience. At least, that is, for those of us who call ourselves normal. The stress of maintaining a lie can cause anxiety, guilt, and even physical symptoms like headaches or stomachaches. Remember that time when you lied about being sick to get out of having to go to work, and then bumped into one of your workmates at the shopping center? The fear you felt, the racing heart, the need to quickly produce another lie—the whirlwind of emotions it can cause can be truly exhausting.

These are the kinds of things that keep people up at night. It can make you lose your appetite. It can make you panic when the wrong person enters the room. Lots of studies have shown that even hardened criminals reduce their internal stress levels when they confess to a crime. They begin to sleep better, regain their appetite, and find it easier to smile. Now, although they might soon be back on the streets and back to their wicked ways, the correlation is still interesting.

Everyday Life Can Get Incredibly Complicated

As we've discussed, one lie will often lead to another just to cover up the initial deception. Before you know it, you can find yourself entangled in a messy web of lies, and it can get difficult to keep all your stories straight.

Imagine that you've lied about having a certain level of expertise on your CV and then being asked to demonstrate your knowledge of the subject. Not only will it soon be plain to all that you're out of your league, but you'll probably have to invent even more lies to cover up the first one.

Or suppose you tell a fib to Emma, who then retells it to Karin, who ends up coming to you to ask what's going on? After all, she knows the truth of the matter. This can get really messy, and you might well end up having to maintain a spreadsheet in your phone just to get through your everyday interactions.

That's not good. That's not good at all.

Lying Can Damage Your Opportunities

In a world of social media and instant communication, things can move quickly. Being labeled a liar can damage your reputation and make it difficult for you to form new relationships or even advance your career. A businessman who's been caught inflating his company's profits will have to fight an uphill battle to regain the trust of his investors. They know he's lied once, and they wonder if he'll lie again.

There's a story that illustrates this very clearly. Unfortunately, I can't remember where I heard it. A businessman has been approached by a new contact and they decide to go for a round of golf to get to know each other. The wife of the businessman sees the new prospective partner cheating—he moves his ball to a better spot. She tells her husband not to do business with this person. The businessman doesn't think too much of it. It was only a golf ball.

But the wife insists. And quite rightly so. When they investigate his background, they learn that he's a serial con man whose only intention was to rip them off.

We often perform this analysis subconsciously. You might see or hear something somebody does and experience a negative reaction you can't quite define. It's a dangerous business. This is especially true if you value your reputation. What bigger asset could you possibly have in business than your good name? Lying can make you miss out on opportunities in many different areas of life. For example, lying about your qualifications during a job interview could result in you not getting the position. In relationships, being perceived as insincere could cause you to miss out on getting to be with somebody who values your true self.

Of course, landing a job by lying is possible (and, I should emphasize, certainly quite common). I don't know how many recruiting interviews I've done over the years, but I've had several occasions where I had a hunch that something just wasn't right. It may take some digging, but if there's something there, it will be uncovered eventually.

At the end of the day, you have to demonstrate your ability to perform the tasks you claimed you were able to do. Suppose you fibbed just a little too much because you were just so keen to get that cool job?

Your fall from grace could be a hard one.

You May End Up Struggling with Your Own Perception of Reality

In chronic liars, the lines between truth and fiction will eventually tend to blur. As time goes by, they find it increasingly challenging to distinguish between the lies they've told and the actual truth. This distortion can cause personal confusion and further isolation. Unless your mind is extremely well organized, things—reality and fiction alike—will blend together and leave you helpless.

What did you tell whom, and why? Our memory is a fascinating instrument, but it's far from perfect. It stores pieces of information and allows us to recall them instantly. However, reality is a lot more complex and imperfect.

Our memory operates in three stages: encoding, storage, and retrieval. Encoding is the process of taking in information, storage involves maintaining the information over time, and retrieval is the process of accessing and recalling the information as the need arises.

Research has shown that our memory is seldom as accurate as we like to think. To put it briefly, our memories fade with time and grow increasingly inaccurate. Moreover, our memories are subject to interference from other information, both old and new, and this can cause further confusion and distortion.

A common truth among mental trainers and coaches is that the brain can't distinguish between our experiences and our thoughts. This ought to mean, then, that you could think your way to success, for example. Now, that's not entirely possible, of course, but there is still a point to this idea.

If you have a thought a sufficient number of times, it will eventually become so familiar to you that it *feels* real. It will *feel* more like a memory than like something you made up in your own head. While you can hardly put a Bentley on your driveway just by thinking about it, you can certainly think of being confident in a certain situation, and thus make yourself a little better prepared to cope with this situation than you would be if you had kept thinking of how unconfident you would be.

But what does this mean in practical terms? Well, that it's actually quite easy to fool yourself.

I've been through this myself, and it can be incredibly disturbing to realize that your memory of something is incorrect. I had a memory of having a certain bicycle as a child. I knew that it had been given to me when we lived in a certain house. This memory was so vivid! I remembered cycling down this street or that street on that particular bike. However, my father—who, by the way, never threw anything away—had photographic evidence that this memory simply couldn't be true. It felt confusing, to say the least. I believed I had spent so much time riding that bike! It *felt* true.

Moreover, the memory is reconstructive in nature, meaning that every time we recall a memory, it is essentially reconstructed based on different fragments of information that are stored in our brain. This process is in turn influenced by our beliefs, expectations, and experiences, which can bring us to create false memories or distort real ones.

In a famous experiment conducted by the psychologist Elizabeth Loftus, participants were shown video footage of a car accident. Afterward, they were asked questions about what they had seen. However, it turned out that the wording of the questions affected their memories of the event. Some participants were asked this question: *About how fast were the cars going when they smashed into each other?* These participants' speed estimates were higher than the estimates of those asked this question: *How fast were the cars going when they hit each other?*

Our memory simply isn't some perfect record of events, but rather a reconstruction influenced by various external factors. False memories, for example, are events that never actually happened, but are still recounted by witnesses. Research suggests that up to 20 percent of us have detailed personal memories that never really happened (Mazzoni, Scoboria, and Harvey, 2010). It's quite appalling, really.

To put it bluntly: If you repeat a lie often enough, you'll start to believe it. And this can lead to some rather surprising realizations when you discover that it's not actually true.

Lying and Deception in the Gulf of Tonkin

Of all the things we've heard and learned, which ones are really true, which ones are in the gray area, and which ones ought to be considered outright lies? One example that I'd like to mention comes from the Vietnam War, a terrible war that caused horrendous suffering for millions of people. Of course, raising questions about a historical event of this significance can cause some controversy, but I'd still like to bring up the Gulf of Tonkin incident, a controversial and decisive moment in the history of the Vietnam War, as it provided the

United States with a pretext to escalate its military involvement in the region. Indeed, this event is often said to be the official starting point of the war.

According to contemporary official sources, the incident involved two separate confrontations between the US Navy and North Vietnamese forces in the Gulf of Tonkin. On August 2, 1964, the USS *Maddox*, a US Navy destroyer, was attacked by North Vietnamese torpedo boats. Two days later, on August 4, the USS *Maddox* and another destroyer, the USS *Turner Joy*, came under attack again.

However, the events of August 4, 1964, have been the object of considerable controversy and skepticism. Officially, there is general consensus that the August 2 attack actually occurred, but that it was very probably provoked by covert US operations.

These events led the US Congress to pass the Gulf of Tonkin Resolution, which authorized Democratic president Lyndon B. Johnson to use military force in Southeast Asia. By presenting the US forces as the victims of an unprovoked attack, the government was able to gain the support it needed to pursue a protracted conflict in Vietnam.

The resolution also boosted President Johnson's popularity and contributed to his winning reelection. One thing we know for sure about American voters is that they always rally behind their president in times of war. Whether you like this fact or not, it remains beyond dispute.

There's also a theory that claims that once a bureaucratic body, like the military or a government agency, begins to move in a certain direction, it can quickly gain so much momentum it becomes difficult to stop or redirect. Various branches of the US government and military were already preparing for increased involvement in Vietnam, and the Gulf of Tonkin incident was simply a catalyst for these plans.

The Gulf of Tonkin incident provided the US government with sufficient support for an escalation of its military involvement in Vietnam, and strengthened the political support for President Johnson and the war. An understanding of the potential motives behind the deception and disinformation that surrounds the Gulf of Tonkin incident is vital for any comprehensive analysis of US involvement in the Vietnam War.

Lying as a Violation of Social Agreements

The philosopher Jean-Jacques Rousseau introduced the concept of the social contract. This is a theoretical construct based on the idea that we ought to give up some of our freedoms in order to function better as a collective in various contexts. However, it also hinges on the assumption that others will do the same. It's all a matter of compromise.

Lying can be considered a violation of this contract. When someone lies, they're failing to adhere to the social contract, thus exploiting the trust that others have faithfully placed in it.

Example: In a professional environment, a group of colleagues is given an assignment by a client. They define the project, divide the various tasks among themselves, and agree on a deadline when they will deliver the work to the client. Everyone does their part except for one member of the team who has chosen to lie and say that he has completed his tasks even though he hasn't. Instead of doing his work, he has spent his time checking out vintage cars on the internet. The project is delayed, and the whole team loses face with the client.

Employees who consistently lie about having finished tasks aren't just jeopardizing the project in question; they're also violating the unstated agreement that each team member is going to do their part of the work. Who can we genuinely rely on?

An Evolutionary Account of Dishonesty

Humans cooperate far more than other species, and there is a lot of evidence to suggest that this ability of ours has played a particularly significant role in our evolution. However, a certain degree of predictability is necessary for effective cooperation. Lying will immediately introduce some degree of unpredictability, and this may have had detrimental effects for survival in the early phases of human evolution. Thus, an aversion to dishonesty could actually be in our DNA. I haven't found any research that offers clear support for this idea, but it seems quite reasonable.

Example: Fifty thousand years ago, if somebody lied about the location of a freshwater spring because he wanted the water for himself, he would put the whole group at risk of dehydration—this illustrates how harmful deception can be when it comes to survival. In extreme cases, a lie could potentially wipe us all out, and that wouldn't exactly be great, would it?

THE IMPACTS OF LYING ON DIFFERENT PERSONALITY TYPES

Now, let's go even deeper and look at the specific consequences that lying can have for some different groups of people. We went through the DISC theory and the four colors earlier, and we'll be revisiting them a few more times. We're all different, and it's quite possible that you don't care about your reputation as much as I care about mine. We don't all react the same way to the same things, and maybe that's just as well. I'd like to return to the four colors now to discuss the particular risks that some of us may face.

Reds Experience a Loss of Trust and Credibility

What consequences can a Red person suffer from having a lie exposed? Well, as we discussed earlier, trust is a fundamental component of any relationship, whether it be personal or professional. When someone is caught lying, they can lose trust and credibility, and this can be difficult or impossible to rebuild. For Reds, who rely on their authority and influence to achieve their goals, a loss of trust and credibility can be particularly damaging.

Lying can damage relationships, in both the personal and the professional domains. When individuals feel deceived or manipulated, this can cause them to feel betrayed and resentful. For dominant individuals who may already face struggles in their interpersonal relationships because of their pushy and competitive nature, lying can further exacerbate these challenges and make it even more difficult for them to form and maintain meaningful connections with others.

A particular challenge for Reds is that they aren't relationship-oriented, but rather task-oriented. Losing a few friends on the path to success isn't the end of the world. At least not for a Red person. They know that it's lonely at the top, and they're prepared to live with that. The worst thing that can happen to them is to lose control of a situation. That'll sting.

Yellows Suffer Both Socially and Psychologically

The social consequences of lying are worse for Yellows because of their extensive social life and their desire to be loved wherever they go. Lies can spread like wildfire, and when the truth is finally revealed, it's not only the liar who tends to get burned.

Psychological consequences like guilt or stress will often follow and negatively impact their overall well-being. It will make them awful in the moment. However, and this is worth knowing, their ability to recover quickly, brush this discomfort right off, and move on is most impressive. All the while, of course, they work hard to convince themselves that the unpleasantness never actually happened. Never underestimate the Yellow's capacity for self-deception.

The challenge for a Yellow person is rather that they are

quite prone to going astray. They like to make the experience special for everyone, and they want to tell good stories. I can't tell you how many times I've listened to a Yellow person's embellished stories and thought to myself that I'd love to find out what really happened. But it's entertaining, in any case. Is it a proper lie, though? Well, that depends on who you ask. If you were to ask a Blue person, anything less than 100 percent true is by definition a lie. The terms of communication are always set by the recipient. That's just the way it works.

Greens Get Into Conflicts

The fact that Greens lie just as much as any color means that their lives can be very dangerous, particularly if they choose to lie to Red people. They won't hesitate to subject the Green little liar to harsh censure when they finally find out the truth. Since Greens tend to shy away from conflict, this can cause major problems.

Change and conflict are the most difficult things for Greens to deal with. They'd love to please everyone, but as that's impossible, they often end up not pleasing anyone. This means that danger looms practically everywhere. They don't cope with stress as well as the other profiles. They're sensitive to criticism, loud voices, and being questioned. Being outed as a liar in front of a whole group can do serious harm to a Green, and this is something a Red or a Yellow wouldn't hesitate to subject them to if they lost their temper.

The consequences of their lies could well end up giving them post-traumatic stress issues.

Blues Can Lose Their Stature as Specialists

For a Blue person who might have lied to cover up a mistake they didn't want to admit, for instance, the very concept of lying can cause difficulties. However, although I can't prove it, I think these people are safest for us to trust. They aren't essentially relationship-oriented, and this probably makes them quite prepared to fib to people they are loosely connected to. Being found out wouldn't cause any great loss in terms of what others think about them.

On the other hand, if they were to be caught fudging data or being wrong about something because of an incorrect assumption—oh, the horror! It would be wrong to say that Blues don't care about status. It all depends on the kind of status we mean.

Just look at the world of academia, where things can get quite brutal. Blue researchers in virtually any field fib quite freely, and are happy to stab some backs if it can protect what they hold to be the truth. Some of them do get exposed as cheaters. That's a real status killer. They end up as pariahs, and they might not even be able to find new jobs.

However, this is even worse: Their phones will stop ringing. They'll be completely ostracized if they're exposed as frauds. While it won't bother them that they won't be invited to any more cocktail parties, the fact that their skills will no longer be in demand will be devastating to them. It's a tough loss for a Blue.

THE CONSEQUENCES OF LIES
IN THE MEDIA

In several of my books I have mentioned the fact that I don't watch TV and that—above all—I don't consume news unless I absolutely have to. There are several reasons for this. In part, it's because the overwhelming majority of all reporting is negative, but it's also a result of the fact that I no longer trust the media. I don't have the time to study with four different perspectives on a single event just to be able to triangulate an idea of what actually happened.

What do I mean by that? Well, we discussed the issue of biased news earlier. Because I find it hard to imagine that there are any completely neutral journalists, I always find myself assuming that something has been left out of the story whenever I read something online. I try to focus on my own concerns and engage in things that are meaningful to me and might be of benefit to others. Like writing and lecturing. I'm not trying to say that this is the right way to live. It's just how I've chosen to do things.

In any case, the media can be a lot of different things these days. There's a lot of it out there to avoid, and you can't always avoid it all. However, I do know a lot of people who refuse to take in what's going on in the world for the simple reason that they don't trust the reporting. Or because of the heavy emphasis on negative news in the media.

What are the consequences of this?

Well, a lot of people simply don't know what's happening in the world anymore.

Cambridge Analytica

While we're on the subject of serious consequences in the media . . . Cambridge Analytica was a political consulting firm that came into the spotlight after its involvement in the 2016 US presidential election and the Brexit referendum that was held in the UK in the same year.

Cambridge Analytica claimed to be able to profile individual voters and tailor political messaging to the profiles they produced. It combined data from various sources, including social media, to create profiles of millions of voters. These profiles were used to deliver personalized political messages and potentially influence the votes people ended up casting.

The company's operations came under intense scrutiny after reports emerged that it had improperly obtained the personal data of millions of Facebook users without their consent. This was done with an app that didn't just collect information related to the person using it, but also extracted data from that individual's Facebook friends.

But wait, there's more. With the use of personality tests on Facebook, it managed to manipulate the outcome of the Brexit referendum. The idea was simple: People were convinced to reveal their personalities by taking a fraudulent personality test that was—importantly—based on genuine research. It used a model called the Big Five, or OCEAN. This way, it gained access to data that revealed the personalities of these individuals.

What did it do with this data? It used it to target specific individuals with tailored, shameless propaganda intended to persuade them to vote in favor of the UK leaving the EU. We haven't yet seen the full consequences of the referendum play out.

Why did this work? Well, there are some fairly reliable correlations between personality and political orientation. Of course, they aren't 100 percent reliable, and there is cause to reflect on the accuracy of the test. But no one can deny that the campaign it orchestrated worked a lot better than anybody ought to be comfortable with.

Concerns were raised about the impact this kind of data mining might have on democratic processes. This led to a broader debate on the roles of personal data, privacy, and disinformation in political campaigns.

But what exactly constituted deception here? Essentially, Cambridge Analytica wasn't forthcoming about how it intended to use its users' data. There are also serious ethical concerns about sending targeted messages to people in that way.

The question is whether campaigns like this are currently being run elsewhere without anybody even knowing about it.

Facebook was fined for failing to adequately protect its users' data. Cambridge Analytica confessed to its misdeeds, even bragging about them at first. I've even seen a video clip online in which one of the executives proudly explains how good they were at it.

In May 2018, Cambridge Analytica and its parent company, SCL Group, filed for insolvency. The official reason given was their loss of customers and the burden of legal fees incurred as a result of the Facebook data scandal.

My guess? The owners could see monstrous lawsuits looming ahead in their crystal ball and decided not to chance anything. Take responsibility for a rigged presidential election? Acknowledge that they had a hand in causing one of the most influential nations in history to take a giant step in a completely new, uncharted direction?

Who knows what that could have cost them.

The Filtered Reality of Influencers

Imagine this: You're scrolling through your feed on your favorite social media platform when a photo pops up. A well-known influencer, tanned and looking confident, is sipping a very expensive detox tea and showing off their almost unrealistically perfect physique. The caption praises the miraculous weight loss benefits of the beverage.

Would you be tempted to give it a try? Hold that thought. We're about to dive into the world of influencers and the various ways to stretch reality to its very limits.

In our digital age, scores of influencers have become powerful opinion leaders, shaping opinions, driving trends, and influencing people's purchasing decisions. With great influence comes great responsibility, but unfortunately not all influencers are fully committed to honesty. Some of them actually peddle misleading recommendations, filtered realities, and curated lifestyle content that's often nowhere close to the truth.

What are the consequences of this deception? Their followers get distorted views of reality. When influencers present their fictionalized, gilded lives to us, this can set unrealistic standards, cause insecurity, and even mislead consumers. And while using a selfie filter might not seem like a huge issue, the consequences of recommending untested products or presenting fake identities as real can be serious and profound.

Would you like an example? No problem.

In 2015, Essena O'Neill, an Australian influencer, decided to reveal the truth about her fictional online persona. O'Neill, who had over half a million followers on Instagram, appeared to live the perfect life: beautiful beaches, fashionable clothes, and a radiant smile.

One day, though, she started editing her posts with pictures and revealing the actual truth behind each one. She opened up about the pressure to post, the countless retakes to achieve a "sincere" posture in every picture to gain her followers' trust, the pressure from sponsors, and the insecurities she struggled with. Having fallen victim to the stress of this herself, she decided to come clean. In a video, she explained her decision and highlighted the difference between her real life and the staged one she presented on social media. Her revelations caused a public debate about the potential for fraud in influencer culture.

Strangely enough, there's also no shortage of examples of

people doing the exact opposite. Plenty of people want to draw attention to the challenges of living with mental illness, and help bring about a more open discourse on the subject by laying bare their own sufferings. However, there are also quite a few rather narcissistic influencers who make a big song and dance of claiming to suffer from some psychiatric diagnosis or other that they don't really have. Why would anyone want to feign illness like that? Well, who knows? Attention is an important asset these days.

How can we tell who's sincere and who isn't?

Well, at this point, it's important for me to emphasize that not all influencers engage in practices like this. Many of them are genuine advocates for the brands they believe in and work hard to make their interactions fully authentic. I know this firsthand. But the case of O'Neill does bring to light a segment of the industry in which the desirability of likes, shares, and sponsorships has given rise to a murky, less than honest culture.

The challenge facing consumers and followers who wish to navigate this space can be likened to walking through a minefield. How can you distinguish genuine recommendations from paid campaigns? How can you tell if something is a genuine moment or a staged one?

Critical thinking is key here. Always take what you see with a hefty grain of salt, and always do your due diligence before deciding to buy something.

While social media offers windows into the lives of influencers, it's important to remember that this window often presents a filtered view. When we engage with different kinds of content, it's our responsibility to distinguish fact from fiction and make sure that our perceptions, beliefs, and decisions will be based on the truth rather than retouched photos. In the ever-changing world of social media, a discerning eye is always the best defense against the mirages of false representation.

Disinformation and Biased News

We've already taken a look at the phenomenon of biased news, and I'd like to mention here that social media is a huge part of the problem. The speed and ease of dissemination that social platforms offer makes them ideal breeding grounds for every variety of deception. In moments, a catchy but fully fabricated headline can travel across the world and receive countless likes, shares, and comments, even if the content of the story is no more real than a mermaid.

Remember that viral story that went around about the pope endorsing a certain candidate in the US presidential election of 2016? Millions of people believed in it and shared it, and some people even changed their decision about who to vote for because of it. The problem? Every word of it was made up. It really only takes three seconds of reflection to figure it out—what possible reason could the pope have to interfere like that? It doesn't take a devout Catholic to realize that the pope isn't actually that stupid.

The danger of disinformation and fake news lies in the power it has to influence people's perceptions, decisions, and even actions. And while social media platforms all claim to be taking measures to combat this issue, the primary responsibility will inevitably fall to us, the users.

In a world that's more connected than ever, all kinds of media play crucial roles in shaping our perceptions, our opinions, and ultimately our decisions. Conventional news broadcasts are still held to be reliable sources of information by many—useful guides that can help us understand the world we live in. However, the rise of biased news reporting has become a major problem, and has undermined the objective news reporting that is so crucial to any well-informed society.

News Is Rarely "Neutral"

By *biased news*, I'm referring to the presentation of news from a particular point of view rather than one of absolute objectivity. This bias can manifest itself in various ways—from the choice of stories to cover to the way the news stories are framed and the way that headlines are phrased. This can be done subtly or blatantly, and the choice of mode can be influenced by various factors including the target audience's interests, the political orientations of journalists, the agenda of the owner of the media company, or pressure from advertisers.

For example, during the 2020 US presidential election, different media outlets presented events in significantly different ways. Some conservative media outlets, like Fox News, were criticized for downplaying the dangers of the COVID-19 pandemic and for promoting unfounded allegations of electoral fraud. On the other hand, liberal channels like CNN were accused of being too critical of the current president, Donald Trump, and of giving more favorable coverage to his opponent, Joe Biden.

Biased news can have serious consequences for society. It can reinforce preexisting beliefs and prejudices, contribute to the polarization of public opinion, and undermine trust in the media and other institutions. It can affect public discourse and decision-making because people might not have access to all the information needed to make informed decisions. It can pit communities against one another—history is full of particularly appalling examples of this.

Besides all that, biased news can also have a degenerative effect on democracy itself. In democratic societies, the media is often referred to as the fourth estate—an independent institution that holds those in power accountable and checks their actions. But if the media and its representatives give in to bias, they can become tools for manipulating public opinion.

As a consumer of news, it's important to be aware of the potential for bias. Here are some tips that can help you become a more discerning news consumer:

Consume news from a variety of sources: Don't rely on a single news outlet for all your information. Instead, consume news from a variety of sources that present differing points of view.

And always remember that the news—I think this is still true—is written by people. People are very rarely neutral. I know I'm not. I, like anyone else, unconsciously project my own opinions and values onto everything I read. There's nothing wrong with that as such, but it does mean you have to be vigilant.

DO YOU ALWAYS TELL THE TRUTH?

Well, what's the story in your case? Now that we've gotten to know each other and I've admitted to being less than absolutely truthful from time to time—would you allow me to challenge you with some questions? If you don't want to engage in self-scrutiny right now, I can respect that—just skip this section. However, if you'd like to take something away from this that will benefit you and help you earn a reputation as somebody people can trust—read on.

Think about the last five times you can recall when you were less than truthful. We could be talking about anything from a blatant lie to the slightest fudging of some inconvenient truth.

It's entirely possible that you had very good reasons for your decision. I don't know that, of course.

Ask yourself these questions:

Why did I do it?

What was the precise reason why I didn't speak the exact truth?

Do I fully grasp the consequences that this or that little lie might have?

Would I have been okay with reading about that behavior in the newspaper?

Would I mind having my name associated with that behavior?

And, perhaps the most important question of all, before we rush on:

Am I answering these questions honestly?

Only you will know the answer to that.

HOW TO DODGE A LIE

As we've established, lying isn't just a matter of spreading untruths. It can invade the very heart of human interaction, eroding trust and creating doubt. In essence, to lie is to disregard the unspoken agreement on which all societies and relationships are based. While there may be scenarios in which dishonesty will appear to be the easiest path to take (and, as we've seen, we're all guilty of making that choice at times), the long-term consequences, both for the individuals involved and the societies they live in, can be profound and far-reaching.

As usual, there's more to this problem than this. However, and this is my point: If keeping track of reality and everything that actually happened or didn't happen is such a complicated task, how much worse will things get if we add a bunch of lies and fabrications to the recipe? No wonder liars tend to get entangled in webs they have a difficult time extricating themselves from.

While lying may seem convenient in the moment, the repercussions can be long-lasting and far-reaching. The immediate relief of avoiding a difficult situation by lying will often be overshadowed by the potential negative consequences.

As we make our way through life interacting with one another, it's important for us to remember the value of honesty. It doesn't just simplify our lives, it also helps us build genuine, lasting relationships. After all, in an age of fake news and online personas, truth can be more precious than gold.

At least, I think it can.

What Have We Learned So Far, Then?

How should we sum all this stuff up? Lying willy-nilly can have huge consequences. Besides the more immediate effects it can have on those around you who might feel deceived, I'd like to remind you that liars often find themselves in precarious circumstances. These range from the obvious risk of being exposed and gaining a reputation for untrustworthiness, with all that this might entail, to the fact that it can actually damage your own brain in the long term.

Evaluating the use of a tool like lying can only be done by peering into the future to consider all the possible outcomes. Most of us prefer to get our rewards as soon as possible, and lying can sometimes seem like the quickest way to get where we want to go. But any claim to that effect would also be a lie. The future is surprisingly similar to the present, even if it doesn't feel that way.

Presumably, the various media groups, for example, have people on their staff who are tasked with considering these aspects when they plan their strategies. Wouldn't you think? Considering all the stuff we just went over about bias in the news, I suppose it's possible that I just made a fool of myself. But if they had employed a strategist who really took the longer view, I wonder if much of the stuff we see now wouldn't have been scrapped while it was still on the drawing board. Assuming, of course, that anybody listened to what this strategist had to say.

So what long-term consequences are we talking about here? Biased news could, for example, reduce trust in the media, reinforce delusions and prejudices, increase polarization of public opinion, and impact public discourse and decision-making. All in all, it poses an obvious and real threat to democracy. Future generations will suffer the consequences of the choices made by conventional media outlets, from their choices of which stories to cover to the way they frame the news, all the way down to the headlines they set.

On top of this, influencers are skewing perceptions of reality, setting unrealistic standards, and misleading consumers. Social media is actually a breeding ground for disinformation, and it has a real impact on people's perceptions and decisions.

Who knows where all this might lead?

INFAMOUS LIARS

Lance Armstrong

Well, talk about the consequences of lying . . . Perhaps you've heard of Lance Armstrong? At the age of twenty-five, this promising young cyclist was diagnosed with testicular cancer, a serious variety that had also spread to his lungs and brain. Miraculously, Armstrong survived his ordeal after undergoing a series of aggressive treatments.

After finishing his recovery, he returned to professional cycling. He founded the Lance Armstrong Foundation, which was later renamed Livestrong, to give support to cancer survivors and raise awareness about the disease. Along with his achievements in cycling, this made him a global symbol of resilience and hope. Understandably, he was greatly acclaimed and a role model to many.

Armstrong's most significant wins were claimed in the Tour de France. Between 1999 and 2005, he won seven consecutive Tour de France titles, forever cementing his status as a legend of the sport. Armstrong became an international icon. He was praised, not just for his sporting achievements, but also for the way he had overcome cancer and other setbacks. He was as good a hero as anybody could hope to find. His survival story, his philanthropic work, and his charismatic personality made him a role model for millions of fans all over the world.

However, some people were less enthusiastic. The dramatic improvement in Armstrong's performance had triggered speculations about the possibility that he was using performance-enhancing drugs. He angrily denied these allegations and claimed to be the victim of a witch hunt. He consistently emphasized that he had never failed a drug test, and he even threatened to sue anybody who would accuse him of cheating.

Armstrong's former teammate, Floyd Landis, who was stripped of his own Tour de France title after a failed drug test, eventually came out to accuse Armstrong of the systematic use of PEDs. The US Anti-Doping Agency launched an extensive investigation into Armstrong's alleged drug use, and the evidence it uncovered against him was devastating. Testimony from former teammates, physical evidence, and financial transactions made it plain that his drug use was supported by an extensive network.

Armstrong's carefully crafted façade was falling apart. Finally, in a television interview with Oprah Winfrey, he admitted to having used drugs throughout his cycling career. This confession represented a seismic moment in the world of sport, because Armstrong actually came out and admitted to having lied and cheated on an epic scale.

Shockwaves reverberated around the world, and Armstrong's fall from grace was profound. He was stripped of his Tour de France titles, banned from professional cycling for life, and abandoned by all his sponsors.

This doping scandal is often used as an example of how far some athletes are willing to go in their pursuits of victory and fame. It also highlights the challenges anti-doping organizations face in their struggle to secure fair competition.

Some people felt that Armstrong deserved a new start in life and a chance to make a positive contribution to society, while others considered his actions an unforgivable betrayal of the ethos of sports. However the story will end, his name will remain associated with a complex legacy that spans remarkable achievement, deep disappointment, and, ultimately, a sincere and, I suspect, painful admission.

Now that's a proper case of suffering the consequences: having the whole world know you as a cheater.

6

How to Construct a
Believable Lie

He who tells a lie is not sensible of how great
a task he undertakes;
for he must be forced to invent twenty more
to maintain that one.
—ALEXANDER POPE

S o how is it done? Well, seeing as you and I don't know
the first thing about lying, I thought it might be useful
for us to learn a thing or two. We, the last remaining
truth tellers of our nations, need to up our game, basically.

No, I'm not being serious. But do you really know how
to construct a good lie? That might be useful to know. Why?
Well, to help you recognize it the next time somebody tosses
one at you.

A few years ago, I published a book on psychopathy and
the effects it has on us all. Among many other things, *Sur-*
rounded by Psychopaths contained descriptions of a set of manipulation techniques. I received some negative comments
for being a best-selling author with a large audience who had

chosen to demonstrate how people can be manipulated, but really there was no way around it considering what I wanted to do: teach people to recognize manipulation. To be able to protect yourself from manipulation, you need to know how manipulation works first. Otherwise, you wouldn't know what to look for.

I'm about to take a similar risk right here. In order for you to understand how to recognize and detect other people's lies, I need to show you how to construct a really believable lie.

I have to rely on your good judgment here and trust that you won't ever use these strategies for personal gain. Can we agree on that?

STEP BY STEP

So how do you construct a really good lie? It's a multi-step process.

To begin with, it'll help if you know why you want to lie. I'm assuming that you're not a psychopath or narcissist who lies just to amuse yourself, so let's presume here that you have some real reason for telling lies. Just doing it out of habit won't do for our purposes.

Find Your Motive

Suppose you find yourself in a situation of some kind. It could be absolutely anything. The point is simply that for some reason or other, you're not going to tell the truth. What do you stand to gain from not telling the truth in this moment?

Every lie starts with a motive. Understanding the under-lying reason is the first step in constructing a lie. This is only to be expected: Without a good enough reason, why would you lie at all? Assuming you know why you're lying, it's go-ing to be easier to keep things consistent.

As the inspirational speaker Simon Sinek put it, and very well in fact: start with *why*. He wasn't talking about lies, of course, but the same thing applies here, as it happens. What-ever you happen to be doing, you need to know why you're doing it. If you don't, there will be an obvious risk that you might make a mess of things.

Is there something you need to protect yourself from? Punishment, unpleasant consequences, the condemnation of others? Anyone who aspires to be a good liar needs to know these things, or they won't be able to keep their story straight.

Maybe you're looking to protect certain relationships? Is there someone, or some people, who you really don't want to lose? Consider whether these relationships are important enough to motivate an elaborate lie.

Is it perhaps that you want to gain certain benefits? Are these benefits important enough to make it worthwhile? There's a huge difference between getting a free cup of coffee and stealing someone's job.

Maybe constructing a good lie can help you increase your own power. It could be power over yourself, over others, over the situation, over the meeting, over the agenda, over the decision-making. You need some power in your life like every-body else, or the world will soon run you down. Make sure you genuinely understand if this is one of your motives.

This is where it all begins. With 100 percent clarity on your purpose.

Choose a Credible Lie

For a lie to be effective, it needs to be rooted in some kind of truth. Truly advanced liars often say that a good lie should be as close to the truth as possible.

There are several reasons for this. First of all, it will make it easier for you to get out of the lie if it's ever uncovered. You can always claim to have misunderstood something, some detail you overlooked that changed the whole situation. However, another reason why sticking close to the truth helps make a lie effective is that it will make the lie seem plausible. It reduces your chances of being immediately caught out by whoever it is you're lying to.

Mixing truth and fiction can confuse the people who hear the lie and make it more difficult for them to tell what's real and what isn't. People tend to act on their emotions, and their decisions aren't as frequently based on rational thinking as they imagine. This is true of pretty much everyone, so there's no point trying to convince yourself that you're some shining exception here. If somebody recognizes that what you're telling them is true, they will tend to feel that you're credible, and this will make it easy for you to sprinkle some elements into the middle of your story that completely alter the narrative about what happened.

Now, some people certainly adhere to the opposite claim. Their idea is that if you're going to lie, you should make your lie so big that nobody would ever suspect you might be stupid enough to try such a ridiculous attempt at deception. However, I think this only applies to people who are looking to pull one over on an entire society. Like political leaders with questionable intentions.

I would recommend that you stay as close to the truth as you can. It won't just seem more credible. You'll also end up with far less to keep track of in your head.

Focus on the Details, but Don't Overdo It

There is a common misconception out there that suggests that the most effective lies are full of details. The idea is that this will somehow cleverly prove that everything you're saying is true. But that's only a good idea if one condition is fulfilled: You need to be the kind of person who sprinkles lots of details around in ordinary situations, too. If you can barely remember what day it is most of the time, it will immediately arouse suspicion if you're able to give a detailed account of a night out in three-minute intervals. The person you're telling your made-up story to might not be able to tell which part of what you're saying is untrue, but they'll still sense that something is wrong. This isn't how you normally sound.

Overloading a lie with excessive or unnecessary details can definitely trigger suspicion. A good lie should contain just the right amount of detail to make it convincing without overcomplicating the story. And as usual, the more details you decide to include, the better you're going to have to plan your lie. On top of having to remember it all. As we all know, remembering the things that really happened can be difficult enough. Having to keep track of a bunch of things that didn't happen can simply be too much.

So keep the level of detail in your lie manageable.

Be Consistent in Your Behavior

This is one of the most important tools for making a lie believable. The power of consistency is enormous. For instance, take Goebbels's comment that a lie, if repeated sufficiently often, will become a truth.

One of the fastest ways to expose a lie is through inconsistencies. Because of this, it's essential to keep the story consistent when fabricating a lie. This applies both to the details and the way the lie is told over time. You need to be able to repeat it several times without ever stumbling. You might even need to deliver it to several different people.

At the heart of every lie, of course, there is a desire that people will believe your made-up story. Consistent behavior ensures that the lie will remain credible over time. If you claim to have had a latte at the coffee shop in one moment, and say you had an espresso in the next, you'll immediately attract suspicion. This produces completely different images in the mind's eye, and that won't seem right. You ought to know what you had to drink, because that choice says something about who you are.

The more consistently a lie is repeated, the better it will stick in the memories of both the liar and the listener. It's a well-known fact that some people who start out to deliberately lie can end up repeating a lie so often that they will eventually come to believe that what they're saying is true. This is because of how our brains work. Eventually, it will become part of the perceived memory.

The brain has difficulties distinguishing between the things we say or think and the things that really happen. A repeated lie will eventually become true in the brains of both the perpetrator and the victim. It won't literally be true, of course, but this is a well-known fact about how the mind works. Politicians and agitators of various kinds are highly aware of this.

You also need to consider the risk of contradicting yourself. Every time a story changes—however slightly—you will risk contradicting some previously mentioned detail. Latte or espresso—which was it?

Contradictions are obvious warning signs. And many people notice these kinds of things. They simply remember that you said you were sitting in a Ford. If you tell them it was a Toyota later on, you'll be in trouble. Consistency minimizes the risk of accidentally contradicting yourself. And that requires preparation, basically.

But there's more to this. Besides the actual contents of the lie, the emotional tone of your delivery will also need to be consistent. If you tell a tragic but fictional story with tears in your eyes one day, and then retell the same story quite nonchalantly the next day, this can definitely raise questions.

Maybe you're thinking that time heals all wounds? That's fine, but the brain sorts things by similarity. It makes me sad to think about my mother's funeral, even though it was more than ten years ago now. Anyone who hears me talk about it can tell that it was a tough day for me, even though my emotions have calmed a lot now compared to the week after it happened.

There are other reasons why you'll need to lie consistently.

Lying is mentally stressful for most of us. Each lie creates a potential loose end that may have to be dealt with in the future. By keeping your lies consistent, you'll reduce your cognitive load and save yourself from having to remember multiple versions of a single event. If, for some incomprehensible reason, you didn't want to admit you were riding in a Toyota (maybe your friend sells a competing brand)—decide what kind of car it was instead. Don't tell Emil it was a Ford one day, and then tell Sara it was an Opel the next day.

Ironically, consistent behavior is also often associated with trustworthiness. We're more likely to trust somebody whose behavior is consistent, even if the consistent story they present is completely made up. Some people can simply get away with more because we've already learned to think of them as credible. History is full of good people who have been considered to be the epitome of credibility. When they are later exposed as liars, people will experience this as far worse than they would have if they gave a shifty, unreliable impression.

In essence, consistent behavior is a shield that can protect you from future problems. It minimizes suspicion and ensures that your fictional story remains credible.

Anticipate Counterquestions

Before you tell a lie, you need to anticipate any potential questions that might arise. The bigger your lie is, the more likely it is that somebody will actually challenge you and question your story. Preparing some well-thought-out answers will ensure that you won't be too surprised.

A thoughtful and well-crafted lie will take into account any natural follow-up questions that may arise. Otherwise, you'll risk stuttering, contradicting yourself, or inadvertently revealing the truth you don't want to let slip.

Moreover, your ability to answer questions smoothly, without hesitation, will make your story seem even more credible.

On the other hand, lengthy answers and hesitation can be taken to indicate that you're making up your answer on the spot. That's where a lot of people get caught.

I mentioned earlier that lying is cognitively taxing. Anticipating questions and rehearsing answers in advance will allow you to preserve energy in the situations where you'll be telling your lie. Preparation reduces your stress, essentially. This is how many people claim you can beat lie detectors. You simply train yourself to give plausible answers to all the questions you anticipate. Eventually, you'll get used to saying these things, and there won't be any inconsistencies in your behavior. A problem will arise, of course, if you're asked a question that you couldn't predict.

The idea, then, is to control the narrative by preparing answers to potential questions. This will help you develop a strategy and direct the conversation. You could craft your initial lie in a way that will guide the victim toward certain questions and away from others that you know you'll have greater difficulty answering.

Basically, you want to anticipate questions to ensure that your deception will be as watertight as possible. This is a strategy that will make you less vulnerable to scrutiny, and increase the likelihood that your lie will be believed.

Master Your Body Language

Skilled liars are often good at controlling the physical signals they give off. They will maintain just the right amount of eye contact, keep their voices steady, and sit or stand without so much as a tremble. They have mastered the art of seeming sincere, even when telling a lie. In particular, they have trained

themselves to behave as *they normally behave* in ordinary situations.

Speaking of eye contact, the common idea that liars cannot
look people in the eyes is a myth. The idea is that constantly
averting your gaze is somehow a sign of lying. A solution to
this dilemma would seem to be to keep staring at the other
person, but it doesn't work that way at all. Maintaining eye
contact for more than five or six seconds at a time feels very
unnatural. Try it yourself, and study the reactions you get.
You'll make everybody's skin crawl.

It's also not true that liars who aren't prepared with things
to say will tend to make a quick glance up and to the left whenever they're about to tell a lie. Oh, and that one's supposed to
apply to right-handed people. People who are left-handed look
to the right, not to the left. But no. There isn't much in the way
of evidence to support this idea.

This myth is probably caused by the idea that lying requires
the brain to fabricate new information, and this engages the
imagination rather than the memory. When we search through
our memories, we tend to look downward much more.

Anyway, remember what I just told you about consistent
behavior: A good lie doesn't just sound right; it *feels* right, too.
You need to make sure that your emotions will be consistent
with the story you are telling. Genuine emotions can lend credibility to a lie, while fake emotions can act as warning signs.

If you want to tell people that you're afraid of snakes, and
that this is why you refuse to enter the forest, you'll need to
illustrate what you say in a similar fashion every time. And
I don't just mean the words you choose. You could say that
snakes are very frightening, and that they scare the life out
of you, and that's why you stay inside . . .

. . . But your emotions will be evident from your body language. They will be evident from your voice. Also, bear in mind that your body language transmits hundreds of thousands of signals. Not everyone understands all of them, but many will react if something feels off.

You've probably experienced this yourself. Somebody told you something, and afterward, your whole body was telling you that something was off somehow. You didn't have a clue what it was, but your hunch was confirmed later on. How did you know? It's a miracle!

Reinforce the Lie

One challenge you'll face is that people forget things. Often, they won't even remember the lie you told them. For an important lie to really take root, you might need to reinforce it over time. This reinforcement can be subtle, like casually referring to your false story in later conversations to entrench it in your collective memory. It also works in the same way as the consistent approach I mentioned earlier. As I have written before: The more frequently a lie is repeated, the truer it will appear to be.

It's also possible to tell your fabrication to others and get them to retell the same lie to the original victim. That will really make it seem like it actually happened.

Plan Your Exit Strategy

Of course, any experienced fraudster is aware that there is always a risk of getting caught. Because of this, they will often have an exit strategy worked out in advance. This could be a diversionary tactic, some way to shift suspicion to someone else, or even a way to turn people's attention to the accuser. This can be done as a preventive measure or saved for when they feel the truth is closing in on them. The Nazi propaganda minister, Joseph Goebbels, is said to have stated that a good strategy for dealing with your enemies is to accuse them of what you are guilty of.

For example, you could accuse the person who's trying to smoke you out of being a liar themselves, to lay down a further smoke screen and shift the focus from yourself. However, like many other stratagems, this requires advance planning.

The more you can stir the pot, the harder it will be for others to determine what's true and what's false.

RECOGNIZING THE SIGNALS

Eyes. Sometimes liars will engage in unusually prolonged eye contact, overcompensating for their deception. Other times, quick blinking or dilated pupils might be tell-tale signs. The challenge here is to notice some kind of change from the person's usual eye behavior.

Microexpressions. These are quick, involuntary facial expressions that reveal a person's genuine emotions—even if they only manifest for a fraction of a second. While someone might smile and reassure you that everything is fine, a brief flash of anger could hint at the truth that's hiding beneath the surface.

Defensive physical posture. Crossed arms, leaning away, or forming barriers (e.g., by placing a bag or a book between you) can be indications that something isn't right. They can be signs that the person in question is subconsciously seeking to shield themselves from the consequences of a lie.

Constantly clearing their throat or swallowing. The anxiety lying causes can produce physiological changes, one of which is making the liar's throat feel dry. If somebody clears their throat or swallows repeatedly before answering a question, this could be a sign of deceptive behavior. However, it could also just be ordinary stress.

Pursed lips. Many people will purse their lips slightly just before they tell a lie. It's easy to miss it, but it does happen.

Changes in vocal pitch. Stress and nerves can cause the vocal cords to tighten, which will raise the pitch of their speech. If somebody's tone of voice becomes noticeably higher when they discuss a certain topic, that's a good reason to be vigilant.

Fingering their face or neck. This could be what is known as a self-soothing gesture, a subconscious way to comfort oneself in the face of the anxiety brought on by the lie. It's almost as if they are literally trying to "hide" their deception.

Of course, they could just have a genuine itch. But why do they have an itch? When you lie, you'll be subconsciously aware of the fact that this could be dangerous. Blood will rush from your head to your hands and feet in case you have to flee the scene. When blood quickly vacates an area of skin, like the nose, this can cause an irritation. And an urge to scratch it.

Strange pauses. If someone frequently pauses or seems to be trying to think of what to say, this can be a sign that they're fabricating or modifying their story right in front of you.

Interpreting these clues will require careful observation and a good knowledge of the context. A single one of these signs in isolation will not necessarily indicate deception. It's important to look for combinations of clues and, more important, deviations from the individual's normal behavior.

The Exemplary Liar

To give you an even better grasp of how you can spot a lie, I'm going to illustrate the eight steps I've written about above. An imaginary character, Sam, will serve as our example.

Sam had always been the go-to guy at the IT company whenever something went wrong. He was responsible, hard-working, and reliable—in short, he had the kind of reputation that could make his colleagues jealous. His credibility was unquestionable. However, one night, everything changed. He made an unfortunate mistake and accidentally deleted a whole month's worth of the company's financial data. He stared at the screen, unable to accept that it was true. His panic intensified when he realized that his team had to give a presentation to some heavyweight investors in just three days. If they couldn't present the financial data he had just deleted there, it would seriously harm the company, on top of not knowing where it stood financially. What he had done was nothing short of disastrous, and it was likely to be considered sufficient grounds for dismissal if the CEO found out what he had done.

FIND YOUR MOTIVE

Sam was, understandably, very shaken. His impeccable reputation was at stake. His motive was clear: He needed to protect his reputation, and possibly even his job. The temperamental CEO of the company wasn't known for leniency when things went wrong. Owning up to his mistake could cost Sam dearly, especially in light of the upcoming investor presentation.

CHOOSE A CREDIBLE LIE

So Sam decided that he was going to tell his team that a system error had occurred, and that the recent data had been corrupted as a result. There was no way he could hide the fact that it was lost, so there was no way he could just pretend nothing had happened. He was determined not to take the blame, however. The IT team started to look into the issue. Unfortunately, things disappearing from servers wasn't an entirely uncommon occurrence, and this made his desperate lie quite plausible.

FOCUS ON THE DETAILS, BUT DON'T OVERDO IT

Sam explained that the error was an unfortunate event, and that it appeared to have been caused by a recent software update. Everyone knew that updates could sometimes cause problems. However, instead of getting into the technical details, which Sam didn't really know much about, he kept things relatively simple, and his explanation was just detailed enough to be convincing.

BE CONSISTENT IN YOUR BEHAVIOR

Whenever he was asked, Sam repeated the same story—there was a system failure after a software update. He claimed to have no idea how it had happened. Regardless of whether he was talking to his colleague Julia about it during a coffee break or discussing it with his manager, the story stayed consistent. Sam expressed genuine frustration and concern about the system failure, and made sure that his displays of emotion were consistent with the story. He spent hours in the office trying to *recover data*, which further reinforced the sense that he was genuinely concerned. And he *was* worried, so that part was completely genuine.

ANTICIPATE COUNTERQUESTIONS

Now Julia, a team member with a keen sense of curiosity, sensed that something didn't add up. She asked Sam why it was only the financial data that had been affected and not any of the other files. Sam was ready for this, though. He had anticipated that particular question, and he explained that the financial software was more sensitive to system updates, which made it particularly vulnerable.

MASTER YOUR BODY LANGUAGE

A series of sleepless nights and general anxiety had an impact on Sam's behavior. While his anxiety actually had a different cause (having to lie to his colleagues' faces), the effects still played into his lie very well. He maintained just the right amount of eye contact whenever discussing the incident, and he practiced in front of a mirror to make sure that he would look credible when he answered questions about it.

REINFORCE THE LIE

A day after the incident, Sam subtly reinforced his lie by sending an email to the entire team. In it, he updated everyone on his progress with the *recovery process* and thanked them for their patience. He even included a note from a fictional IT consultant in which he recommended specific backup measures that might prevent future mishaps.

PLAN YOUR EXIT STRATEGY

As the day of the investor presentation approached, Sam knew that he needed to bring his lie to some kind of end. He informed the team that while much of the data was still inaccurate, he had managed to recover some of it, and he was going to use older data to fill in any gaps for the presentation. He promised to arrange a full recovery soon afterward.

While the presentation wasn't perfect, it still went well. The investors were understanding, and the crisis was averted. The CEO stayed calm because he had been given Sam's word that the problem would soon be resolved.

We have to assume that Sam, a generally nice and decent guy, was quite drained of emotional and mental energy by this point. But he actually got away with it.

A Commentary on The Exemplary Liar

The lesson to take from the case of Sam we've just looked at is we need to study people's claims along consistent dimensions. Can we spot a liar by figuring out their strategy? Maybe, or maybe not.

What I can tell you is this: The vast majority of people are unable to prepare this kind of deception. They certainly lie effortlessly enough, but they don't do so with much skill, and this is a good thing for the rest of us. Instead of behaving consistently, they will constantly change their story and fabricate details that nobody ever asked for—details that they will subsequently go on to forget themselves. Taken together, this will give us the impression and the feeling that we're being lied to.

I have personally interviewed an incredible number of people in various recruitment contexts. I can confidently assure you that very few people are 100 percent truthful on those occasions. Apart from embellishing the truth regarding their previous experience—an assistant office manager might become an office manager, a bank clerk who dealt with ordinary, uninteresting customers will suddenly have worked on major, complex accounts, and a recently gradu- ated systems administrator will claim to be able to learn to run any system you could imagine—the most common way they lie is probably that they withhold some parts of the truth. Not mentioning certain problems they've had or not wanting to reveal the things that really stress them out. It's all totally understandable and very human. However, it's not too helpful when somebody is trying to find someone for a very specific key role.

In some cases, I've not been able to pinpoint what the problem is. I've just had a feeling that something wasn't quite right. Also, these days, many people have a lot of experience and training applying for jobs. They might have visited a con- sultant who helped them clean up their act and look their best in an interview—much like that long example about Sam that we just looked at.

The challenge here is that it takes a great deal of practice— not to mention incredible presence of mind—to present yourself as somebody who isn't quite you for up to ninety minutes. Few are able to do that well.

It might be something I notice about their body language. A tense look in the face of somebody who claims to have been very happy with their previous employer. For no obvious reason, the person begins to move around in their chair in a completely new way. Or their speech suddenly becomes very vague and evasive after previously having been very clear and distinctive. Or vice versa.

The point here is that everyone has things they'd like to hide. Everyone understands—this includes the recruiter, the job seeker, and everyone else—that people cover their blemishes and try to present themselves in their best light in these situations. The trick for me as a recruiting manager is to try to penetrate all the embellished experiences and platitudes and get a clear view. Whenever a candidate starts talking about the importance of cooperation and the value of getting everyone involved, I quickly move on to some more questions.

That's it! You have all the equipment you need to become a better spotter of liars now.

UNDERSTANDING THE LIE

Obviously, the fact that you understand the anatomy of a lie in no way exempts you from the ethical considerations involved. Lies, as we have seen earlier, can erode trust, and even the most skillful liars have to contend with the moral implications of their actions. It's important to remember that although lying may offer short-term benefits, the long-term consequences will often outweigh those benefits.

In summary, the art of deception is an intricate and multi-faceted one. While this review can certainly be turned into a good checklist for constructing useful lies, it also highlights the complexity and potential pitfalls that lie ahead if you embark on that path. The age-old adage is still a good one: Honesty is the best policy.

Now, you mustn't use this knowledge for the wrong purposes, okay? Understanding the background of a lie is mainly useful for detecting the crooks that we can sometimes find ourselves surrounded by. Looking for just the right amount of detail and all the other things that make for a good lie is all a matter of staying on the right side of the ethical line. But you already knew that.

It's important not to be constantly looking for signs of lies in other people. Staring excessively in an attempt to detect any microexpressions, grunts, weird pauses, and all the other stuff can make you seem rather crazy, to be honest. However, if you should get the feeling that says something isn't quite right, it's a good idea to start paying more attention to all those details. If you like, you can reread this chapter and add some notes to the margins. Yes, you're allowed to write in my books.

I wish you all the best in your attempts to recognize and decode people's lies.

INFAMOUS LIARS

The Tinder Swindler

Online dating can be a dodgy business. The growing number of dishonest individuals looking for opportunities for personal gain has become quite a concern to those who seek to navigate this complex landscape of personal preferences of all varieties. There are quite a lot of creeps out there, but I wonder if the individual who has become known as the Tinder Swindler doesn't take the prize. This person used the the unverifiable nature of dating apps to manipulate and exploit other people's sincere feelings.

The scammer created fictional personas that were designed to be personifications of the victims' ideal partners. Charming and attentive, this pseudo-personality would very skillfully form relationships that initially seemed incredibly meaningful and promising. However, much darker intentions were operating beneath the surface.

The Tinder Swindler was, in fact, a man who claimed to be the son of a wealthy diamond magnate named Lev Leviev. He went by the name of Simon Leviev. This scammer, who was originally named Shimon Hayut, was born in Israel. He successfully convinced women from all over the world to give him their money. Many even took loans from banks to give the money to him.

He used various psychological ploys to attract women's attention. On his Tinder profile, he would post pictures of himself traveling on a private jet and leading a luxurious life in expensive and famous restaurants and hotels all over the world.

However, that was only the beginning. He also created the website LLD Diamonds so that anyone who googled his name would discover a link to the site and be convinced that he really was the son of a multimillionaire who had made his fortune dealing diamonds. Why a guy like that would need to look for dates on Tinder is a very good question, but the scam nonetheless worked perfectly for quite some time.

He would form an emotional bond with the women he matched with on Tinder, date them for a few months, and then proceed to ask them to lend him money that he needed because his "enemies" were coming for him. Who these enemies really were remained shrouded in mystery. He then proceeded to spend the significant sums these women lent him on other women. Needless to say, he never repaid those loans.

To prove that he was in danger, he would send pictures of his supposed bodyguard, bleeding and with stitches on his forehead, and then follow this up with a video of himself in a blood-stained T-shirt during an ambulance ride.

The women he conned believed that he was rich because he had taken them on dates that gave them a taste of his lavish lifestyle. The thing is, he was paying for that lifestyle with his past victims' money. It was basically the same kind of scam that Bernie Madoff engaged in, a Ponzi scheme.

Mr. Leviev is believed to have stolen about $10 million over the years from women in various European countries. When he was finally arrested in Finland in 2015, authorities discovered two fake Israeli passports, three fake Israeli driver's licenses, two fake Israeli flight permits, and five forged American Express credit cards.

Mr. Leviev was sentenced to two years in prison for fraud in Finland in 2015. He's also wanted for the same crime in several other countries.

When Netflix made a documentary about his life, he relished the attention and wrote this message on Instagram: "I will share my side of the story in the next few days when I have sorted out the best and most respectful way to tell it, both to the involved parties and myself. Until then, please keep an open mind and heart." Whether this request seemed convincing to his victims is questionable, of course.

LLD Diamonds also sent a statement to *Newsweek* in which it stated: "LLD Diamonds has been a well-regarded leader in the diamond industry for three decades. Our company has no connection whatsoever with Shimon Hayut. He is a fraud who has tried to exploit our good name to con victims out of millions of dollars."

What motivated this guy, then? Money, I suppose. It must have been great to live in luxury and always let other people pick up the tab, and $10 million is quite a lot of money to steal in just a few years. The Tinder Swindler was quite willing to lie about absolutely anything to get to live that way. If he hadn't been caught, he would probably still be at it.

I don't expect that he would have changed his ways. There's probably a significant risk that he'll carry on deceiving people to finance his lavish lifestyle.

He's currently a free man who's struggling to rebuild his reputation. We'll have to see how that works out for him. If I were you, I'd make a point of remembering his face and steering well clear of him.

7

How the Four Colors Deal with Lies

The trust of the innocent is the liar's most useful tool.
—STEPHEN KING

An interesting question whenever you're trying to expose a liar is, of course, what variations you might expect to encounter based on the type of person you're dealing with. Since our basic assumption is, unfortunately, that everyone lies, it might be interesting to see if we could predict what kinds of lies a certain person might be likely to tell. After all, not everyone tells the same lies in the same way. Also, people tend to lie about different things, too. It would be convenient if we had a simple basis for predictions. However, people differ in their predictions, too. How might the different colors, for example, actually react when they find out that someone is lying to them?

Let's pretend that the liar is standing right in front of you. What should you really expect?

REDS LIE WITH PURPOSE

Dominance, the main trait of Reds, is characterized by confidence, authority, and a desire for control. Individuals who exhibit a high degree of dominance tend to be ambitious, competitive, and results-oriented. Red individuals are very purposeful and highly motivated to achieve their goals.

Their desire for power and authority can influence their attitudes to lying and deception. They might think of lying as a means to an end, a tool for overcoming obstacles, gaining advantages, or achieving desired outcomes. For example, a Red person might exaggerate their qualifications or achievements during a job interview in order to secure the position they want. While they do recognize that lying is unethical, of course, the drive they feel to achieve their goals can cause them to disregard their moral reservations.

Power and Control

A strong desire for power and control is characteristic of the Red profile. These individuals often seek to assert their authority and influence over others, and this can lead them to manipulate the truth to maintain or increase their power. For example, a Red leader might downplay a problem or withhold information to stay in control of a situation or make it difficult for others to question their authority.

Competition

Highly dominant people are often competitive about everything, and feel a strong drive to outdo others. This competitive spirit can bring them to deceive others to gain an edge.
Red athletes might lie about their training regime or their
physical fitness to mislead their competitors and give themselves a psychological advantage.

Rationalizing

Reds might rationalize their behavior and convince themselves
that lying is necessary or justified in a particular situation.
They might view deceptive behavior as a strategic act, almost
like a chess move, a necessary step toward achieving their
goals or overcoming some challenge. This rationalization can
help them ignore any feelings of guilt or moral reservations
they might have about lying.

Self-Confidence

Confidence is a key characteristic of the Reds. They tend to feel
like winners even before the race has begun. They'll often be
direct and forthcoming in their communication with others,
and I would argue that this can often make them more sincere
and honest than other people tend to be. They rarely see much
point in using white lies, for example. However, their self-
confidence can also push them to offer some rather bold and
convincing fibs when they feel that it's necessary. They can be
more likely to lie with confidence and conviction, which can
make it more difficult for others to detect their deception.

Risk Acceptance

Although lying can sometimes help Reds achieve their goals, assert their authority, or gain a competitive edge, it always involves a degree of risk and potential consequences. Lying can lead to a loss of trust and credibility, damaged relationships, and a tarnished reputation. Moreover, this can turn into a slippery slope where one lie leads to another, resulting in a web of deception that grows increasingly difficult to unravel. The problem for the rest of us is that Reds are often fully prepared to accept a degree of risk in order to advance their plans. They reason that since controlling everything is impossible, they might as well take some chances.

Loss of Trust and Credibility

What can the consequences be for a Red person who lies? Well, as we've already mentioned, trust is a fundamental part of any relationship, be it personal or professional. If someone is caught lying, this can lead to a loss of trust and credibility— which can be difficult or impossible to rebuild. People who fall victim to deception or manipulation can end up feeling betrayed and resentful. Since Reds rely on their authority to achieve their goals, this kind of loss can be very damaging to them. They may already struggle in their interpersonal relationships as a result of their pushy, competitive nature. Lying can exacerbate these difficulties and make it even harder for them to form and maintain meaningful connections with others.

A particular challenge for Reds is that they aren't relationship-oriented, but rather task-oriented. Losing a few friends on the path to success isn't the end of the world. At least not for a Red person.

A Summary of Red Liars

The Red profile is associated with a strong desire for power, control, and achievement, and these can make highly dominant individuals more willing to lie in certain situations. While lying can sometimes help them achieve their goals, assert their authority, or gain a competitive edge, this won't come without risks and potential consequences. Deceptive behavior can cause a loss of trust and credibility, damage relationships, ruin somebody's reputation, and bring all sorts of other problems.

If you're a Red person, my recommendation to you is to be aware of these potential pitfalls, and lie only with the utmost care and consideration.

YELLOWS LIE TO BE ACKNOWLEDGED

As we're discussing deception and lying, I feel I have to point out that these behaviors aren't unique to any specific personality type—they are general human tendencies that can manifest themselves in different ways depending on the situation in question and the individual's core temperament. Within the framework of the DISC theory, the Influence (*I*) personality type relates to lying and deception in fascinating ways. This personality type is most distinguished by the social skills, outgoing nature, and persuasiveness it is associated with, and these characteristics also tend to make these individuals interesting to consider in relation to lying.

Social Skills: A Double-Edged Sword

People who exhibit Yellow behaviors tend to be social chameleons. They can adapt their behavior to different situations and different types of people, mainly because one of their main characteristics is their desire for harmony in interpersonal relationships. However, this characteristic can also make them likely to resort to small (or white) lies to protect someone's feelings or social standing. The important question to answer is whether this kind of deceptive behavior is actually rather harmless, or whether it is likely to develop into more serious kinds of dishonesty as time goes by.

The Fine Line Between Influence and Manipulation

Being persuasive is one of the most noticeable characteristics of Yellow people. Their ability to convince people of things can serve many different purposes: from selling stuff to influencing people to considering something from a different point of view. But how far can this be taken before it crosses the line to actual manipulation and deception? I can tell you that in the many training sessions I've given, I've often heard people comment that Yellow people sound downright manipulative. That's not exactly flattering.

It's important for anybody who holds a lot of influence to recognize this. The distinction becomes particularly crucial

in situations where the stakes are high, like business negotiations or personal relationships in which lying might have
serious consequences.

The Need for Acknowledgment

Yellow people need to be acknowledged. They want to be
liked, recognized, and accepted by everyone. This desire for
acknowledgment can sometimes drive them to embellish the
truth or even lie outright to protect the social status they enjoy. This kind of lying is often a subconscious act, and it can
be viewed as a reaction to deep-rooted insecurities. However,
the effects of these lies can sometimes negatively impact both
their relationships and the trust they enjoy.

Emotional Intelligence and Deceptive Ploys

People with Yellow traits often possess a high degree of emotional intelligence. They're good at reading the room, predict-
ing people's reactions, and adapting accordingly. This insight
into human emotions can be used for good (e.g., in empathic
communication), but it can also be turned to more deceptive
or manipulative ends. Yellows can sometimes use their emotional acumen to detect when someone is lying to them, or
even to identify the best opportunities for them to lie. They
tend to play things by ear, and something that can cause
problems for the rest of us, of course, is that most of what
they say sounds phenomenal.

Lying to Yourself: Internal Deception

Interestingly, Yellows aren't just capable of lying to others, they're also particularly likely to lie to themselves. Any bad news might be filtered out and replaced by far brighter, more enjoyable memories. This form of self-deception can express itself as hubris or inflated self-confidence. Recognizing this inclination is the first step toward mitigating the internal and external effects of these lies—but, unfortunately, Yellows seldom decide to take that step.

They can't tolerate being criticized, and any accusations of misbehavior come as a bolt out of the blue to them.

I don't know how many times I've confronted Yellow individuals about their nonsense and pointed out all the things they have claimed that don't match up with reality. It often surprises me how surprised they look at hearing this. The picture I'm presenting obviously doesn't match their own self-image.

Who? Me? That doesn't sound like me at all!

Then they simply turn a deaf ear.

A Summary of Yellow Liars

The Yellow profile possesses incredible power, but with great power comes great responsibility. Understanding the nuances of when, how, and why a Yellow person might resort to lying is crucial for the individual and ultimately for society as a whole. Their willingness to lie doesn't make them bad people; it makes them human. What distinguishes Yellow truth tellers from Yellow liars is their degree of awareness about this characteristic, and their ability to keep their lying and themselves in check. However, we can't ignore the fact that Yellow people tend to tweak the truth they present as it suits them in the moment. The people who keep having to say things like *I never said that* are most often Yellow. Their main challenge here is that they simply don't remember saying it. And when they say these things, they genuinely believe them, because the words *feel* so right when they pass their lips.

GREENS LIE TO AVOID ARGUMENTS AND DEMANDS

People who exhibit high degrees of stability are usually cooperative, reliable, and easygoing. They value harmony, and often act as mediators when conflict arises. They prefer stable and predictable environments, and they tend to resist change. People who score high in the *S* dimension of the DISC model are characterized by a desire for consistency, patience, and a willingness to help others. They are empathetic, will often be perceived to be good listeners, and are generally considered nice people. These are the ones I call the Greens.

At first glance, one might presume that individuals who exhibit Green behavior would be less likely to lie. Their quest for harmony and their empathetic mindset ought to make them avoid lying in order to maintain positive relationships and avoid conflict. Conflict is one of the worst things you can expose a Green person to. They'll often go out of their way to avoid raised voices and angry looks. This, however, is often how they get themselves into trouble.

White Lies

White lies, as we said earlier, tend to be told with good intentions, usually in order to protect someone's feelings or to defuse an uncomfortable conflict. For example, telling a friend that their new hairstyle looks great, even if that's not your honest opinion, would be a typical white lie. This means that Greens, who value harmony and positive relationships, are more likely to tell white lies to maintain a positive atmosphere and avoid hurting anybody's feelings. They tend to profess to agree with whoever spoke last, regardless of what they actually think. Of course, this isn't always a workable strategy, but it is nonetheless their instinct to behave that way.

Lying to Bring Harmony

In some situations, lying can be thought of as a way to maintain harmony and prevent conflict. If a group of friends is trying to decide where to go for dinner and one person states a strong preference for a particular restaurant, an individual whose profile is highly dominated by Green might lie about their own preferences to prevent conflict and maintain the group's harmony.

I like sushi, too. They might say that even if they find the idea of eating raw fish anything but appealing.

Lying to Prevent Change

People who feel a strong need for stability prefer predictable environments and tend to resist change. I should clarify that: They actually *hate* change, particularly rapid change. The good old days *were* good. In any situation where the truth might disrupt the status quo, a Green individual might well be inclined to lie just to maintain stability. I have seen this behavior reach extreme heights, when Green people have struggled to an almost pathological degree to avoid having to state their feelings about an impending change. It might even have been funny to see if it wasn't so sad.

Situations Where Greens Avoid Lying

However, there is some good news. There is also reason to believe that individuals who exhibit Green behavior are less likely to lie than others in some situations. They value long-term relationships, and they tend to be loyal and trustworthy in general. They may be less likely to lie to their close friends and family members, because they value these relationships so much and wouldn't want to jeopardize them by behaving dishonestly. The fear of being caught in a lie and the potential negative consequences that could follow can serve as very strong deterrents for Greens. They prefer to stay honest, even if this might cause conflict in the short term, in order to maintain their integrity and retain the trust of others.

A Summary of Green Liars

The relationship between the Green profile and the willingness to lie is rather complex and multifaceted. Although there are some situations where people with Green traits are more likely to lie—for example, to maintain harmony or prevent change—there are also situations in which they are less likely to lie. For example, in long-term relationships or other contexts where lying could bring major consequences or cause a serious conflict. Understanding the nuances of this particular "game" can help you predict and make sense of Green people's behavior. Ultimately, of course, their willingness to lie will be influenced by countless factors.

BLUES LIE TO GAIN OTHER PEOPLE'S TRUST

Individuals who score high for analytical behavior in the DISC model are usually characterized as careful, conscientious, and systematic. They are often thought to be detail-oriented and quality-conscious, and they often have an extensive personal set of internal or external standards that they strive to uphold. People with high conscientiousness generally value accuracy, reliability, and integrity. They tend to carefully weigh up the pros and cons before making decisions, and they often take a meticulous and organized approach to their work and everyday activities. I like to call these individuals Blues, as a learning aid.

Their propensity to deceive others is influenced by a wide range of factors, ranging from the current situation to the potential repercussions that deception might bring. A conscientious behavioral pattern will play an important role in determining an individual's willingness to engage in deceptive behavior.

Lying to Maintain Standards

Blue individuals often follow a set of internal or external standards. In situations where lying might help them establish or maintain these standards, they will be more likely to resort to deception. If an individual believes that punctuality is extremely important and they find themselves arriving late to a meeting, they might lie about the reason for their late arrival in order to uphold their image as somebody who values punctuality.

Lying to Avoid Mistakes

Blues are often very reluctant or even fearful when it comes to making mistakes or being perceived as incompetent. In situations where admitting to a mistake or a lack of knowledge might bring negative consequences, a Blue person might be more inclined to fudge the truth in order to maintain their reputation as a competent and knowledgeable person.

Lying for Perfection

The desire to achieve the best possible results, if not absolute perfection, and avoid all kinds of criticism can be a strong motivator for conscientious individuals. They may resort to lying if they believe that it will help them achieve a perfect result or deflect criticism. When Blue people realize that they have made a mistake that might attract criticism, they might be inclined to try to cover up their mistake or lie about it to protect their reputations as perfectionists.

Compliance With Moral and Ethical Standards

Now, there is also reason to believe that a Blue behavior profile will make people less likely to lie in certain situations.

Blues often subscribe to a strong moral and ethical code. They value honesty and integrity, and they may be less likely to lie because it simply conflicts with their moral convictions. In situations where lying might bring personal gain but would be ethically questionable, a person who exhibits high conscientiousness might choose to be honest even if this would have negative consequences for them personally.

Fear of Long-Term Consequences

People who exhibit high degrees of conscientiousness tend to consider the long-term consequences of their actions. In fact, they often consider so many potentialities they can sometimes end up unable to bring themselves to act. Trying to predict every eventuality can be quite draining. However, they have sufficient powers of imagination to assess the risks they might face. They may be less likely to lie because of their awareness of the potential negative repercussions that can follow an act of deception.

A Summary of Blue Liars

The relationship between conscientiousness and willingness to lie is multifaceted and usually depends on the context. While there are some scenarios where Blue people can be more likely to lie, like situations where they're seeking to maintain standards or avoid mistakes, there are also situations where they would be less likely to do so. These might be when they act in accordance with their moral and ethical codes, or when they consider the long-term consequences of behaving deceptively in some way. Ultimately, the choice between deception and honesty will be determined by a variety of factors, and these people's conscientious personality traits will only ever be one piece of the puzzle. Understanding the nuances of this interplay can help you predict and make sense of conscientious individuals' behavior and grant valuable insights into the complex nature of deception.

HOW DO THE DIFFERENT PERSONALITY TYPES REACT TO LIES?

I thought it might be interesting to take a look at what might happen in the opposite situation. How do people with different behavioral profiles react when lied to? Since we have already established that lying is wrong but that it sometimes happens when people get carried away, it might be useful for you to know for which people the stakes are the highest. Is it the Reds, the Yellows, the Greens, or the Blues? And how are the consequences best handled in each case?

Lying to Reds

Being lied to is an insult that can trigger a range of emotions and reactions, from feeling betrayed and hurt to getting angry and confrontational. A Red's behavioral patterns will definitely influence their reactions in that kind of situation. They will rarely overlook a slight, and these cases are no exception.

Analyzing the Situation
Reds are determined and pragmatic. With a bit of luck, they will manage to stop themselves before they erupt. If they dis-

cover that you have lied to them, they are likely to quickly analyze the situation to try to understand your motive for lying, and then assess the impact of your lie on their goals and plans. They might consider whether the lie was malicious or well-intentioned, and whether it might have significant consequences or is likely to be relatively insignificant. This will all happen in a matter of moments, and if you're lucky, you might just get away with it.

Taking Charge

People with Red behavior profiles like to be in control. When they find out that they have been deceived, they will sometimes take immediate action to regain control of the situation. This could involve trying to uncover the truth, correcting the situation, or taking action to minimize the impact of your lies.

Confrontation

Reds tend to be very direct and confrontational. They're also controlling, and tend not to be too relationship-oriented. However, having someone lie to them can still trigger a powerful emotional reaction. They might feel betrayed, angry, or disappointed, particularly if the perpetrator of the deception is someone they trusted. Also, they seldom stop to think. When it dawns on them that you have lied to them, their initial reaction will be to address the situation immediately. Right now. They will confront you and demand an explanation. Their unusually pushy nature will make it easier for them to confront a liar directly rather than avoid the issue or suppress their emotions.

You might as well prepare for battle because they won't

mince words if they consider you an untrustworthy person. The most brutal scoldings I have witnessed in my days have all been delivered by Red people who have lost their patience entirely with someone. *Blind rage* is an apt description, and the main fuel for this anger is their sense of betrayal.

Now, there are some positives here, too. Their pragmatic and results-oriented natures can cause them to focus on resolving the situation rather than dwelling on their emotional reactions. Once the eruption passes, the dust will settle. They seldom hold grudges. They might well give you another chance to prove yourself to them. One chance. You'd best take it.

Reassessing Relationships
Trust is a crucial aspect of any relationship, and being lied to can cause a loss of trust. Reds are fully prepared to reevaluate every aspect of their relationship with somebody who has lied to them. They try to determine whether the deception is a one-off event or part of a long-term pattern of behavior. After making a call on this, they will move on to determining whether the relationship still matters to them or needs to be terminated.

Setting Boundaries
Reds tend to have clear boundaries and expectations of others. When someone lies to them, they might view this as a violation of these boundaries. As a result, they may seek to reinforce their boundaries and clarify their expectations to prevent similar situations from occurring in the future. The consequence of this—if you're the person who lied to them— could be a severe restriction of your freedom of movement

around them. You could well be subjected to an incredible degree of scrutiny and control.

Lying to Yellows

Yellows enjoy interacting with others, they like to be the center of attention, and they are primarily driven by their desire for social recognition, positive relationships, and favorable environments. They are often averse to conflict and do whatever they can to avoid it or set things right. (However, this behavior can also spark conflict, although that's another matter.)

Yellows tend to like most people. Because of their friendly and accepting nature, they will often assume that others share their values and intentions. This disposition makes them particularly vulnerable to deception and betrayal.

Initial Shock and Distrust

For individuals who have, shall we say, distinctive egos—who it makes sense to refer to as Yellows—it will often come as a shock when they discover that someone has lied to them. Given their trusting nature, their immediate reaction may be one of disbelief. They might find it difficult to accept that someone they have placed their trust in has deceived them. This phase can involve some doubt over their own judgment. Despite their creative and imaginative nature, this possibility never crossed their minds. *Have I lost it?*

Emotional Pain and Disappointment

The next stage of a Yellow's reaction to deception will often be characterized by emotional agitation and disappointment.

They will feel let down and betrayed by the person who lied to them, particularly when that person happens to be someone they considered a friend or close associate. Their essentially optimistic and trusting nature can make them experience this as more painful than other personality types might do in similar circumstances.

The Need to Understand

Yellow people often feel a strong need for closure and understanding. They may seek out the person who lied to them to demand that they explain their actions.

How could you?

Their natural tendency to avoid conflict can bring them to approach this interaction with the aim of achieving reconciliation rather than confrontation. But they can also feel torn between their desire to maintain a positive relationship and their need to address the deception itself.

Forgiveness and Rebuilding Trust

Given their kind and forgiving nature, Yellows will often be inclined to forgive the person who lied to them, especially if they sense that the person in question is genuinely remorseful and committed to making up for their transgression. However, rebuilding trust can take a long time. Yellows may well be more cautious and less trusting in the future, at least until trust is regained.

Mitigating Circumstances

Not all lies are created equal. White lies, or lies told with good intentions, can be easier for Yellows to accept, forgive, and move on from. Lies that constitute more serious betrayals or have caused significant harm, on the other hand, will provoke stronger reactions and be more difficult to forgive. Intentionally misleading a Yellow can cause some real problems. They can take it very personally.

The closer the bond between the Yellow person and the liar is, the more intense their reaction is likely to be. Lies told by a close friend or family member can be more hurtful and disappointing to them than lies told by more distant acquaintances. They might think: *How could you do this to me? I thought you cared about me?*

Past Experiences

Past experiences of deception can also affect how these individuals will react to lies. They may have a harder time trusting their peers if someone has lied to them or betrayed them in the past. On the other hand, if their past experiences have been mostly positive, they may be more likely to forgive. They also tend to have poor memories. After some time, the incident will have faded to some degree.

Lying to Greens

Individuals who strive for stability (S) in the DISC model are usually patient and calm. They are often empathetic and supportive, and they love stability and consistency. Greens also tend to be team players, good listeners, and generally averse to change. They value relationships, trust, and loyalty. So what is it like for a Green to realize that they have been duped by somebody?

Greens Take It Personally

Discovering that someone is lying to you can be a distressing experience for anyone, and of course, people with a strong need for stability are no exception. However, their typical reactions can differ from those of other personality types as a consequence of their core attitudes and values.

As mentioned previously, Greens are relationship-oriented. As a result, discovering that someone they trust is lying to them can be particularly hurtful and cause them to become disappointed, feel betrayed, and lose trust in the person who deceived them. They may also experience self-doubt and question their ability to judge other people's character or wisely place their trust in the future. They also carry grudges. These individuals won't forget an ill deed.

Seeking Understanding

Greens tend to be good listeners and always try to see things from other people's point of view. When they discover that someone has lied to them, their first reaction may be to ask for an explanation and try to understand the reasons for the deception. They may be inclined to give the person who lied to them a chance to explain themselves, and they are likely to be willing to consider the context and circumstances in which the lie was told. However, this is mostly about gaining an understanding, which is *not* the same thing as forgiveness.

Avoiding Confrontation

Individuals who score high for stability usually prefer to avoid arguments and confrontations. To put it more directly, they fear conflict. They can be reluctant to address a lie immediately, and they may internalize their feelings and reactions at first. However, their quest for stability can eventually bring them to address the problem, as leaving it unresolved will cause tension and instability in the relationship. However, it's clear that many of them need help getting this process started because they belong to one of two so-called passive profiles. This means that they are more reactive than proactive.

Reevaluating Relationships

Trust and loyalty are crucial for individuals whose profiles have a lot of Green in them. Being lied to can cause them to reevaluate their relationship with the liar. They may question the person's reliability and consider if the relationship can actually continue now that their trust has been damaged. But their natural inclination to maintain stability can make them start to look for ways to rebuild the relationship and reestablish their trust rather than ending things immediately. It all very much depends on the particular circumstances.

One reaction you can expect to see from a Green person is that they will simply stop contacting you. They might also start exhibiting passive-aggressive behavior.

Seeking Support

Another thing that can happen is that Greens might look to their close friends and family for support in a challenging situation like this. Feeling cheated and betrayed can be emotionally painful for them, which makes them likely to seek support from their most trusted inner circle to help them process their emotions and determine the best course of action. But this is all likely to be limited to a fairly small circle of people. They won't be posting about it on Instagram.

Resistance to Change

Greens are usually opposed to change and favor stability. This resistance can also play a part in their reactions to lies. They may be reluctant to make drastic changes to their relationships or their attitudes to trust, and they may prefer to work through the problem and restore things to the way they used to be over making significant changes.

Lying to Blues

Blue individuals are usually analytical, detail-oriented, and systematic. They value accuracy, consistency, and reliability. These people prefer a structured environment, and they are naturally inclined to follow rules and established routines. They are usually reserved and private people who prefer to keep their emotions in check. Blues try to maintain high standards for themselves and others, which makes them particularly sensitive to deception and dishonesty. So what happens when you lie to someone like this?

Analyzing the Situation

When they discover a lie, Blues will usually engage in a thorough analysis of the situation. They might replay conversations in their mind, evaluate the evidence, and consider different points of view in order to ascertain the full and ugly extent of this insidious deception. Their analytical nature will drive them to gather all the relevant information before they make a judgment or take any kind of action.

Relevant Circumstances

The nature of the deception can have a significant impact on how a Blue will react. They can quite easily understand and forgive a white lie or a lie told with good intentions. On the other hand, a lie that involves deceit or causes significant emotional damage might provoke a stronger reaction and be more difficult for them to move on from.

Past experiences of deception can also influence the reactions of Blue individuals. If they have been lied to or betrayed in the past, they may find it more difficult to trust others and adopt a more cautious approach. If, however, their experiences of other people have been mostly positive, they will be more likely to forgive.

Feelings of Betrayal and Disrespect

Once these detailed analyses have confirmed that a lie has been told, Blue people will often feel betrayed and disrespected. After all, they value honesty and integrity, and being made the victim of some filthy liar constitutes a direct challenge to these core values. The high standards they set for themselves and others make it particularly hurtful to them when someone deceives them.

Seeking Clarification

After processing their feelings, Blues will often seek clarification from the person who lied to them. They may demand that the villain offer them an explanation that can help them understand the reasons for the lies. Their systematic approach allows them to address the problem directly and rationally, even though this can certainly be emotionally challenging for them.

However, being lied to is something they can quite easily move on from.

Reassess the Relationship

A Blue person is certainly going to reevaluate their relationship with the person who deceived them. They will question whether they can ever trust the person again, and whether the relationship is worth maintaining. After all, they aren't particularly relationship-oriented to begin with, so why should they cling to something that doesn't even seem to work? They don't maintain large numbers of friendships, but tend rather to stick to fairly limited circles. Their decision might depend on the nature of the lie, the person's response when questioned, and the history of the relationship. Also important is whether they deem it to be a one-off offense or something that will happen more frequently in the future. Being deceived by a close friend or family member can be more hurtful and disappointing than being told a lie by some more distant acquaintance.

The Importance of Setting Boundaries

If they should choose to maintain the relationship, Blue people will often set new boundaries after having been tricked by somebody. They may become more cautious and reserved in their interactions with this individual. In fact, the silence is likely to be deafening at first. Setting boundaries helps them protect themselves from future deception and reinforces their demand for honesty and integrity.

THE COLORS LEAD THE WAY

As you can see, things can go quite differently depending on who you're dealing with. And, as always, understanding people who don't function and think like you do can be very valuable. Sometimes it can feel as though someone isn't playing fair, when in reality, they just think in a different way than you do. Sometimes it can be fruitful to address these differences. Maybe you don't even define lies or untruths the same way. As always, it will help if you can communicate rather than trying to read each other's minds.

INFAMOUS LIARS

Bill Clinton

"I did not have sexual relations with that woman."

That's one of the most infamous quotes in the history of the world.

When the history of the American presidents is written in the distant future, it will probably state that few scandals have left such a deep echo in the soul of the United States as this one did. The affair between President Bill Clinton and White House intern Monica Lewinsky happened in the late 1990s. It eventually caused the House of Representatives to impeach Clinton, making him the second US president in history to face this ordeal (although he was subsequently acquitted by the Senate). But beyond the actual scandal itself, it was Clinton's lies about it that made it so remarkable.

Monica Lewinsky accepted an internship at the White

House in 1995. Over the course of the next year and a half, she and President Clinton had several . . . intimate encounters. Both parties would later admit that their relationship had been most inappropriate. Up to this point, I think most people would agree.

In late 1997, rumors of the affair began to circulate. When these rumors eventually reached the attention of the press, Clinton quickly denied them. During a press conference, he uttered the words that live on in infamy: "I did not have sexual relations with that woman." This outright denial was echoed by his close advisers, who probably believed him at first.

However, Clinton's denials weren't limited to press conference appearances. In connection with a separate sexual harassment lawsuit filed by Paula Jones, a former Arkansas state employee, Clinton was questioned under oath in January 1998. When he was asked about Lewinsky, he denied having "sexual relations" with her, using a very narrow definition of the term. This would later become a significant issue, as lying under oath—perjury—is a serious crime.

However, Lewinsky had told a colleague, Linda Tripp, about her relationship with Clinton. Unbeknownst to Lewinsky, Tripp had recorded their conversation. Details of Lewinsky's encounters with Clinton soon reached lawyer Ken Starr. After initially being appointed to investigate the Whitewater controversy, which also involved the Clintons, he was soon given the authority to investigate the Lewinsky affair, too.

On top of all this, a blue dress belonging to Lewinsky turned up that was stained with the president's . . . DNA. Now, there was physical evidence of their intimate relationship.

When all this evidence started to appear, Mr. Clinton changed his story. In August 1998, he testified in court. In a televised address to the nation, he subsequently admitted to having had an inappropriate relationship with Lewinsky and recognized that this had been "wrong." However, he maintained that his statements during the Paula Jones trial had been "legally correct." I can only assume that there was a whole team of expensive lawyers involved here to help him tread this fine line between truth and lies. The whole story is a sordid affair from start to finish, and I have no intention to even try to recount all of its twists and turns.

The House of Representatives initiated impeachment proceedings spurred on by Clinton's evasive lies. In December 1998, they voted to impeach Clinton on two charges: perjury and obstruction of justice. The primary basis for the perjury charge was the Paula Jones case, while the obstruction charge was linked to his attempt to keep the affair with Monica Lewinsky secret. The Senate subsequently acquitted Clinton.

Mr. Clinton finished his second term as president, but this scandal still defines his legacy.

The affair and the lies that followed it deeply polarized the American public. In the eyes of some, Clinton's behavior was an unforgivable breach of trust. To others, it's no more than a regrettable mistake that shouldn't be allowed to overshadow his political achievements.

Clinton had and still has a reputation as an extremely charming and engaging man. He could easily charm his political opponents thanks to his undeniable charisma. There's no shortage of testimonials from people, both men and women, who were completely enchanted by his mere presence. But nobody on the planet has forgotten this embarrassing episode, of course, and it's a glaring blemish on his record.

In a study of psychopathic traits in US presidents carried

out by British psychologist Kevin Dutton, Bill Clinton scored the second highest of all presidents. Only John F. Kennedy scored higher, according to Dutton. Yes, that's the truth. This might explain the fact that Clinton still seems quite unembarrassed to move around in his usual circles. He simply doesn't appear to be particularly affected by the scandal. Somewhere inside, he seems to be able to rise above the whole thing.

In his memoirs, and in more recent interviews, Clinton recognizes that he has some serious personal flaws. He has repeatedly apologized to Lewinsky and the American people for his indiscretions, and for the choices he made as the scandal unfolded.

To err is human, as they say. And that's probably true. But it doesn't mean that everyone will forget. Or forgive.

8

How Psychopaths and Narcissists Lie

There were lies we told to save ourselves,
and then there were lies we told to rescue others.
What counted more, the mistruth, or the greater good?
—JODI PICOULT

Speaking of Bill Clinton, why don't we take a look at some of the world's most effective liars? Narcissists and psychopaths.

Understanding the manipulative techniques that psychopaths and narcissists often use is essential if you want to be able to recognize and protect yourself from them. They often resort to a combination of lying, playing the victim, and various other tactics to gain control over others and alter situations in ways that favor them. Their lack of remorse and guilt in combination with their ability to lie convincingly can make it extremely difficult for the people around them to recognize that they are being manipulated.

Their lies are often concealed under appealing layers of superficial charm, which is another significant characteristic shared by psychopaths and narcissists. The allure of a charming individual can be quite intoxicating, and this behavior, which is really quite superficial, can be very disarming even to the most discerning of observers.

These are the people you need to be watching out for. They aren't victims and they don't deserve your pity. They are evil incarnate. And they can tell any lie you could imagine. The problem with these people is that they often lie just because they can. They don't need a real reason to lie. It amuses them, basically.

MASTER MANIPULATORS

Psychopathy and narcissism are two distinct personality disorders, each with their own unique set of characteristics. Psychopathy is characterized, among other things, by a lack of empathy, remorse, and guilt, as well as superficial charm, a willingness to manipulate others, and impulsive behavior.

Narcissism, on the other hand, is characterized by an inflated sense of importance, an excessive need to be admired, a lack of empathy, and an apparent inclination to exploit others for personal gain.

Although these two disorders—which aren't mental illnesses as such, but rather two distinct varieties of personality disorders—are not identical, they do share several key characteristics.

The most obvious of these are their lack of empathy and their propensity for manipulative behavior. Lacking empathy means that psychopaths and narcissists are unable to imagine what other people are feeling, and this can cause a whole host of problems. Most commonly, of course, for the people they encounter, as we will soon see.

Manipulative behavior is a common trait of both psychopaths and narcissists. It involves misleading people to gain control over them and turn various situations to their own advantage. I have written about both psychopaths (*Surrounded by Psychopaths,* 2016) and narcissists (*Surrounded by Narcissists,* 2021) before. In those two books, I give detailed accounts of the techniques they use to manipulate the people around them. Here are some of the most common manipulation techniques that psychopaths and narcissists often use.

Gaslighting

You may have heard of this one. This is a manipulative tactic in which someone makes another person question their own reality, memory, or perceptions. It is a way of gaining control over somebody by causing them to doubt their own sanity. For example, a narcissist might deny having said something hurtful, or accuse the other person of being overly sensitive, or of misremembering the whole situation.

Victimhood

Psychopaths and narcissists will both often play the victim to gain the sympathy of the people around them so they can continue to manipulate them. They might exaggerate their problems, pretend to be hurt, or claim that they are being treated unfairly. These approaches are all attempts to manipulate others into giving them support or something else they desire. Note that they don't actually feel victimized in the slightest, quite the contrary, but they do understand the value of posing as victims.

Love Bombing

This involves showering someone with affection, compliments, and gifts to win their trust and affection. Once the target has been snared by this, the manipulator can start to use them in various ways in a continuous cycle of mental abuse. People who suffer from low self-esteem are particularly vulnerable to this.

Triangulation

Another popular technique involves pitting two people against each other to cause conflict and gain control of a situation. For example, a narcissist might tell one person that another person said something bad about them, even if they never did, just to create animosity and give themselves a psychological advantage.

Playing Dumb

This is just what it sounds like. It involves pretending not to know or understand even simple things in order to avoid responsibility for something or to manipulate other people into doing something for you. Funnily enough, it can be extremely effective for a manipulator to play dumb because most people would rather try to appear smarter than they are.

The Silent Treatment

This means ignoring someone, or acting very dismissively to punish them or gain control over them. It is a way of exercising power by withholding attention and affection.

FORMIDABLE FRAUDSTERS

These are just a few simple examples from the repertoire that virtually all narcissists or psychopaths rely on. To state the obvious: Naturally, this can manifest very differently from one individual to another. There are tests used by the criminal justice system to grade how serious somebody's condition is. All these behaviors can be graded on a scale. The higher somebody scores, the greater the problems they will cause for the people around them.

So what's the story with lying and these two most unpleasant types?

Well . . . lying is an essential key component of the manipulative strategies used by both psychopaths and narcissists. Pathological lying, or the tendency to lie compulsively for no obvious reason, is a standard mode of behavior among the people who suffer from these disorders.

This could include lying about their own actions, feelings, and intentions, but also lying about others. I can honestly say that if I knew somebody who had been clinically diagnosed with psychopathy or narcissism, I would *literally* not trust a single word they said. Not one. None.

Psychopaths lie just because it amuses them. They lie even

when they have no reason to do so. It's just what psychopaths do. Moreover, psychopaths will never take responsibility for their actions. They will always blame other people.

The lies told by psychopaths and narcissists will often be elaborate and remarkably convincing. They might fabricate intricate narratives that are difficult to refute, and they are able to lie so believably and with such conviction that it's very difficult to tell if they are lying or not. This knack for lying convincingly can make it difficult for the rest of us to recognize that we're being manipulated.

A Lack of Remorse or Guilt

One important characteristic of both psychopaths and narcissists is their lack of remorse or guilt. They are aware that these emotional responses exist in others, but they don't experience them personally. Brain scans have revealed to us that the amygdala, the part of the brain that regulates stress and many other reactions, differs from the norm in these individuals. And you can't fix that. In other words, psychopaths and narcissists simply don't feel bad at all about lying or manipulating others. This lack of remorse and guilt contributes to the ease with which they can lie and manipulate others.

A Lack of Empathy

In simple terms, empathy is the ability to understand and identify with another person's feelings. It is a fundamental aspect of all human interaction that allows us to connect with one another on a deeper level and form meaningful relationships.

Empathy is a key component of our capacity to tell the truth and maintain honest relationships. When we empathize with someone, we're able to understand how our actions and words affect them. This understanding often discourages us from lying, as most people don't want to hurt or upset their fellow human beings. However, in individuals who suffer from psychopathy or narcissism, empathy is largely absent, and this fact contributes greatly to their propensity to lie and manipulate. If we aren't fully able to understand or care about other people's feelings, there won't be any real reason for us to tell the truth or even consider the effects that lying might have on others. This is the reason why these individuals lie with such ease and with no remorse. They simply don't feel anything at all.

It's worth mentioning that many people believe that psychopaths, for example, actually have a very good understanding of the feelings of others, it's just that they don't feel anything themselves. This is what allows them to manipulate others so effectively.

Anyway, trust is a fundamental aspect of any healthy relationship, and constant lying and manipulative behavior will naturally erode this trust as time goes by. These emotional abuses can cause a breakdown in communication and may ultimately bring about the end of the relationship.

But there's more. This lack of empathy also means that individuals who suffer from psychopathy or narcissism don't care at all about the emotional impact their lies might have. Accordingly, they don't take any responsibility for making amends or repairing damaged relationships.

Understanding the role that empathy plays in lying and manipulation can help us recognize and protect ourselves from the manipulative tactics of psychopaths and narcissists. If we can notice their lack of empathy and their propensity to lie, we will be able to set boundaries, seek support, and take steps to protect our own emotional well-being.

Self-Centeredness

Self-centeredness is a prominent characteristic of both psychopaths and narcissists. It also plays a significant role in their use of lying and manipulation. Psychopaths and narcissists both possess an inflated sense of importance—their self-absorption is all too often the thing that fuels their behavior. Their own needs and desires are always the most important things, and the needs and feelings of others don't "exist."

Emotional Abuse

This one can get a bit tricky. Psychopaths will often be so convinced of their own superiority that things can get rather unpleasant. On the other hand, many narcissists actually have rather fragile self-images, which they go to great lengths to protect. The consequences are similar, however. They lie about their own actions, achievements, and feelings in order to maintain a façade of competence, superiority, and desirability.

For example, a narcissist might exaggerate their achievements to gain admiration, while a psychopath might lie about their past to seem more sympathetic or trustworthy. Both scenarios involve lying to manipulate the perceptions of others and maintain the specific self-image this individual has decided to hold up as the truth.

The self-centeredness of psychopaths and narcissists will often cause them to completely disregard the feelings and needs of others. This can turn into emotionally abusive behavior as they manipulate and lie to achieve their goals without any regard for the emotional impact they have on their victims. Ultimately, self-centeredness, lying, and manipulation can simply lead to relationships breaking down, as people choose to distance themselves from these problematic individuals in the interest of their own well-being. At this point, the question is one of whether the psychopath or narcissist will agree to end the relationship. It's far from certain that this will be a painless procedure.

When Mark Lied to the Police

Let me give you a simple, everyday example taken from a real-life experience of one of my former clients.

Mark is a charismatic, successful businessman who has a well-hidden secret: He is a high-functioning psychopath. He has never been diagnosed because he has the ability to blend into society and manipulate everyone around him. Mark doesn't feel remorse, guilt, or empathy like most people do. He often engages in deceptive behavior, sometimes without gaining from it in any tangible way—his main reason for it is the thrill of doing it. He also often finds it hard to believe how gullible people can actually be.

One day, while attending a business conference, a crime occurs at the hotel where he is staying. A prominent entrepreneur is found dead in his room. The police start to question all the guests.

When asked where he was at the time of the crime, Mark calmly replies: "I was in a bar in the city center with a friend. We were there from 9 P.M. until midnight."

However, the hotel security camera footage clearly shows Mark entering the hotel at 10:30 P.M., shattering his alibi. When confronted with this evidence, he just shrugs and says, "I must have been confused about the times. I was in the bar earlier and then returned to the hotel."

Mark wasn't involved in the crime, and the security footage eventually proves his innocence. His fabricated alibi, then, wasn't just unnecessary; it also raised unnecessary suspicions against him.

What normal person would lie to the police when they genuinely had nothing to hide? You and I are bound to ask, Why this pointless lie?

But Mark doesn't wonder that. His question would rather be this: *Why not?*

For a psychopath like him, lying is a game, a way to test his own abilities. He doesn't need any obvious reason to deceive people. The thrill of misleading others, the challenge of maintaining a lie, and the dynamics that surround the whole thing feed him positive energy. In this scenario, Mark lies just for the sake of lying. He thus exemplifies the erratic and sometimes aimless behavior that can be characteristic of psychopathic individuals.

And yes, this really happened. Guess who the person was in this story who revealed the truth to the police? Yes, I was at the hotel that night, and, of course, Mark isn't his real name.

RELATIONSHIP DANGERS

Naturally, the manipulative and deceptive behavior that's associated with psychopathy and narcissism has extremely far-reaching effects on what could otherwise have been normal relationships. It can lead to constant betrayals of someone's trust, emotional abuse, and ultimately cause the end of the relationship itself. It's not uncommon for individuals who were in a relationship with a psychopath or narcissist to feel betrayed, hurt, and confused for a long time after things end. Their victims can suffer emotional, physical, and financial harm.

My book, *Surrounded by Psychopaths*, is the one I receive the most personal—private, really—reaction to. Victims of psychopaths can often be quite severely damaged. It's often almost physically painful to read the stories my readers send me.

As I have already written entire books about psychopaths and narcissists before, I don't want to get too long-winded here. However, due to the number of questions I keep receiving from readers all over the world, I want to share an insight I have arrived at myself after my interactions with people who had distinct psychopathic traits.

What should you do if you realize that you're being targeted by a psychopath?

Answer: Walk away.

There is no other solution. These individuals will never change. They can't change, or they don't want to. It doesn't matter what they tell you. I realize this may sound rather dramatic, but the reason for that is that it *is* rather dramatic.

If a colleague is targeting you—switch departments.

If a manager is manipulating you—find another employer.

If a "friend" turns out to behave psychopathically enough to make you feel uncomfortable—change your phone number. Stay away from them.

If it is your parent—painful as it may be, if you're old enough to leave home, do it. If you have already left home—minimize your contact with them.

Yes, I can hear myself. But all the serious research points to the same conclusion. These people are never going to change. They might very well promise to change. They might act all remorseful. They might make all kinds of promises to keep you entangled in their web. In the short term, they can even make you feel hopeful. That's what they're good at. It's called manipulation for a reason.

Write this down: You mustn't listen to them. All you should do is pay attention to their actual behavior.

If it feels wrong, it *is* wrong.

Get out of there.

Charming Manipulation

Here's something you hear quite often: *She was so charming. He was so charming. They were charming every step of the way.* But what exactly is charm?

Charm is often described as the ability to make other people feel liked, admired, and listened to. But to a psychopath or a narcissist, charm is a dangerous tool that is specifically designed to facilitate manipulation.

By appearing to be friendly, attentive, dedicated, and committed, these individuals can quickly establish relationships and feelings of closeness with people. There are plenty of women who have related how they encountered a male psychopath and were thoroughly charmed from the very first moment. There are also lots of accounts from men who have been fooled by ladies who seemed very nice. Afterward, the victims can't quite understand how they could have been so fundamentally deceived.

Once trust has been established, charm can be used to exert influence over the victim. Many people who have been in close encounters with this personality disorder, when discussing the events after the fact, will describe a strange feeling of superficiality that is difficult to put into words. Superficiality is a lack of depth or substance within an individual, and it probably presents quite differently from one individual to the next, but in the context of psychopathy and narcissism, it tends to present as feigned emotions and an emphasis on interactions that lack any kind of depth. They show no genuine interest in anything. Other than their own self, of course.

The emotions they express are often fabricated and designed specifically to manipulate the beliefs and responses of their victim. For example, an individual like this may pretend to be sad to elicit sympathy, or express outrage in order to manipulate others into taking their side in a conflict.

The interactions of psychopaths and narcissists are often focused on the surface level. There is little or no genuine interest in the thoughts, feelings, and well-being of others. This superficial engagement is sufficient to allow them to maintain a façade of interest and involvement while remaining emotionally detached and entirely focused on their own goals.

At the end of the day, all these things end up being useful when these people set out to exploit others. By gaining trust, exerting influence, and masking their true intentions, they can manipulate others to help them further their personal agenda.

IS IT TREATABLE?

Sometimes people ask why I express so much negativity about psychopaths. Am I being overly, perhaps even unfairly, critical of them? After all, it's not as though they asked to be that way. Okay, slow down there.

Psychopathy is thought to be caused by a combination of genetic and environmental factors. Some studies suggest that there is a genetic predisposition to psychopathy, while others indicate that trauma or neglect in early childhood might play a role in its development. As I mentioned earlier, psychopaths exhibit differences in terms of brain structure and function, particularly in the areas associated with empathy, emotional regulation, and moral reasoning.

In other words, someone or something created the psychopath. Not their own fault, you tell me? But psychopaths' behavior still has serious consequences for those around them. Because they so often exploit others to benefit themselves, without any regard for anybody else's well-being, they end up harming people. Their lack of empathy allows them to do this without ever feeling any guilt or remorse.

Treatability and Potential for Change

Perhaps this is a bit of an aside, but there is an ongoing debate among researchers and clinicians regarding the potential for treating psychopathy and narcissism, and whether psychopaths are actually able to change their ways. In short, none of it works. Not only will a psychopath never see anything wrong with their own behavior, but they will also use everything they learn against the people around them because that's what they are—psychopaths.

It's like telling a cat to stop chasing mice—why would it listen to you? It's a cat. It chases mice. End of story. We find cats cute, but to mice, a cat is a bestial and lethal killing machine.

What Lessons Have We Learned, then, about Psychopaths and Narcissists

We need to bear in mind that psychopaths and some narcissists completely lack empathy, are extremely self-centered, and never show any signs of remorse, no matter what they might have done. On top of that, they unfortunately tend to be very charming and not at all afraid to lie to people. Lying amuses them, in fact. All this combines to make them excellent liars.

Their lies are often used for manipulative purposes—gaslighting, love bombing, victimhood, triangulation, and a whole host of other tactics that I won't go into here. The more you can learn about these rather unfortunate human beings, the less likely you will be to end up victimized by them.

I wish this wasn't the case. But we can't afford to turn a blind eye to reality here.

There is no way of curing them. In other words, we simply have to try to avoid them as best we can.

Feeling pity for a psychopath—or a narcissist—is complicated. On the one hand, psychopathy might result from a combination of genetic and environmental factors that are beyond the individual's control. The differences in brain structure and function that are associated with psychopathy and narcissism contribute to these people's inability to feel empathy and remorse, and this can make it difficult for them to change their behavior. When you look at it this way, you can, of course, raise the argument that both these types are really the victims of their own biology and upbringing, and that they are thus deserving of sympathy to some extent.

On the other hand, the behavior of these individuals inevitably causes significant harm and suffering to others. They consistently fail to take responsibility for their actions. Feeling sorry for them can actually maximize their potential for causing harm and serve to enable their manipulative and deceptive behavior.

No, I don't feel sorry for them. I don't believe in capital punishment because I don't think the state should be entitled to make that kind of decision concerning an individual's life.

But I absolutely do believe in isolating those who repeatedly commit serious violations of the norms of society, preferably for life.

INFAMOUS LIARS

Bernie Madoff

Now that we've already used a bunch of ink to discuss psychopaths, we might as well take a look at one of the most horrific examples in history. This man's name has become synonymous with fraud on an epic scale. Bernard Madoff was an American financial trader and former chairman of the NAS-DAQ stock exchange. During his influential career, he orchestrated one of the largest and most notorious Ponzi schemes in history, and cheated thousands of investors out of billions of dollars.

Madoff set up his own investment firm, and at first, he appeared to be engaged in legitimate investment brokering. However, as time went by, the business became a front for his complex pyramid scheme.

Psychologist Robert Hare, who is probably the greatest expert on psychopathy in the world, says that some psychopaths are well-mannered, physically attractive, verbally sophisticated, highly educated, and well connected. Once the psychopath has been allowed in, they can manipulate, lie, cheat, and scam their way to the top.

Bernie Madoff consistently misrepresented the investments that his clients entrusted to him. His funds consistently yielded very high returns, leading thousands of wealthy individuals and prominent organizations to move their money over to him.

He promised annual returns ranging from 10 to 12 percent or even more, but meanwhile, in reality, what he presented as profits were funds taken from the constant influx of new investors' money. In fact, the money never actually left Madoff's own pockets.

The fund claimed to possess a diversified portfolio of stocks that mirrored the S&P 100 index—a major US stock market index—and this was designed to minimize risk for the investors. In reality, however, no shares were ever purchased; instead, Madoff fabricated reports that inflated the funds' fictitious assets.

In addition, he produced fraudulent bank statements, business confirmations, and tax forms, all carefully designed to look like original documents issued by legitimate financial institutions, and presented them to his customers.

Madoff also cultivated the notion that his services were only available to a select few, and he sometimes chose to reject certain potential clients in order to give the business an aura of prestige. This exclusive approach, underlined by his alleged connections and influential clientele, helped him keep this scam going for a very long time before he was exposed.

His immediate family protected him at first, actively participating in the fraud. They cooked the books, falsified financial records, and played complicated roles in the deliveries of false bank statements. However, in December 2008, his sons finally confessed to suspecting fraudulent activities in their father's company. One of his sons took his own life in 2010.

The sheer scale of Madoff's massive fraud was made possible by his appealing personality, his role in various charities, and his memberships in various prominent organizations. He also held leadership roles in various stock exchange organizations, and he used this influence to derail potential investigations into his shady business.

He leveraged his reputation to build relationships with many high-profile individuals including politicians, celebrities, and philanthropists. Madoff's polished façade caused many people to trust without any doubt that he was an honest and impeccable financial trader, and this allowed him to expand the scale of his fraud even further.

Elie Wiesel, a Holocaust survivor and Nobel Prize winner, whose Foundation for Humanity lost about $15 million to Madoff's fraud, said this: "We thought he was God, we trusted everything in his hands."

In late 2008, his house of cards collapsed after decades of lies. After a sharp dip in the economy and a wave of redemption requests from investors who wanted to get their money back, his carefully constructed pyramid scheme collapsed. Madoff admitted that the whole thing had been a massive fraud.

An interesting question here, of course, is this: What were the real motives that fueled this scam? Money or power, or money *and* power? After watching the Netflix documentary about Madoff's life, I personally feel that he possessed distinctively psychopathic traits. He could be generous and charming one moment, and ruthlessly destroy a coworker the next.

And I may well be right. A recent study found that Madoff's personality traits scored close to 100 percent on a pair of checklists for psychopathic traits (PM-MRV2 and CAPP). "He was a financial serial killer," said Joe Berlinger, the director of the Madoff documentary.

Madoff seems to have enjoyed being able to scam all those people, especially the ones who had lots of money. It gave him a kick, basically. What we know for sure is that Madoff's huge web of lies didn't just ruin people financially, it also destroyed countless lives and harmed people's confidence in the financial system.

There are probably plenty of people in the financial industry who have psychopathic traits very similar to the ones Bernie Madoff had. There's simply too much money in circulation there for them to be able to stay away. The challenge for the financial industry—if they want to give themselves the best chance of steering clear of crises like this one—is to learn to identify the psychopaths in time. Before they gain too much power. But that's true of any arena that they stick their ugly faces into.

Madoff's ego, it is reported, remained intact even in prison, and he never showed any remorse toward the thousands of victims who lost their investments, homes, and even their lives as a result of his lies.

Madoff died in prison.

He's missed by very few—if any.

9

Exposing Liars

To a liar, the most dangerous individual
is the person who catches lies but
doesn't say anything about it.
Then the liar isn't sure
which lies are compromised.
—JESSE BALL

If there really are liars lurking under every rock, it might be useful to know who is the most able to uncover and smoke out a liar. Before I started writing this book, I had my suspicions about which categories of people would be best placed to see through fraudulent behavior, but I wasn't quite sure. So let's take a closer look at how to recognize a lie and identify a liar. My presentation of these ideas will be somewhat different from the approach a psychologist would take. I'm not claiming that their approach is wrong as such, I'm simply giving you my own way of looking at it.

WHO'S THE BEST AT IT?

Detecting various kinds of fraud is a complex task, and people's ability to detect lies varies greatly. However, some groups tend to be better at detecting lies because of their training, experience, or natural abilities. So I googled it.

And indeed, there is research being done on which kinds of people it's best not to lie to. Of course, this list is hardly exhaustive and the suggestions will vary slightly depending on who you ask. But here are five categories of people who are thought to be better at detecting deception:

Police officers. This isn't exactly a shocker. Professionals like police officers and detectives are often trained to detect deception by paying attention to verbal and nonverbal cues. However, their accuracy can vary greatly, and they aren't by any means always significantly better at it than the population at large.

Judges and lawyers. Well, this group is similar to police officers in this respect. Dealing with crooks all day long is bound to make you better at recognizing a fraudster. Judges and other legal professionals often develop their skill for detecting fraud through training and experience—naturally, they need to be good at assessing the credibility of witnesses, for example. They also have to evaluate lots of different types of evidence. Over time, I guess this category of professionals learns what to look for.

Professional interrogators. These people are also lawmen, and many of them are basically police officers. Those who are employed by intelligence agencies often receive specific training in advanced techniques for lie detection and confrontation. I will describe that process in a moment. Regular people like you and me can learn a lot from this.

Deception researchers. Well, why not? Of course, researchers who specialize in deception and lie detection ought to have a more nuanced appreciation for the clues that are associated with deception. After all, it's what they do. Right? But is knowing *how* to perform a certain task really the same thing as being able to do it yourself? That's an interesting question. I know how to put a new roof on my house, I know what equipment I'd need and which materials I should use. But does that really mean I could actually do it? That's not at all obvious. Particularly if you ask my wife.

This is where things get interesting, though.

Clinical psychologists. They are are on the list of people who are most apt at detecting lies. At first glance, this certainly seems like a no-brainer. Specialists of the human psyche! Shouldn't they really be at the top of the list? After all, clinical psychologists are trained to observe and interpret subtle signs in human behavior, and this obviously ought to make them better at detecting lies.

Why don't we take a look at what they themselves have to say on the matter.

HOW IT'S DONE

In 2009, the US government formed a focus group called the High-Value Detainee Interrogation Group, or HIG, and tasked it with developing a new methodology for identifying lies and general deception. It spent more than $15 million on over one hundred research projects that were led by top psychologists. A lot of the work it has been doing is extremely fascinating.

Good Cop, Bad Cop?

So what do people who are highly skilled when it comes to catching liars actually do? For simplicity, I have adapted HIG's results below and phrased them in plain English.

A good trick is to think of yourself as a friendly journalist, these psychologists suggest. What does a friendly journalist do? Good journalists do their homework before they ever write a single word. The more information you can bring to a conversation, the better calibrated your internal lie detector will be.

And then there's the "friendly" part. The HIG report found that the bad cop approach isn't really all that effective, but that the good cop approach actually is. Everyone wants to be treated with respect, even a hardened liar. And when people feel respected and like they're being treated considerately, they will be more likely to speak openly and honestly.

Basically, you should be kind and nice. Not necessarily overwhelmingly sympathetic, but friendly. You need to get the liar to like you. To open up. To talk a lot. And, importantly, to slip up in some way that exposes their deception.

A Hardened Liar's Body Language Won't Necessarily Give Anything Away

A skilled human lie detector doesn't rely too heavily on body language. Aldert Vrij, a psychology professor and leading expert on lies, claims that body language is rarely completely predictable. I agree with him. There is a section on body language in a different part of this book, and while there are helpful patterns to look for in ordinary people who may not be hardened liars, I agree that the importance of gestures and physical mannerisms shouldn't be overestimated in the cases of hardened criminals. A seasoned liar will probably have learned how to keep from leaking any of the information they don't want to give up.

I mentioned a common myth earlier: Liars won't look you in the eyes. And no, that's not a reliable method. There are plenty of people who, for some reason or another, won't meet your gaze. Some of them are simply shy. HIG's review of the research on this showed that eye contact isn't a reliable indicator.

And if that's not enough to dispel the myth, I also read a study on the interpersonal behavior of incarcerated psychopaths. Guess what? They look people in the eye *more* than nonpsychopaths do. How about that?

Ask Unexpected Questions

People who are good at detecting lies often ask unexpected questions, questions that might not even be relevant to the conversation.

For example, ask somebody who isn't old enough to drink in a bar they have no business visiting at their age, and they will confidently tell you, *I'm twenty-one.*

But what if you asked them this instead: *What year were you born?*

This is an incredibly easy question for someone who is telling the truth, but a liar will probably need to pause to do some calculations. And like that, you caught them.

So the idea is to begin with questions that anyone would expect. These questions aren't at all threatening, and while they might give you plenty of information, their most important purpose is to give you what an interrogator calls a baseline. Next ask them a question somebody who was telling the truth would have no problem answering, but a liar is unlikely to be prepared for.

Assess their reaction. Did they respond calmly and quickly, or did they suddenly pause for an unusually long time before responding?

You should ask for verifiable details, too. *So if I called your boss, would she be able to confirm that you were at that meeting yesterday?* Truth tellers can quickly and easily answer that question. Liars, however, will be reluctant.

Here's another example: *What was Peter wearing at the meeting?* Again, this would be easy for honest people to answer, but an absolute nightmare for a liar. The answer is verifiable—and they know it is.

The report also reveals that interrogators often use strategic evidence. *You did your homework in advance, right? That's right.* Build rapport. Get the other person to talk. Get them to offer you something that contradicts the information you've uncovered.

Ask for clarification, to commit them to their words. And then: *Sorry, I'm confused now. You told me you spent yesterday with Lena. But she's been home sick all week.* Ask yourself these magic questions: Do they look like they're thinking hard? Do their hastily constructed answers contradict anything else they've said? Are they digging a hole for themselves, or can they explain what they were doing in a sick person's home, too?

Feedback Helps the Liar

I read a study by psychologists somewhere that showed that Swedish police officers could detect lies about half the time on average. However, police officers who had been given training in something called *strategic use of evidence* detected more than 85 percent of all lies they were told. That's quite an impressive difference.

A good method here is to reveal evidence piece by piece. An approach I often use myself is to avoid raising any challenges to the person I'm talking to too early in the process. Many people will only be more cautious if you pounce on them right away and reveal that you don't trust them. There is a great danger that they simply won't say anything at all if I hit them with that abrasive attitude. A gentler touch is much better.

If you start questioning what someone says right away, or immediately accuse them of lying, they might just switch off. Alternatively, they might start to change their story.

Why would you want to help them lie better? Rather, your goal ought to be to make them want to put everything out there themselves, thus painting themselves into a corner. Only then do you strike. So relax. Let them talk.

This is the problem with dealing with slippery people: They get feedback from you, but you don't get any feedback back from them. If I lie and I *don't* get caught, I learn what works. If I lie and immediately get caught, I learn what *doesn't* work.

Don't help them get better at lying.

PSYCHOLOGISTS AND LIARS

While we're on the subject of studies on how to spot a liar, as I mentioned earlier, that particular study was conducted by psychologists. This ought to mean that psychologists are the professional group you would least want to have to lie to. Right?

As usual, nothing is as simple as it seems. Many of the tips I just shared certainly sound very good, and I have spent about six months conducting my own experiments to evaluate them before finalizing this book. And there are undoubtedly some real gems in that material.

But then, there is also the real world. Practicing psychologists usually believe their practices to be places where patients can feel comfortable about sharing their deepest, most intimate thoughts and feelings without being judged. Places where they can work with their patients to bring them closer to healing. And yet, a surprisingly high percentage of patients—in fact, almost every single one—reports having either lied to or been less than truthful to their therapists. This actually sounds rather strange. They go there for help. What's the point of visiting a psychologist to discuss your problems, and then not being completely honest with them about what's going on?

Barry Farber, PhD, a professor with the clinical psychology program at Columbia University's Teachers College, has stated that this *isn't just common, it's something that happens constantly*. For example, people in couples counseling apparently lie a great deal.

Everyone hides the truth sometimes, and it seems that therapy sessions are no exception.

It also seems to be completely true: In one survey, 93 percent of psychotherapy clients said they had knowingly lied at least once to their therapist. In another survey, 84 percent said that this dishonesty continued on a regular basis.

And while therapists ought to be able to at least suspect that their patients might be less than truthful, research has shown that this actually isn't the case at all. In one study, 73 percent of respondents reported that the truth about their lies had never been discovered during therapy. Only 3.5 percent of patients confessed to their lies of their own volition, and in another 9 percent of cases, the therapists discovered the lies. Therapists, then, might not actually be very good at detecting lies.

What's Left Unsaid

Patients tend to lie or not be completely truthful to their therapists about quite a few subjects, but the researchers were surprised to learn of some of the more common areas where deception was used. The most common subjects were quite subtle ones. More than half the respondents in one study reported that their psychological distress hadn't actually been reduced by the therapy, and that they pretended to feel happier and healthier than they really did. The second most common lie was to pretend that their problems weren't really too serious. The third most common lie was failing to share suicidal thoughts (reported by a third of the respondents).

Psychologists are bound by confidentiality. They can't tell anyone what is said during a patient consultation, just like a doctor can't. So what is the actual point of telling lies when you're supposed to be getting help with your mental issues? You have to agree that it sounds rather farfetched.

People spend both time and money on therapy, so what's the point of hiding the truth? For patients who are hiding suicidal thoughts, the main reason is probably a fear of what the consequences might be if the truth is revealed. You could, of course, end up hospitalized if your condition is deemed to be really serious, but above all, it can be hard to deal with your own problems. This might sound illogical, but sometimes, the solution can seem more frightening to these people than the condition they need help with.

Better the devil you know than the one you don't know, and all that.

The same can be true of addictions—patients might fear being forced to go into rehab. Letting a therapist know that you smoke pot might not be a huge deal, but you might not want to tell them about all the cocaine or OxyContin you're doing. Shame is also a factor here, particularly when it comes to sex. Many clients are afraid that their therapists simply won't understand them—and so, they lie.

Studies of Personality Types

Naturally, working as a police officer and interrogating hardened criminals is bound to improve your ability to recognize lies. Whether that will make you the world's best lie detector, I couldn't say, but I can't see why it couldn't. On the other hand, which people have the best natural aptitude for finding and smoking out liars?

There have actually been some attempts made to find the answer to that question.

In a very small study conducted at Lindenwood University in the US, it was found that introverts seem to have an edge here. They have a natural ability to stay in the background during a conversation and let the other person take more space. This gives them more material to evaluate.

An extrovert will tend to talk more and often control the dialogue. This, according to this study, can make it easier for a liar to go undetected. An extrovert simply won't pay as much attention to the details.

My own thesis, which I can't present any actual data to support, is that people with Blue personalities—those who are both introverted and task-oriented—must have an unquestionable advantage. They pay attention to details, their brains are often extremely organized, their memory is generally very good, and they ask an awful lot of questions.

It's not uncommon for the partners of Blues to actually feel like they're being interrogated when this behavior kicks in. It just happens to be in their nature to dig around in search of further details. To keep from being caught out by that, a liar will really need to know what he's doing.

However, as I mentioned, I have no scientific evidence to support this idea. It's simply based on my personal experience as a coach and behavioral specialist who has a good understanding of how people function. I have also mentored and coached thousands of people, and I've seen it all by now. I also happen to have a very high Blue bar in my own professional profile. What I gave you just now was more or less a description of myself. My wife even tells me that she sees it in my face whenever I realize that someone is playing loose with the truth. She also says that she's reluctant to tell me even the whitest of lies because I'm almost certain to detect them.

Personally, I'm quite pleased about this. Except, of course, when I ask her what she thinks about my new jacket and she—honestly, without hesitation—asks me if I kept the receipt. Ouch.

THE POSSIBLE UTILITY OF LIE DETECTORS

People have always been looking for clever ways to detect liars. Back in the 1920s, psychologist William Moulton Marston, the man who devised the DISC theory, actually introduced the first lie detector.

Many people question whether technological gadgets like these actually work, and while that's highly debatable, of course, they are nevertheless an interesting phenomenon. From time to time, you come across a story about polygraphs, particularly in American police investigations, and about people who are subjected to a polygraph test—that is, a lie detector test—before being given employment by the FBI or CIA. The accuracy of these tools has been strongly questioned, and this methodology has been rejected entirely in many parts of the world. But since we're discussing how to detect a lie, it might be interesting to take a quick look at how these mythical machines really work.

How Does a Lie Detector Work?

The purpose of a lie detector is to determine if a person is telling the truth or lying when answering certain questions.

When somebody takes a polygraph test, four to six sensors are attached to their body. A polygraph is a machine in which the multiple (poly) signals from the sensors are recorded onto a strip of paper (graph). The sensors usually record four kinds of data:

- Breathing rate
- Heart rate
- Blood pressure
- Sweat levels

Sometimes a polygraph will also record things like arm and leg movements.

When the polygraph test begins, the interviewer will ask three or four simple questions to determine the normal levels for this person's sensor signals. They simply look at how the four parameters listed above appear when the person is telling the truth. Now they have a baseline to make comparisons with.

After this, the actual test questions are asked. Throughout the interview, all of the person's sensor signals will be recorded on a moving sheet of paper. Both during and after the test, the reviewer can study the graph to see if the vital signs change significantly in relation to when responses are given to any of the questions. In general, a significant change (such as a faster heart rate, higher blood pressure, or increased sweat level) will indicate that the person is lying.

A well-trained examiner who uses a polygraph will be

able to detect lies very precisely. However, since the examiner's interpretation is subjective, and since different people react differently when they lie, polygraph tests aren't perfect, and they can certainly give misleading results.

How Accurate Are Lie Detector Tests?

Like most people these days, I wondered if lie detectors actually work. However, the estimated accuracy of polygraph testing, according to FBI data, is 87 percent. That sounds very high to me, and if it's that accurate, shouldn't these instruments be used a lot more often? However, I'm also aware that there are researchers who claim that lie detector tests are not at all credible. In other words, they claim that the accuracy is actually 0 percent.

I find that just as doubtful, to be honest. Let's just say that in many cases, the test can contribute important indications that can aid police investigations and the like. The results might simply indicate that a suspect is lying about *something*, without conclusively determining what.

And, of course, some people have definitely beaten lie detectors. For example, it wouldn't be much of a challenge for a psychopath because their brains don't function like your brain or mine.

Could an innocent person fail a polygraph test? Could someone who is actually telling the truth be falsely detected to be lying when they weren't?

Yes, and there are several examples of this happening. Innocent people can even fail the test just out of sheer nervousness. This is why the results of these tests are often dismissed by courts. The margins of error are simply too large.

THE TRUTH WILL OUT

Is it possible to become a living lie detector? It could be. But remember, different people have different talents when it comes to detecting lies.

And liars are all different, too. You can never generalize to the point where it's correct to say that all liars do this or that particular thing. You have to look for patterns. It takes time, but if it concerns someone in one of your close, important relationships, it might be a good idea to pay some extra attention, especially early on. At least that's my personal opinion.

I'm not saying you should go around being suspicious of everyone. But you should dare to trust your own gut feeling. If it feels wrong, it might *be* wrong. Or, maybe, there's a perfectly reasonable explanation for it. The important thing is essentially not to allow yourself to overlook things for too long.

INFAMOUS LIARS

Richard Nixon

Of course, history is full of stories of power, ambition, and blurry lines that separate great leadership from manipulative behavior. However, few events exemplify unchecked authority and mendacity as well as the Watergate scandal does. After this event countless scandals have been given names that end with "-gate," and this story is the one that the whole expression originated with. The Watergate scandal will probably remain a stain on the political landscape of the US.

Richard Nixon was quite a promising figure early on in his career, and he demonstrated a good blend of charisma and political acumen. His political star began to rise when he was elected to the US House of Representatives and eventually, he went on to become the thirty-seventh president of the United States.

So what was the Watergate scandal all about? The June 1972 break-in at the Democratic National Committee headquarters in the Watergate office complex in Washington, DC, was a sad tale from beginning to end. The actual break-in itself could have been dismissed as a relatively minor incident, but what led to Nixon's eventual downfall was the subsequent attempts to cover it up.

The break-in was organized by people associated with Nixon's reelection campaign, and it was carried out to gather important intelligence and potentially sabotage the Democratic Party's campaign. To put it bluntly, they wanted to spy on their political opponents.

Although the whole thing was denied by the Nixon administration, of course, evidence soon began to trickle to the press, revealing increasingly serious links between the burglary and some key individuals within the president's inner circle.

The Nixon administration (not to mention Nixon himself)—soon became entangled in an absolute mess of lies and contradictions. One thing led to another. After a series of embarrassing revelations, leaks, and journalistic investigations, the full extent of the cover-up began to come into view. Bob Woodward and Carl Bernstein of *The Washington Post* played a crucial role in unraveling this deception, relying on an anonymous informant known as Deep Throat who provided them with inside information. This, too, has given rise to a phrase often used for inside informants who reveal secret information.

Soon, Watergate had grown into a full-scale scandal, and a complex network of illegal activities including wiretapping, bribery, and political espionage was uncovered. The Nixon administration's attempts to obstruct the investigations raised even greater suspicions.

Central to the Watergate scandal were White House recordings that had been made of conversations that took place in the Oval Office of the White House. These recordings revealed the extent of the president's involvement in the embarrassing attempted cover-up. The case eventually reached the US Supreme Court. The court ruled that Nixon was obliged to hand over the recordings, and that ruling ended the whole game. The recordings revealed a shocking conversation between Nixon and his chief of staff in which they discussed using the CIA to obstruct the FBI's investigation of the Watergate break-in—an incident that has since come to be referred to as the *smoking gun*.

Nixon eventually threw in the towel and announced his resignation. This was the first time in American history that a president had voluntarily resigned from office. Well, perhaps not entirely voluntarily, I guess. Nixon claimed to have acted in the best interests of the nation, but recognized that continuing his presidency would do more harm than good.

When Nixon left the White House with his tail between his legs in August 1974, many Americans breathed a sigh of relief. Finally, the country would be able to get back to normal after months of strange revelations concerning the break-in at the

Democratic campaign headquarters at the Watergate Hotel in June 1972.

To this day, Nixon's legacy remains dominated by lies and contradictions. He did actually initiate diplomatic relations with China and ease tensions with the Soviet Union—two significant international achievements. He was also one of the first, if not the first, modern politician to seriously shift the focus from issues of economics and justice to value issues, and he was the first to make law and order the dominant political issue.

Nixon was, in many ways, a political cheat, a charlatan of democracy, and a fraud. The Watergate scandal was just one of his many transgressions against democracy. In fact, few American politicians have behaved as recklessly in office as Nixon did.

By now, Nixon has been reduced to a mere political villain. He has epitomized the most disturbing aspects of modern politics, even to those of us who weren't old enough to follow the story at the time, or hadn't even been born. It's very likely that the Watergate scandal will forever loom large over his legacy.

10

Confronting a Liar

*Don't lie to me unless
you're absolutely sure
I will never find out the truth.*

—ASHLEIGH BRILLIANT

n the complex universe of human relationships, lies can
create a treacherous web, one that threatens to trap not only
the deceiver, but also the deceived. As we travel through the
terrain of interpersonal relationships, which are often fraught
with danger, we will come across cases that bring us face-to-
face with this question: Is this person lying to me? This very
suspicion is already loaded with implications. It raises doubts
about the trust we place in others, and it can force us to struggle with our own values and judgments.

As I mentioned, philosophers, psychologists, and poets
have been contemplating lies since the dawn of time. At its
core, lying is an adaptive behavior that can even be a survival
mechanism. Our Paleolithic ancestors may have used deception
to outwit predators and competing tribes. In modern times,
lying can serve multiple purposes—from preventing conflict
to protecting people's feelings, from cultivating one's public

image to evading punishment. The reasons to lie are as varied as the individuals who lie. This complexity arises when we, the recipients or observers of these possible lies, have to decide on a course of action.

Confronting somebody who we suspect of lying is a lot more involved than a simple fact-checking mission. It's a delicate process that involves understanding motives, ensuring that trust won't be irrevocably broken, and ultimately seeking clarity. Behind every lie, of course, there is a human being—somebody who has their own fears, ambitions, and vulnerabilities, and may even have motives we can't predict. When you choose to confront somebody, you won't just be addressing the lie itself; you'll also be questioning the sincerity of the person you suspect may have lied. That's why the term "confront" mustn't be taken to refer to an act of aggression in this context, but rather an approach in which we seek to enter into a situation with sensitivity, tact, and genuine engagement.

UNDERSTANDING THEIR MOTIVE

I have already touched on this in earlier chapters, but I want you to remember that if you intend to confront a liar, nothing will be as simple as it seems.

William Shakespeare once wrote, *"No legacy is so rich as honesty."* To properly approach someone we suspect of dishonesty, we must first enter the labyrinth of human psychology and seek to understand the central motives they hold for taking a particular action.

Are they lying for self-preservation—might that be the explanation for what you just heard? Our instinct to protect ourselves, physically and emotionally, is powerful. For example, when children are caught with their hands in a cookie jar, their immediate denial is often a defense mechanism. They are seeking to protect themselves from the potential consequences. This instinct doesn't go away in adulthood, it just takes on more complex forms. An adult might lie about a mistake at work because they fear retribution or judgment.

Could it be a matter of social pressure? The society we live in comes with plenty of expectations and norms. We are all under enormous pressure to fit the mold, to look a certain way, and to conform to certain values. The fear of social judgment or ostracism can bring people to create false narratives. Somebody might lie about having a prestigious job to gain the acceptance of a status-conscious social group.

It could also be some form of altruistic deception—as we have seen, not all lies are motivated by purely selfish intentions. Many of them are born from a desire to protect someone else's feelings or take responsibility for someone else's problems. Telling a friend that their new haircut looks great when you actually think otherwise is a basic example of this. These "white lies" occur frequently in our everyday interactions and serve to maintain harmony and prevent harm.

But, of course, your liar may be looking to gain some kind of advantage. Whether it happens in business negotiations, politics, or personal relationships, personal gain is, after all, the most common motive for lying.

Emotional complexity, fear of conflict, the thrill of lying—it could be anything, really. My point here is just that it might be a good move on your part to consider the motives that might be behind the lie you suspect you've told before you take things too far.

Understanding isn't a matter of excusing anybody's dishonesty, but it does hinge on being able to approach the liar with empathy and insight. When confronting someone who might be entangled in a web of deception, it can help to recognize the potential reasons for their lies, and frame the conversation in a way that makes it plain that what you're seeking is understanding and closure, not an opportunity to level accusations at them.

Lies, as I have stated repeatedly, are rarely entirely black and white. They come in many different shades of gray, and can be colored by human vulnerabilities, desires, and fears. As you navigate this intricate terrain of truth and untruth, then, remember this: Your understanding is the compass that will guide you on your journey.

HOW TO PROCEED

Okay, you have determined that the liar's motives are unacceptable. I would assume that this conclusion is the most common one. So now you want to have a chat with this person and find out what's really going on. Here are some ideas on how you might go about finding out the truth with as little friction as possible.

Create a Space That Encourages Honesty

When navigating these tricky waters, you need to create a safe environment. This environment must comfort rather than complicate, and reassure rather than accuse in order to serve as a good foundation for open dialogue. Here are some tips for how to establish such a space.

Neutral Territory

Choose a place that neither party will think of as their home turf. A quiet café—as long as you can have an undisturbed conversation there, of course—a peaceful park, or any other place that seems sufficiently neutral can make the conversation feel less confrontational. Familiarity can sometimes engender defensive behavior, so feel free to depart from *business as usual*.

Active Listening

I cannot overemphasize this. Listening is more than just hearing. It involves absorbing, understanding, and reflecting. Don't interrupt, and don't jump to conclusions. Let the person tell their side of the story from beginning to end. This act alone can make people feel valued and make them more willing to open up.

Open Body Language

Keep your arms open, and maintain gentle eye contact—don't stare, but don't avoid meeting their gaze, either. Lean forward a little. This will nonverbally signal to them that you're open to their point of view even if you may not agree with it.

It's worth bearing in mind that many people tend to imitate

the body language of other people subconsciously. And open arms actually make it easier to tell the truth. If you want to show engagement and get the other person to relax, tilt your head a few degrees to one side. This will make you appear to be favorably disposed.

Avoid Casting Blame

To the best of your ability. Rather than leading with an accusation like *You lied about* . . . , try to describe your concern in terms of your own personal feelings, for example, *I felt hurt when I discovered* . . . This can prevent the liar from becoming defensive and promote a more constructive dialogue.

Be Honest About Your Intentions

If you really want to understand them, say so. If you're looking to clear the air, let the other person know. Being open about your intentions can make you more likely to gain similar insight in return.

Ask Open Questions

Rather than questions that can be answered with a simple "yes" or "no," choose questions that invite detailed answers. *Could you help me understand why you felt the need to do that?* provides more space for honesty than *You lie all the time, don't you?*

Assure Them of Your Absolute Confidentiality

If you can, that is. If someone believes that their confessions might be used against them or shared with others, this will make them less likely to be sincere. Reassure them that the conversation is just between the two of you, and mean it.

Cultivate Empathy

Understand that everyone, including yourself, has experienced both sides of deception before. Approach the situation with empathy. Show them that you understand the fear, shame, or pressure that may have motivated their lie.

Lies are, essentially, often there to cover up deeper wounds. By ensuring an open dialogue, you won't just be exposing a lie, you'll potentially be addressing deeper issues, healing your relationship, and promoting personal growth for both parties. No, this isn't easy, but if you really want to get the whole thing straightened out, and this is a person who is important in your life, it's definitely worth a try.

Read Between the Lines

As you try to understand and confront a serious lie that has had some kind of real consequences, it's important that you keep in mind that lying is every bit as much an emotional act as it is a rational one. This is where your emotional intelligence will enter the picture.

Emotional intelligence, or EQ, is the ability to perceive, evaluate, and respond to your own emotions—and those of others. More than just a buzzword, EQ represents a real ability to understand human emotions and the impact they can have on communication. When confronting a lie, this ability can help you move past the surface level and notice the more complex emotions that lie beneath.

Empathy, a cornerstone of EQ, is, as we mentioned earlier, the ability to understand or identify with what another person is experiencing.

Ask yourself again: Why did they lie?

Was it out of fear? Shame? Some protective instinct?

If a child lies about who stole some cookies, an empathetic response might affirm the child's fear of punishment. Similarly, if a colleague lies about completing a task, acknowledging the potential pressure or stress they may be under might pave the way to a more honest conversation.

Intuition, another aspect of EQ, is that gut feeling or internal voice that will often suggest what has been left unsaid. We have all been in conversations like that at some point. Something's off, we don't know what it is, but we can instinctively tell that something isn't right. Intuition is far from foolproof, of course, but it is underpinned by a lifetime of experiences and observations. Sometimes we just *know* that something is wrong even if we can't quite explain how we know this. Recognizing and trusting this instinct can be valuable, and I firmly believe that it can be trained and improved.

Imagine a friend who assures you that he's fine, but something about his behavior doesn't add up. Emotional intelligence can help you probe deeper, ask the right questions, and offer a listening ear. This intuition will often reveal hidden truths.

When confronting a lie—whether it be white or otherwise—

or when someone chooses not to tell the whole truth, what you want to do is not so much interrogate somebody as open up a channel for them through which truths, fears, and vulnerabilities can flow freely. We use empathy and intuition not only to seek the objective truth, but also to gain an understanding for the subjective realities within which the deception occurred.

CONSIDER THE CONSEQUENCES

When is addressing a lie worthwhile? Of course, the decision to confront a liar is not always entirely black and white. There is a delicate balance to be struck between trying to get at the truth and making sure to preserve your relationship. Before you dive headfirst into any kind of interrogation, it's crucial that you consider the consequences and ask yourself: Is this confrontation really necessary?

Some lies are like quicksand; the deeper you dig into them, the more likely you are to find yourself stuck and the more difficult it will be to get out. Not all lies are equally important. If your friend lies about her plans for the weekend because she needs some alone time, confronting her might cause unnecessary friction in your relationship. But if a colleague lies about a crucial project, addressing the lie won't just be justified, it will be necessary.

Consider the emotional consequences for both parties. Confrontations can be draining for all involved, that's for sure. The accused might feel attacked, become defensive, or feel cornered. At the same time, the accuser may experience anxiety, frustration, and disappointment. It's important to determine whether both parties are actually emotionally equipped to deal with the confrontation and able to make sure that it won't escalate into an emotional maelstrom.

I'm not suggesting that you should always ignore everything just because the conversation might get difficult, but you have to consider the context. Let's say you're with a group of people and you discover that one of them is in denial about something you know very well happened. Addressing it then and there—in front of the group—might make the liar feel humiliated or attacked, and make them defensive rather than open to constructive dialogue. A conversation in private at another time will usually provide a more suitable environment for these kinds of discussions. This will give both parties an opportunity to express their feelings and concerns without the pressure of other people watching.

You should also assess the potential outcomes. If you confront your boss with a lie, even if you happen to be right about it, you might suffer a backlash that affects your professional standing or your relationship. I don't really recommend doing that because it can end up costing you more than it's worth.

Seem unfair? Well, of course it is.

Even in your personal relationships, revealing a lie has the potential to either strengthen your bond or further complicate things between you. It's important to figure out if the pursuit of truth is worth risking the potential outcomes.

Finally, consider the intention behind the lie. Was it malicious, intended to cause hurt or bring personal gain? Or was it a white lie, intended to protect someone's feelings or prevent conflict? Again, understanding the motivation can grant you clarity on whether you should address the lie or let it slide.

It can be easy to feel compelled to confront each and every lie. Particularly when you've just read a whole book on the subject. But sometimes, silence is the best strategy—this is something I've pointed out elsewhere in the book. If you weigh the risks and the consequences, you'll be in a position to decide when to step up and challenge a liar, and when to stay out of it and let the whole thing pass without taking action.

My own personal reflection is that the older I get, the more I tend to let some things pass that I might have taken up the battle for in my younger days. I'm not saying this is the right approach, but I do know that I've come to give my own mental health and psychological well-being precedence over most other things.

DEALING WITH DENIAL

We've all been there. You've done it all right. Asked questions, showed interest and understanding, and offered every thinkable way out to somebody who has lied or acted deceptively. You've read this book, and applied the things it has taught you. But even so, nothing works.

The liar is simply refusing to play along. Typical.

Even when confronted with irrefutable evidence, some individuals will insist on clinging to their fabrications as though they were a lifeline, and raise the stakes of their lies even further. Dealing with this kind of denial can be very challenging, as it interferes with our quest for truth and clarity. Here are some suggestions for how you might handle someone who simply refuses to acknowledge the truth.

It can be easy to let your emotions flare up when someone insists on making a denial that blatantly contradicts what you know to be true. But please, stay calm and collected. Emotional reactions are likely to make the liar defensive, and will only drive them further into their lie. Staying calm will create an environment in which open dialogue is more likely to be achieved.

Repeat your concerns without making accusations. Rather than saying, *You're lying!*, try to express your feelings using phrases like *I'm having trouble understanding this*. This shifts the focus from the lie itself to your concern, and offers the other party an opportunity to give you clarity without having to feel attacked.

This provides the offender with a platform from which to explain themselves, and maybe they will even decide to tell the truth eventually.

Denial is often rooted in fear. Recognizing and acknowledging your own feelings can help break down the barriers between you. Saying, *I can tell that this is difficult for you,* can be taken as an outstretched hand.

Reflect on your own approach: If someone persists in their deception, it may be wise to take a step back and reevaluate what you've been doing. Were you being confrontational? Did you give them space to talk? Sometimes adjusting your approach can lead to more fruitful exchanges.

Be clear about when it's time to give up. You can't save everyone. Not every lie will be revealed, and not every truth will see the light of day. If you've exhausted all your strategies and the person you're trying to save from their own lie refuses to change their mind, it may be time to consider whether this particular truth is worth the emotional price you're having to pay. Sometimes preserving the relationship or your peace of mind might be the greater priority.

Denial is essentially a mechanism intended to protect liars from the potential consequences of their own deception. Sometimes, maybe the right approach is to simply feel sorry for them and do what we can to support or even guide them. Of course, the situation will determine what you want to do, but you should remember that very few matters are completely black and white.

HOW TO OUTSMART A LIAR

It could be that confronting a liar is never going to be easy. All the same, it's something we all have to do from time to time. While doing the research for this book, I came across this comment: *If everybody lies, who am I to judge one of my fellow fraudsters?*

Now, that really isn't the point here.

The problem is how deceptive behavior can affect us. Lies cause messes and problems. And if someone is lying to you habitually, I think you need to address the situation before it gets completely out of hand.

If something doesn't feel good, it isn't good. It's that simple.

Take action, and try to follow the advice I gave you above to the best of your ability. It's better to tell the truth than to live your life with lies hanging over you. At least, that is my own, most personal opinion.

If someone attempts to use these techniques on you, bear in mind that there's something you've done that has caused them to react. And that might produce an equally fruitful conversation.

Good luck!

INFAMOUS LIARS

Pope Joan

Honesty is of God and dishonesty of the devil;
the devil was a liar from the beginning.
—JOSEPH B. WIRTHLIN

The question of whether Pope Joan ever existed is one of the most contentious debates in the history of the Catholic Church. Trying to summarize all the details of this intricate story would be a great challenge as there isn't historical evidence to support all of it. Nevertheless, I'm going to try to give an account of the life she may have lived and of her most significant lies and deceptions.

Let's go! Pope Joan, then, is said to have reigned as pope in the ninth century, at a time when women were excluded from all positions of religious and political power within the Catholic Church. There are no contemporary sources that give any evidence at all that Pope Joan ever lived, but many writers—from the Middle Ages onward—have nonetheless written about her. Historically, there is limited documentation from this period anyway, and this only adds to the controversy over the matter. However, this is a pretty good example of the kind of thing you would certainly hope really happened. A female pope? That's awesome! More than a thousand years ago! Maybe that's why this rather peculiar story is so hard to put to rest.

However, even if it is an amalgamation of various legends and folktales, it can still provide us with insight and understanding. According to some sources, Joan was from Mainz, Germany, and possessed an exceptional intellect. She studied theology and philosophy in her youth. Joan claimed to be a man. She disguised herself, engaged in intellectual pursuits in Athens, and later traveled to Rome.

Joan got involved in theological debates and soon gained the confidence of Pope Sergius II. Soon thereafter, he/she was appointed important positions within the church hierarchy of the Vatican. After the sudden death of Pope Sergius, she was quickly elected as his successor. It is noteworthy that at the time of Joan's ascension, it was customary for new popes to be seated on a stone throne with a hole in the seat, through which a cardinal would be able to inspect his genitals. Why this provision was ever introduced is a very good question. Somehow, remarkably, Joan passed this examination. One hesitates to imagine how.

How can it be that so many people are prepared to believe in and defend the idea of Pope Joan's alleged papacy? In a time when education was limited and illiteracy widespread— the Bible, for example, was only permitted to exist in Latin— authority figures and religious leaders often held practically infinite power over the people.

Pope Joan's time as the pope lasted for almost two and a half years. Her true identity was revealed during a procession from the Lateran Palace to St. Peter's Basilica, where she either went into labor unexpectedly or suffered some other kind of serious complication. Hard to explain away, of course. Either way, it was discovered that she was in fact a woman, and naturally, she was deposed.

What became of Pope Joan after that? Some writings suggest that she died during childbirth, while others claim that she was stoned to death. Still other writings claim that she simply went into exile.

Why did this story—whether fictional or true—actually live on? It's simple: It captured people's imagination. Through the ages, the myth of a female pope challenged gender roles and the power hierarchies of the church, which only increased her significance.

Despite the lack of any formal, historical evidence, the story of Pope Joan, although generally held to be a fabrication, continues to captivate readers, commentators, and historians. And if she never did exist at all, then whoever came up with this story is still a certified, but skillful liar—and perhaps that means that they belong on this list anyway. If only we knew who made the whole thing up. It's a good story all the same.

TEST: ARE YOU A LIAR?

Okay, this might be where we will finally part ways. If you're feeling strong today, feel free to read on. However, if you're not having a good day, it might be better if you came back at a better time. Now that we've gone through all the different aspects of lying and how it can affect us, we might as well rip the final Band-Aid off right now. It's time to find out how prone you are to telling lies. I mean, you're armed to the teeth by this point. What could possibly go wrong?

Here, then, is a simple test that can give you some valuable insights on how you ought to approach truths, white lies, scams, frauds, and—importantly—yourself.

Answer each of the questions that follow by selecting the answer that best describes your behavior and tendencies. Remember that you have to answer honestly to get accurate results.

1. **How often do you find yourself lying in your daily interactions?**
   A. Rarely or never
   B. Sometimes, but only white lies
   C. A little too often for comfort
   D. Often or always, what's the difference?

2. **You drop your new smartphone in the pool and it breaks. Unfortunately, your insurance policy doesn't cover this. You don't want to pay for a new one, so when a salesperson asks you what happened to the phone . . .**
   A. You tell them the truth about the water damage and ask them to make an exception.
   B. You shrug and say nothing.
   C. You talk around the issue without offering any real explanation.
   D. You come up with an elaborate story about how your phone suddenly, mysteriously stopped working.

3. **When faced with a difficult situation that you would prefer to avoid, how likely are you to lie or hide the truth?**
   A. I always prefer openness and honesty, even when it isn't in my own interest.

B. On rare occasions I will resort to lies to protect myself from discomfort.

C. Sometimes I get carried away and lie.

D. Lying is basically my strategy.

4. You hope to receive a grant, but you don't actually have all the required qualifications. During the application process . . .

A. You write a cover letter in which you address the gaps between your experience and the requirements, and explain why you still think of yourself as an ideal candidate.

B. You add some qualifications you don't actually have to make your application more competitive.

C. You add a whole bunch of qualifications, because that's the only way you can get the grant.

D. During the interview, you hand the interviewer a stack of cash and give them a wink.

5. How comfortable are you with lying to protect your own interests?

A. It is against my principles to lie for personal gain.

B. I'm sometimes tempted to lie for personal gain, but I always feel a bit sick to the stomach afterward.

C. I sometimes lie for personal gain. Who doesn't?

D. I have no qualms about constantly lying for personal gain. It's the only way to level the playing field with all those other dirty liars.

6. Your son has been caught cheating at school. You're concerned about what the consequences might be. When his headmaster calls you to discuss the cheating, you respond by:

A. Playing dumb and claiming that you have no idea what might have happened.

B. Vehemently denying the school's accusations and defending your son.

C. Acknowledging the evidence and openly sharing your disappointment about your son's behavior.

D. Ignoring the headmaster's call—you don't want to get involved in this mess!

7. **Can other people generally trust the things you say to be true?**

A. Yes, I am consistently honest, for the most part.

B. I tell the truth most of the time as long as I don't think it will hurt anyone's feelings.

C. I will occasionally distort the truth to avoid conflicts and arguments.

D. I rarely tell the truth.

8. **At a party, you realize that the person who had agreed to drive you home is no longer sober enough to drive. When you're both ready to leave, she looks at you and asks if you've seen her car keys (they are in your pocket). You . . .**

A. Tell her you haven't seen them and proceed to help her look under the sofa cushions.

B. Reprimand her for even thinking of driving in her state.

C. Avoid the question altogether, and distract her with your favorite song.

D. Admit that her keys are in your pocket, and explain to her that you don't think it would be safe to let her drive.

9. How often do you find that you embellish stories or exaggerate facts?

   A. Never, I always stick to the truth, however boring it may be.

   B. Sometimes, for dramatic effect.

   C. Sometimes, to make myself seem more interesting.

   D. I always embellish and exaggerate my stories, I'm just that kind of person.

10. You've been trying to improve your relationship with your boss all year. When she asks you what you thought about the game last night (she's a big sports fan, but you never watch the stuff), you respond by . . .

   A. Nodding enthusiastically, but saying nothing.

   B. Pretending that your boss's favorite team is also your favorite team.

   C. Changing the subject as soon as you can so you won't have to comment.

   D. Acknowledging that you didn't see yesterday's game, but going on to offer to get tickets for next week's game.

11. When confronted over a mistake or error you've made, do you tend to lie to save yourself from having to own up to it?

   A. No, I always confess to my mistakes.

   B. I'm not often tempted to lie to avoid a confrontation, but it would depend on who the other person was.

   C. I sometimes try to evade responsibility by lying, particularly when the consequences might be negative.

   D. I consistently lie to avoid having to own up to any mistake or error. I reckon I'm practically flawless.

12. At a party, a casual acquaintance (whose name you have completely forgotten) comes up to greet you. What do you do?

    A. Tell them you need to make an urgent call (you don't) and leave.

    B. Apologize for forgetting their name and ask them to remind you.

    C. Take your best guess at what their name might be and hope you get it right!

    D. Address them with *Hey there,* and just launch into conversation, hoping that you'll realize who it is eventually.

13. How often do you find that you hide the truth to avoid hurting people's feelings?

    A. Rarely or never, as I prioritize honesty above all else.

    B. Sometimes, if it will really make a difference to them.

    C. Occasionally, if it can prevent an unnecessary conflict.

    D. I consistently hide the truth to make sure that people won't get upset.

14. After you've used the bathroom at a friend's house, the toilet suddenly begins to overflow uncontrollably. Even though you hardly caused this issue, it's most embarrassing, and you can't fix it yourself. What do you do?

    A. Blame whoever used the toilet before you.

    B. Quietly exit the bathroom and decide to deny ever having used it.

    C. Find the host immediately and explain the situation.

    D. Party's over, time to go!

15. Are you generally aware of the lies you tell or the manipulations you use?

 A. Yes, I'm fully aware of all my lies and actions.

 B. I'm mostly aware, but I lose track sometimes.

 C. I'm only partially aware, as it often seems to happen almost automatically.

 D. I have no idea what you're talking about.

16. You have recently learned that you and your partner are expecting a baby when your boss asks you to take an overseas assignment for the next seven months. It's too early for you to share your personal news, but you already know that you won't be able to accept this request, so you . . .

 A. Thank them for the opportunity but clearly decline, offering some other reason for why it wouldn't work.

 B. Tell them that you'll have to answer later, and then avoid your boss (even if you know that your answer isn't going to change).

 C. Offer noncommittal answers like *Maybe* or *That might work* . . .

 D. Agree to go, planning all along to decline at a later date when you're ready to share your news.

17. Do you often make excuses when you don't want to do something or be somewhere?

 A. Never, I prefer to be honest rather than lie.

 B. Rarely. I only do it if I desperately want to avoid some highly unpleasant situation.

 C. Sometimes I find giving excuses easier than admitting the truth—that I don't feel like it.

 D. Excuses are my constant companions. I often promise to go before I've had a chance to think things through properly, because I find saying no to be quite difficult.

18. Your daughter wants a kitten, but a cat is the last thing you want in your house because you don't like furry animals. What do you tell your daughter?

    A. You tell her firmly that getting a kitten is out of the question and that's final.

    B. You tell her that because of your severe allergy, you can't get a kitten.

    C. You explain to her that keeping an animal is a big responsibility, and that they also tend to tear half the house up with their claws. There's not going to be a kitten.

    D. You tell her that it's not a good idea at the moment, but that she might be able to get a kitten at some later date.

19. Your partner wants to watch yet another film in the X genre (insert your least favorite film genre).

    A. You tell her that you've simply had enough of that stuff, and you have to draw the line somewhere.

    B. You tell her that you'll agree, as long as you get to choose the next film.

    C. You tell her you'd love to see it, but once the film starts, you spend the whole time on your phone instead.

    D. You agree to her choice of film, and then proceed to spend two hours on the couch grinding your teeth with frustration. You spend the rest of the evening sulking, and when your partner asks you what's wrong, you simply say, "Nothing."

20. Would you say that you've answered the first nineteen questions honestly?

    A. Absolutely, why wouldn't I?

    B. More or less. I act honestly most of the time, and I did in this case.

    C. I've tried to be honest, but I've probably fudged a few answers.

    D. No, I chose the answers that sounded the best to me, not the most truthful ones.

Results

Calculate your score using the following scale:

1   point for each *a*
2   points for each *b*
3   points for each *c*
4   points for each *d*

Add up your score to calculate the total.

Note: This test, of course, can only give a general indication and you should treat your results with caution. It can't provide any definitive or foolproof determinations of someone's degree of honesty or dishonesty, but it can give some insight into a person's general behavioral tendencies.

Pass—20 to 33 points

If you scored between 20 and 32 points, we can safely assume that most people can definitely trust you. Even if you occasionally, out of consideration for others, might slip a minor fib or two in, you're unlikely to hurt anyone's feelings with your occasional white lies. You're an essentially honest and sincere person who would return a wallet you found to its owner with all the money left inside. I would presume that you also miss out on the occasional opportunity in life because you value honesty as greatly as you do. This life is quite cruel in the way it rarely gives the saints among us any particular advantages.

Near pass—34 to 49 points

If you scored between 34 and 48 points, you're probably a lot like most of us. You prefer telling the truth over twisting it, but you're also a realist who realizes that sometimes, making life work smoothly will require more than an occasional white lie. Withholding certain unnecessary truths can be a good way of avoiding boring and—especially—unnecessary conflicts. It can be difficult for you at times, but you realize that life is tough all over. And your intentions are actually good, so what's the issue?

Fail—50 to 65 points

Okay, you scored between 50 and 64 points. This makes you somebody who is quite comfortable with telling half-truths and outright lies, probably out of a combination of a desire to not offend people and a realization that it can benefit you. You find it far too easy to fabricate stories that you know are completely untrue, and you probably rationalize most of this behavior by telling yourself that everyone else is doing the very same thing. Everyone else lies, so why shouldn't you? You also don't particularly trust others, and you choose to constantly operate right on the edge of what is actually acceptable.

Alarmingly poor—66 to 80 points

Somebody who scores between 66 and 80 points will undoubtedly be a notorious liar, and have obvious problems adapting to normal circumstances and expectations. Somebody who feels this free to lie to other people's faces is playing hard and fast with their reputation. Many of the people who spend time with this person will be fully aware of the fact that they simply can't be trusted. Lying to this extent could well indicate that the person in question belongs somewhere on the narcissistic spectrum, or perhaps even on the psychopathic one. Of course, there is a possibility that this person lies out of sheer cowardice, but if any of you out there reading this book actually scored this many points based on truthful answers, I think it's definitely time for you to give some serious thought to how you want to be perceived. If this is you, you should know that the people around you know you for the pathological liar you are. The only question is really how long you imagine you'll be able to get away with it.

How did you score?

Remember what we discussed earlier on in this book. Those around you won't necessarily appreciate you the most if you make a point of never wavering from the absolute, unfiltered truth. Sometimes a bit of flexibility can actually get you further. For example, there is definitely something to be said for protecting other people's feelings.

So how complicated is your particular relationship to the truth? What was your score? Was it what you expected? Now, this simple test obviously depends entirely on your honesty and sincerity in answering the questions, which immediately brings us to an interesting paradox.

What reason do you really have to answer truthfully? Who would want to let the world know what a notorious liar they are? There's an old adage that says that only drunks and children tell the truth. Seeing as you can't go back to your childhood, and I have no desire to encourage you to get drunk and take the test again, we'll have to leave this matter unresolved. More research will probably be needed here before we can fully confirm the results.

A consequence of all this could be that the more dishonest a person actually is, the lower their score would be in a test like this as there's every reason to suspect that they wouldn't hesitate to lie about how much they lie. On the other hand, a truly honest person would no doubt admit to lying sometimes since it's true as we established earlier on that practically everyone does lie. A liar would get a lower score than a truth teller. It's all rather unfortunate.

We run quite the risk here of ending up in a confusing meta-level discussion, so I think the best thing we can do about this simple test is probably to admit to ourselves that we should perhaps strive to be more honest than we really are. If you've answered the questions honestly, you'll have indicated roughly how often you actually thumb your nose at the truth, and only then will you actually reap any benefit from this exercise. You don't have to post your results on Facebook, but you might want to take the odd look in the mirror more often from now on.

I hope we're still friends. ☺

A Few Words in Closing and Some Advice for the Road

Wow, what a journey this has been! We have studied the anatomy of a lie in-depth to arm ourselves with the opportunities and insights we need to navigate the landscapes of deception. As we approach the end of our journey together, I'd like to urge you not to just close the book up and set it aside. Instead, I want us to apply the things we've learned to make ourselves more honest people and promote transparency among the people around us.

I don't believe in being ruled by fear, and I'm going to close this book with an account of how I arrived at that conviction. Trying to anticipate every single possible risk and potential problem is probably a bad idea. You'll end up too afraid to take any initiative at all, and you'll soon end up too afraid to even talk to people. That's no way to navigate life.

However, I also don't mean to suggest that we should just walk around pretending that everything is 100 percent as it should be. Pay attention to what goes on around you. Naivete is not a blessing. It's more of a curse, really.

Whether it happens to be a small, seemingly innocent lie that you're suddenly confronted with, or some grand fiction, a near-epic story that you'd love to be able to believe—stay vigilant. If dishonest behavior crosses your path, call it out! Make a habit of questioning people whenever it's warranted, and always make sure to have the courage to speak the truth yourself. Even if it happens to be an uncomfortable one. In fact, especially when it's uncomfortable. It can be most invigorating.

You should also encourage the people around you to value honesty, and set an example for them by living by that principle.

Make a sincere declaration of the thing most people would claim: *I want you to be honest and sincere with me, even when the truths you tell me are painful to hear.*

But don't do what many others seem to do when making that statement: *lie.*

Most people aren't serious when they say that, they're just saying it. This is similar to the thing I mentioned in the introduction to the book about declaring honesty to be one of your core values. Let honesty and truth represent more than just words that sound good in your life. Most people want to be lulled into some oversimplified illusion in which everything is as it should be. They can't face delivering the truth in its entirety all the time. Most people don't even want to hear the truth a lot of the time.

But that's not you. You know better. Mean it, really mean it. When you tell people you want honesty from them and intend to give them honesty—let your actions demonstrate your sincerity. Show them that you can handle difficult truths, even ones that might hurt you. I'd rather have a difficult truth than an easy lie.

I don't know how I could put it any other way.

Learn to recognize the signs of deceptive behavior, wherever and for whatever reason it occurs, but be careful not to let suspicion cloud your perceptions of others. Especially the people who are important in your life.

Instead, do your best to approach potential liars with empathy—try to understand their motives and fears. It's more often vulnerability that drives people to lie than malice. We've discussed all the various motives that people can have for telling lies. Remind yourself that these matters are almost never entirely black and white.

Sometimes a lie can communicate something as painful as a desperate need to be loved.

Confronting a liar isn't something you should take lightly, but it will sometimes be necessary. Do it out of respect for yourself, and out of respect for the other person.

If you can do it without making any accusations, that's good.

If you can understand them, that's even better.

And if you can resolve the issue, that's great.

If you should find yourself tempted to deviate from the truth, pause and consider the consequences—not only for yourself, but for all the people who will be impacted by your words. Ask yourself this: If I lay the truth bare . . . what's the worst that could happen?

More often than not, you'll find that it can't actually do much harm. Now, this depends, of course, on what it is you're about to say. There are situations where the truth won't be at all appealing to yourself or to the person who needs to hear it. In those cases, you need to look inward and focus on who you are. And who you want to become. Each lie you refrain from telling will reduce your need for further lies to cover up your deception, and this will spare you a lot of fear of being exposed. You'll feel more secure in the absence of lies to maintain.

While this all sounds good, I'm sure you're wondering if it's really that easy? Do I follow my own advice, down to the letter?

Of course I don't.

I'm just like you. I'm an ordinary, simple human being, complete with embarrassing faults and obvious flaws.

But I do try. We all know what the right thing to do is, even though we might find it difficult to live up to our convictions at all times. Finding our way through life is a complicated task, I won't deny that.

In a world that can often feel full of nothing but duplicity and presentable masks, it can be tempting to resort to lies as a defense mechanism, as some kind of social lubricant, to demonstrate your friendliness to others, for example. But the consequences, as we have seen, can harm trust and relationships, and the damage it does is sometimes irreparable.

What other solutions are there? What alternatives do we have to lying?

Daring to be vulnerable in front of people could be one of them.

It can be draining to walk through life with your mask on at all times. It requires energy and focus, and it can be tremendously exhausting to never be *able* to or, perhaps, never *dare* to show weakness, always having to maintain a façade that proves to everyone around that we're strong as hell and can handle anything life throws at us. Because that's what things are like out there a lot of the time.

We've all been there. Trying to appear as though we were on top of things. And we often do manage to maintain that mask.

Hi there, you look a bit stressed? Do you need a hand?

Oh, hell no, no, not me. I was just thinking about something else.

There are plenty of situations where we actually lie to avoid having to let people know that we're dealing with some kind of problem.

How is everything now that you have to take care of your elderly mum at home, and are in danger of losing your job?

I'm fine, thanks, it's made us a lot closer actually.

Sometimes we don't want to admit that we just want to be left alone. We don't want to let people know that we're practically boiling over inside over all the stress and pressure.

Is this seat taken?

Not at all, I'd love some company!

Sometimes you probably wish you were strong enough to share your real feelings with people.

Hey, do you mind if I ask you a personal question?

That's actually the last thing I need on a day like today. No chance.

Being vulnerable isn't the easiest thing to do. Many of us have opened ourselves to others at some point only to be rewarded with a slap in the face. We've learned to keep silent about the things that make us suffer the most out of fear of what might happen if we let our guard down. However, it is precisely in our vulnerable moments that we can discover alternatives to lying.

Psychologist and author Brené Brown has done extensive work on vulnerability, courage, and empathy. She argues that vulnerability is not a sign of weakness, but rather a sign of strength. It is the basis of all innovation, creativity, and change. Embracing vulnerability means to be prepared to say, *I don't know, I need help,* or *I'm afraid*.

Relationships based on vulnerability will be more genuine. When we share our truths, insecurities, and fears with one another, this invites more genuine connections and fosters deeper understanding and trust.

Daring to be vulnerable requires us to leave our comfort zone. It teaches us more about ourselves, our triggers, and our strengths, and this leads us on to personal development.

On some level, this is all related to honesty.

Clinging to lies and maintaining a façade is exhausting.

At one end of the spectrum, we have complete openness and vulnerability, and at the other end, we have a heap of untruths. As we move toward vulnerability, we will actually become less reliant on lies. It will become natural for us to tell the truth.

As I said, it takes courage to be vulnerable, especially if you're afraid of being judged. But every time you choose vulnerability over maintaining that façade, you'll strengthen your inner resolve.

Now, I'm not saying this is easy. In many cultures, strength and stoicism are highly valued, and vulnerability is often misinterpreted as weakness. It can still be considered a bit unmasculine to be vulnerable.

How do you do this?

Start out small: At first, start sharing little truths with close friends and family. As you get more comfortable, expand your circle and include others as well. What kind of others, you might ask? Other truths or other people? Well, why not both?

Therapy and counseling can be very helpful when it comes to overcoming barriers to vulnerability. Of course, it's important that you find a therapist who you get along with, but it might be worth a try.

Read books and watch talks about vulnerability. About honesty. About truth and all its benefits. Understanding its effects might help motivate you to act. However, no system is infallible. This is a truth we have to accept.

Keep a diary. Write down your feelings. This is a safe place for you to be vulnerable in front of yourself, which can help you process your emotions.

Embracing vulnerability isn't a matter of simply showing off your weaknesses to the world. It's actually a matter of understanding that your own truths, although not perfect, are an integral part of who you are. Admitting this to yourself will make lies lose a lot of their allure.

As we begin to embrace authenticity, vulnerability emerges as a beacon, guiding us away from the murky waters of deception toward the shores of genuine human connections. Because in the end, our relationships with others are the only things we'll have left. In vulnerability, we won't just find an alternative to lies, we'll also find a path to richer and more meaningful life experiences.

I think that there is an important lesson to learn from daring to let go of that façade that you've been building for so long, maybe even for decades.

Imagine never having to pretend to be someone you're not again. Imagine daring, little by little, to let people see you as you really are?

Don't you think you'd sleep quite well at night?

What could it do for you if you devoted yourself to the truth over all?

Dear reader, thank you for making it this far. Most people never do. Most people are too impatient to make sure to tie up all the loose ends. The majority of people who pick up a non-fiction book never read it all the way to the end. But you did. And I want to thank you for that.

You made it all the way here. That makes you unique.

If we meet somewhere along life's endless highway, I'd love to hear what you thought of this book. But only on one condition: I want your honest opinion. (Even as I read that last sentence, I feel a faint twinge of insecurity: What if you didn't like it? Would I be able to handle that?)

As you move on from here, I want you to carry this simple truth along with you: Every single time you choose honesty, you'll be taking a step toward a life of trust and integrity. It's the small acts of truth that will, gradually, weave a web of trust around us.

Let us choose the truth in this world where honesty has become a priceless commodity. Something unattainable. But highly valued, nonetheless. I hope you will.

So what about choosing not to be afraid?

Many years ago, I found myself in a relationship that started out great, but soon took a turn for the worse and became a mess of pathological jealousy and generally stifling behavior. I spent a lot of time wondering what I could do to change things, but nothing I did seemed to work. And sometimes that's just how it goes. Nobody is a perfect fit for everyone. It may be a bitter pill to swallow, but it's still the truth.

In any case, I remained in this relationship for far too long for one simple reason: I was scared. I was scared of what might happen. Of all the alternatives. Of not making it on my own in the world. Of hurting the other person's feelings.

When I think back to that time now, I can remember it so clearly. My stomach churns whenever I think about how scared I was to make anybody even the slightest bit sad. It ended up taking a toll on my own well-being, and I started to feel terrible about the whole situation. I neglected the rest of my family. My parents, my children.

To cut a long story short, I ended up speaking out. I simply said this: *I don't believe in this relationship anymore.*

And sure enough, emotional outbursts followed. Not quite the ones I had expected, though. After witnessing the physical destruction of our shared home, I had received all the confirmation I needed: This was wrong, for both of us.

Once all the drama died down, I felt so relieved. So relieved. It was a physical sensation that I can't quite describe. But I got a spring in my step, my days turned brighter, I got better sleep, and I suddenly had a future.

My children told me that they had been given their father back.

And the most obvious feeling, which has remained with me to this day, is that I'm not afraid anymore. Not of anything.

The truth had finally set me free.

It could happen to you, too. If you want it to.

That's all for me. Thank you.

—*Thomas Erikson*

April 2022–January 2024

Appendix

Truth and Consistency in Media and Politics

They didn't cheat because of who you are.
They chose to cheat because of who they are not.
—CHARLES J. ORLANDO

Feel free to read this section if you want to explore some more general areas. I've chosen to delve a little deeper into media, politics, and statistics—you might find that to be quite a mixture, but it's interesting to study this stuff when you have a moment to spare. Sometimes lies don't look the way you might expect them to. Sometimes everything just feels dandy, and you're not at all expecting to be deceived. There are many places and situations in this world in which lying and deception are commonplace—and there are some phenomena that some would place in the gray area between truth and consistency. Social media is one such area where it can be difficult to determine whether something is true or false. Statistics is another supposedly "deception-proof" subject, but a wise person apparently said that numbers may not lie, but liars do use numbers.

MORE ON SOCIAL MEDIA

Of course, in any conversation about undue influence and lies in general, we need to take a closer look at social media as well. In this context, I'm actually most concerned about young people's ability to distinguish truth from lies. Sure, Gen Zers are well aware that social media contains unimaginable amounts of fakery, but at the same time, they have—at least compared to my own generation—a lot less life experience. This can present challenges for anybody who's trying to judge what's real and what isn't.

None of the things I'm about to highlight can be said to be absolute truths, but I think it's vital for our mental health that we actually take the time to look at these issues. So stay tuned, and we'll find out what your reaction will be.

Deepfakes and Manipulated Media

In the good old days, the camera was considered an impartial witness. The camera doesn't lie, they said. I'd like to welcome you to a different reality.

Maybe you've seen that Tom Cruise clip? I saw these little film clips myself on Instagram in which Tom Cruise was walking around doing ordinary things. Naïve as I am, I thought that for some unknown reason Tom Cruise had chosen to post bits of his life on social media. I soon realized that this couldn't be true. My next thought wasn't that this must be fake, but instead, *Wow, this guy really looks like Tom Cruise!*

Curtains for Erikson. I had been deceived by a *deepfake*.

In case you don't know, deepfakes are hyper-realistic,

computer-generated video or audio clips that present a person doing or saying something that they actually never did. It's a new kind of technological deception that will allow your Aunt Berit to suddenly "prove" her claims to have been a disco-dancing superstar back in the 1970s. It's deeply disturbing.

The potential consequences of this are almost impossible to fathom. While a disco-dancing Aunt Berit might be a lot of fun, imagine a fictional video of a political leader declaring war, or a CEO announcing the bankruptcy of a company. The real-world repercussions—before the truth has even got its running shoes on—could be catastrophic. And rest assured that many people who possess both technological expertise and psychopathic personality traits are going to try to fool the world.

In 2019, a video of Mark Zuckerberg appeared online in which he seemingly said, "Imagine this for a second: One man, with total control over billions of people's stolen data, all their secrets, their lives, their futures." The video was eerily realistic, from the vibrations of Mr. Zuckerberg's voice to the details of his facial expressions. The post was widely shared, and many believed the video to be authentic.

The problem? It was a deepfake, created by two artists as part of an art project. Their goal? To draw attention to the subject of digital manipulation and its consequences. Although the video was eventually confirmed to be fake, it served its purpose and became a compelling demonstration of the capabilities of deepfake technology and the potential dangers of falsehoods being spread this way.

Last week, I saw the latest Indiana Jones film and I couldn't believe how young they made the eighty-one-year-old Harrison Ford look. The technology is stunningly realistic.

It's nothing short of impressive and terrifying at the same time.

For the savvy web surfers among us, the rise of deepfakes emphasizes the need for a new kind of digital awareness. We can no longer rely on our eyes and ears; we need to equip ourselves with tools that can distinguish genuine content from sophisticated fakes. As technology continues to evolve, a healthy dose of super-skepticism and new verification tools will be our best defenses against digital fraud attempts.

While deepfakes open a veritable Pandora's box full of countless ethical dilemmas, they also serve as a timely reminder. In the ever-changing environment of the digital landscape, it's imperative that we be particularly careful and research everything we see before we trust anything at all. Far from everything we see—however convincing it may seem—has any connection to truth or reality.

My own very simplistic solution? I spend a minimal amount of time on social media, and I spend significantly more time in the real world.

On Echo Chambers, Filter Bubbles, and Confirmation Bias

Imagine snuggling up in a warm, comfortable bubble in which everyone agrees with you, pats you on the back, and assures you that your view of the world is the only right one. Whatever you happen to say about this or that, however outlandish your opinions might be, everyone agrees with you. You never have to listen to anyone who disagrees with you. You can forget everybody like that. It sounds inviting, doesn't it?

Welcome to the world of echo chambers, filter bubbles, and confirmation bias on social media.

At first glance, an echo chamber may seem like an innocent, harmonious, and essentially pleasant community. However, these are places—often on social platforms—where shared opinions are reinforced over and over to the point where if someone were to offer a dissenting opinion, you would be quite taken aback. *What? That group doesn't think like we do? Let's destroy them!*

Dissenting views are muted or excluded altogether. You might think of this as an orchestra in which only one instrument plays and drowns out the rest of the musicians. Someone plays the trumpet so loudly that no other instrument can be heard. Or played.

Should we call this a lie? If we emphasize the deliberate distortion of reality, that is, withholding of the truth (whatever that is), or other related perspectives, then yes, certainly.

Confirmation bias refers to our brain's sneaky bad habit of favoring information that confirms our preexisting beliefs and conveniently ignores everything else. Simply put, it's that inner voice that says, *See? That's what I told you!*, every time we stumble upon a post that agrees with the views we're used to seeing. Whether it be true or false, we want more of what we already know.

Why is this particularly dangerous in social media? Because these platforms—which have algorithms designed to show us more and more of what we "like," turn into breeding grounds for these bubbles. When our feeds are filled with nothing but familiar and pleasant content, it restricts our worldview and makes us more receptive to disinformation.

You've probably noticed that if you spend a lot of time look-ing at pictures of old cars (in my case, vintage Land Rov-ers), you'll start to see more and more of them appear in your feeds. Eventually, you might get the impression that every-one is exclusively preoccupied with these money-guzzling old bangers. That's not the case, though, it's all a trick that social media algorithms play on us.

Do you remember the Pizzagate conspiracy theory? In 2016, a story was spread online in which it was claimed that a high-profile child trafficking ring was operating out of a pizzeria in Washington, DC. The theory caught on in parts of the internet in which like-minded users shared and spread these baseless claims. The more they read about it, the more they believed that the conspiracy was real. For many in this echo chamber, the story seemed to be undeniably true, and this eventually drove an individual to enter the pizzeria in question wielding a firearm. Nobody was harmed, but the in-cident highlighted the tangible dangers of uncontrolled echo chambers and the ways that confirmation bias can cement false beliefs.

What can we do about these bubbles, then? The respon-sibility probably lies with the users in this case. Actively questioning our own beliefs before sharing anything with anybody else would be a step in the right direction. It's im-portant to remember that a simple click of the share button ought to require us to take responsibility for spreading noth-ing but verified, balanced information.

Imagine that you read a three-word newspaper headline on your way to work, and then went on to send an email to every-body you know based on those three words—without know-ing anything about what was behind them. You would never do that. But sharing things in social media without giving it any thought at all has exactly the same effect. If not worse.

Fake News

The term "fake news" has been popularized in recent years to the point where it has become a buzzword in politics, media, and public discourse. While disinformation and propaganda are as old as human communication itself, the digital age has boosted the speed, scale, and reach of misleading stories. Today, the term "fake news" is mainly used to refer to intentionally false information that's widely disseminated, often to serve some political agenda or cause polarization.

If we take a closer look, we'll discover several theories offering explanations for the emergence and distribution of fake news.

The internet, and social media in particular, allows news— both real and fake—to spread faster than it should. Algorithms prioritize sensational and preferably negative content, as this generates the most clicks and reactions. Controversial or entirely fake stories often end up at the top of users' feeds.

At the same time, we're seeing a general erosion of trust in conventional media. A perceived bias in the established channels has made many people highly skeptical of conventional news sources. People of all political colors seem to feel that their own particular cause is consistently and deliberately portrayed unfairly.

Is fake news a new phenomenon? Not at all. For the longest time, learned Europeans believed that there was a very special fruit growing in India: little, delicious lambs that grew on trees. The lamb plant was described in several writings.

Eventually, people discovered what ought to have been obvious from the start: that the plant didn't exist. There's a shock. Okay, that one was fairly harmless, I guess.

This one's a bit worse: During the coronavirus pandemic, there was a lot of fake news in circulation. Like the story about how Bill Gates had some insidious plan to inject microchips into people who were getting vaccinated against COVID-19. This story was first published on something called Biohackinfo.com, and then, of course, it spread on social media, YouTube, and finally—amazingly—in the conventional news media. Exactly what these microchips were supposed to do was fairly unclear, but I've read claims that they did everything from steal people's money to make people jump off cliffs, like lemmings in Lapland. On the one hand, the claim is so crazy that it could just be true. The world is a weird place. On the other hand, maybe Bill Gates was just looking to make money off his shares in various pharmaceutical companies. But what do I know?

I was the subject of a kind of fake news a few years ago when I was given a less than flattering award for my books, and the justification for the award was about 90 percent a fabrication. You could call them lies if you were so inclined. Either way, it made for some great headlines, and it brought me a large new group of followers. The question, I suppose, is whether this could even be considered a negative incident in my career? The story made such a good splash in several of my foreign markets that it was ultimately a positive for me, I think.

In this age of digital hyperconnectivity, the impact of fake news reaches beyond shaping public opinion, and can even cause tangible harm—whether it makes a man enter a pizza restaurant with a firearm or induces individuals to consume dangerous substances in the hope that they can cure COVID-19. What can individual media consumers really do about all this?

That's a good question. We need to take a multipronged approach in the fight against fake news. Technological platforms need to refine their algorithms to enable them to identify and deprioritize fake content. Educational systems need to emphasize critical thinking and teach students to assess and verify sources. Government agencies and civil society need to promote transparency and restore trust in credible news channels. The problem with all these ideas is that all these control mechanisms need to be programmed by humans, and humans, unfortunately, are simply never neutral. We just aren't able to completely disregard our feelings, attitudes, and perceptions. Some degree of bias will always remain, no matter what measures we take.

Perhaps the most important thing for us to do as consumers of news is to remain vigilant, discerning, and engaged, and strive for truth in an age in which everyday life is inundated with various digital scams.

Above all, you have to remember that nothing is true just because you read it on Instagram.

Catfishing

The world of online dating is an absolute minefield. Here, Romeo meets Juliet by swiping to the right, and Cinderella can find her prince in an ocean of filtered selfies. Beware, however! In these waters, a strange creature called a catfish is on the prowl. I'm not talking about a whiskered aquatic animal here, but rather a cunning digital imposter who hides behind a false identity.

In the digital sphere, catfishing is the practice of creating a fake profile to deceive people on social media or dating platforms. People's motives for doing this vary—they might just want attention, they might want to perpetrate fraud, they might want a release from everyday life, or they might even just want to experience the thrill of stringing people along. Sometimes it's all quite innocent, but other times it can end up having profound emotional, financial, and even physical consequences for the unsuspecting victim.

Imagine this: You've met someone online. Their photos look like they just stepped out of a magazine, their interests are a perfect match with your own, and their stories are incredibly fascinating. Does that sound too good to be true? Well, it just might be.

Do you remember Manti Te'o, the American football player who was tricked into having a relationship with a woman who never existed? That's a case of public catfishing. The emotional turmoil and shame he went through when the fraud was revealed is evidence of the damage that this kind of deception can cause.

While the digital world is a great big playground for our social and romantic dreams, it also, unfortunately, grants a degree of anonymity that is quite easy to abuse. The screen that allows us to connect with someone from another continent also has the potential to shield scammers from any immediate consequences.

So how does one safely navigate the dating seas?

The general principle is to believe what you see, but try to verify it. While it's certainly wonderful to believe in people's good nature, a healthy dose of skepticism can protect us from a great deal of evil. If a story seems too outlandish or somebody's life appears to be a little too perfect, do some digging. Reverse image searches can help you determine whether somebody's stunning photo is actually unique, or has simply been stolen from some random website.

Limit the amount of personal information you share about yourself. Manipulators will often fish for information that they can use against you later on.

In the technological age, there is no legitimate reason why somebody can't make a video call. That's an easy way to verify that the person you're chatting with actually matches the profile you've seen. Camera not working all of a sudden? Watch your step.

Trust your gut: If something feels wrong, it probably is. Listen to your inner voice. It has evolved over millennia, and it's there to protect you!

Sometimes someone else's point of view will notice things that lovestruck eyes might miss. Share your online interactions with a trusted friend and ask them to help you analyze the situation.

Computerized Social Proof

In today's world of likes, shares, and followers, digital popularity seems to have become the new currency. With just a wave of a magic wand (or the click of a button), your social status can skyrocket. But what exactly is "social proof"? Essentially, it is a psychological phenomenon where people mimic the actions of others in an attempt to emulate "correct" behavior. If a social media account has a large number of followers or a post has many likes, we will often perceive it to be trustworthy or credible. This is the digital version of trusting that a restaurant that always has a line outside must be good.

However, these numbers can be manipulated. With the emergence of digital tools and platforms, it has become alarmingly easy to purchase followers, likes, and comments. This can create an illusion of popularity, which gets the snowball rolling.

Consider this example: Sofi is an aspiring travel blogger who's struggling to get her business off the ground. Frustrated by her failure to attract interest, she buys ten thousand followers, which suddenly makes her page seem influential. Different brands, mistaking this for genuine engagement, approach her for promotions. A casual visitor to her profile who sees these collaborations will assume she must be a trusted and important figure in the world of travel.

Do you think I'm making this up? As a writer, I receive offers to buy followers at least twice a week. I consistently decline as I know that what I'm being offered has nothing to do with real people.

So Why Is This a Problem, Exactly?

It's a jungle, that's what it is. When brands and individuals use these deceptive tactics, it means that the rest of us need to be more careful. This produces a general atmosphere of distrust where genuine, honest influencers and well-run businesses might end up being questioned or doubted for the simple reason that these kinds of scams have become so common.

While our fictional Sofi's follower count may have increased, it's not an indication that any real individuals really care about her content. Naturally, this doesn't mean that her posts weren't created from a place of genuine, meaningful engagement on her part. But it's still just a scam.

Social media platforms that know about these dodgy practices have started to crack down on this stuff. Their measures range from purging fake accounts to penalizing users who get involved in these fraudulent practices. They have learned that the short-term gains of allowing fake profiles can result in long-term negative consequences.

And, of course, there is an ethical aspect to consider here. Is it right to mislead followers, brands, and even yourself by inflating the numbers this way?

Navigating these treacherous, deep waters requires awareness and good judgment. Whether you happen to own a brand or just be a private individual, you shouldn't allow yourself to be swayed by somebody's number of followers alone. Do your research. Is this a measure of genuine engagement? Are the comments on this profile meaningful or fictitious? Social media should encourage genuine connections and sincere sharing of experiences. Real "social proof" has nothing to do with numbers, it's a matter of authentic interactions, meaningful engagement, and trust that's been built over time. With real, flesh-and-blood people. Not fake digital profiles.

MORE ON POLITICAL CORRECTNESS

As I write this, the concept of political correctness is the subject of much debate. It's definitely a good question whether this is an appropriate subject for a book about lies, but people who oppose political correctness, especially when it goes too far, often argue that if you're not telling the truth, you're lying. I find it interesting that people who dislike political correctness can actually be said to be accusing those who defend it of lying. At the same time, however, the politically correct aren't too inclined to allow other people to express their opinions and thoughts on sensitive issues.

The term itself (often abbreviated as PC) seems to evoke strong emotions, from appreciation and understanding that it can make society more inclusive, to anger and frustration at what some perceive to be hypersensitivity and a willful blindness to the evidence of our own eyes. Fundamentally, political correctness is about refraining from expressions, statements, and actions that may marginalize, offend, or harm certain groups in society, particularly those who have been subjected to discrimination in the past. A wonderful cause, you might think. But like everything else, it has its controversies.

A Lengthy History

The term "political correctness" is actually over a hundred years old, and it has a rather troubling history. It first appeared in the Marxist-Leninist vocabulary that emerged after the Russian Revolution of 1917. There, it was used to refer to strict adherence to the policies and principles of the communist party of the Soviet Union. Essentially, it was forbidden to hold views that didn't conform to party policy.

In the 1960s, political awareness grew in many parts of the world, and political correctness began to involve the highlighting of uses of language and actions that promote more inclusive modes of representation and respect for various groups. Over the years, it has grown to cover a range of topics, from gender and racial issues to issues related to physical abilities, mental health, and a whole host of other phenomena.

The term took on a new, derogatory meaning in the late twentieth century when conservatives in the United States began to call leftist sympathizers politically correct as a way of accusing them of practicing censorship.

Some Examples of Political Correctness

Let's look at some brief examples from recent years. Around the turn of the millennium, for example, the names of American sports teams, especially the ones representing certain educational institutions, became the subject of debate. Why? The use of indigenous names and images in these contexts was thought to be derogatory and to perpetuate racial stereotypes. One example of this is the University of Illinois mascot, Chief Illiniwek, who was finally retired in 2007 after being the target of prolonged criticism and protest. During this period there was a significant cultural change, and focus shifted to the importance of respectful speech. Discussions began about the damage that stereotypes can cause, especially when they are presented in public and influential arenas like sports.

Fast-forward a decade, and we saw an acceptance of trans and nonbinary people come to prominence in the world. Around 2010, the discussion surrounding gender pronouns intensified. This was immediately connected to the fact that the rights of people whose gender identity didn't fit the traditional male/female mold were inserted into the political agenda.

From the rethinking of mascots in the 2000s and the recognition of gender identities in the 2010s to the in-depth examination of systemic racism in the 2020s, political correctness has become a concept that reflects our rapidly changing social consciousness. In these areas, it has served us well.

What Are the Benefits of Political Correctness?

The basic principle of political correctness, as mentioned above, is one of consideration and respect. By encouraging the use of inclusive language, for example, political correctness advocates seek to promote appreciation for and inclusion of marginalized groups. Historically oppressed or neglected communities, like ethnic minorities, LGBTQ+ groups, and people with disabilities all deserve to be treated just as respectfully as the majority does. By adapting our language we can signal to these groups that they are seen and respected—that they are included in the community.

While critics often describe political correctness as excessive or phony, its core principles do serve some very important societal purposes. As the world becomes more interconnected and more diverse, our need for mutual respect and understanding will only grow more crucial.

What Are the Disadvantages?

Are there no problems, then, with political correctness? Oh, there definitely are. There's no shortage of challenges here. The enemies of political correctness often accuse those they consider to be politically correct of lying about how the world is actually organized, and critics say that it would be dangerous to uncritically accept everything that is presented under this umbrella. Because, they argue, there are actually outright lies mixed in with it all.

According to them, the danger of being labeled as politically incorrect, or—even worse—as a conspiracy nut or a full-on racist can discourage people from daring to express their views. This, they claim, can stifle public discourse. PC opinions produce an environment where individuals feel compelled to censor themselves, which deprives society as a whole of its full diversity of points of view. People simply don't dare to be honest when they discuss certain topics. So instead, they stay silent.

Others argue that an excessive emphasis on PC culture might foster an atmosphere of hypersensitivity. People will be more likely to take offense, even when nobody has any intention of questioning or hurting them. Some universities have gone so far as to set up "safe spaces" where anyone who feels marginalized or like a member of a minority group can be left alone to avoid discomfort. This is a form of voluntary segregation, in other words. Is this a good thing? Does it actually promote diversity and understanding?

This increase in sensitivity can also make honest dialogue more difficult and lower people's tolerance of opinions that don't align with their own. In the long run, this can cause intolerance to growth and make society overly cautious. This, in turn, will risk undermining the robustness of public discourse and the trust that citizens have for one another. We are made to fear criticism, perhaps to the point of being angry before we've even opened our mouths.

What Can We Do About It?

There is a growing concern that political correctness might cause signaling behaviors that are simply aimed at demonstrating that you are an ethical and moral person. The consequence would be that individuals express opinions or positions in order to appear to be moral, rather than to communicate their actual thoughts or feelings.

One example of this might be a young influencer who picks up rubbish on the beach and films themselves doing it, but then leaves all the rubbish behind once the camera has been switched off.

Or somebody who films themselves giving money to a homeless person. It's not enough to do a good deed, you have to show it off, too.

This adds further fuel to activism and militant advocacy. When people's main reason for adopting politically correct speech patterns is to fit in or gain social capital rather than a sincere belief, critics argue that something is obviously getting out of hand.

An excessive focus on language and presentation might also divert our attention from the underlying issues themselves. If discussions are more concerned with the "correctness" of the language used than with the actual topic itself, society might lose sight of the pressing issues that need to be addressed. For example, replacing a derogatory term with another one is certainly a step in the right direction, but if we leave the systemic issue that motivated the change unaddressed, any change achieved will really be more cosmetic than it is transformative. George Orwell's *1984* contains countless examples of this very idea.

What Are We Seeing Here?

In George Orwell's modern classic *1984*, he introduced the concept of Newspeak. Newspeak is used by the totalitarian state in the novel to restrict freedom of thought and concepts that pose a threat to the regime, including freedom, self-expression, individuality, and peace. All dissent is made impossible by the elimination of the very words that could be used to express such ideas.

For example, the word "free" still exists in Newspeak, but it is only used in statements like *This dog is free from lice,* which means that it *cannot* be infested with lice. The political and intellectual concept of being *free* doesn't exist, which makes it impossible for people to question whether they are free or not.

Of course, manipulation of language—in fiction and in reality—is a powerful tool used to control populations because of the ways it can limit their range of thought. In *1984,* the idea is that the citizens of Oceania won't even be able to imagine rebellion or criticism of the government because they have no words to express these ideas.

Just a moment, you might be thinking, *George Orwell was a novelist. This is a work of fiction, not a true story.* Unfortunately, nothing is ever that simple. And the expression that truth is sometimes stranger than fiction hasn't come about by accident. While the intentions behind political correctness— the promotion of a more inclusive and respectful society—are certainly benevolent, it's important to approach this concept with a sober mind. When fitting in with a group becomes more important than being truthful, some very problematic contradictions will eventually arise. We can already see them in the media on a daily basis.

Real-World Examples

I'd like to return to the issue of gender and biology here. While it is scientifically established that biological sex is determined by chromosomes, the concept of gender identity is more fluid and covers a whole spectrum of identities. There are also people whose biological sex can't be definitely determined at birth. It's not that common, but it does happen.

Alongside this, there is the question of which gender somebody feels they belong to, that is, gender identity, which is not the same thing as biological sex. Some would argue that political correctness prevents all open discussion about the differences between biological sex and gender identity. They are worried about suffering backlash, or being accused of narrow-mindedness or claims that they suffer from some kind of phobia.

The whole idea of recognizing the right of all people to decide for themselves which gender they belong to can be complicated for people who have grown up being taught that our society is based on gender distinctions. I'm by no means an expert on these matters, and I will willingly admit that I don't understand all the finer points of this. However, suddenly allowing everyone to consider themselves to be anything they like can seem to turn the entire social order on its head. It can cause conflict and further fuel the polarization we are currently seeing.

The Importance of Honesty

So what can we do to stick to the actual truth as much as possible while also showing consideration and respect for dissenting views?

It can be challenging to navigate the minefields of political correctness while also seeking to maintain one's personal integrity. For example, I hesitated over including this section at all for a very long time, as I knew that it might very well upset some of my readers. But don't worry. That's not my intention at all. Remember, this is a book about lies and liars, and we have to dare to examine the areas where people's perceptions of the truth conflict the most. I can only hope that anybody reading this will have the courage to reach beyond the polarized state of discourse and try to view the issues from other points of view. My basic reflex is to engage in dialogue in a respectful manner. When confronted with statements that seem to be politically correct, but also feel questionable to me, I try to seek clarity by cautiously digging a little deeper. Instead of angrily dismissing or, for that matter, blindly accepting a peculiar statement, I prefer to ask open-ended questions to gain a deeper understanding (open-ended questions are questions that cannot be answered with a simple yes or no).

Furthermore—and this is very important to remember— you can't change other people. On the other hand, you don't need to go along with something obviously crazy just because a certain phrase is trending on TikTok this week. You're entitled to have your own opinions. Remember that whatever you might think, you're not alone. It's not always the ones who shout the loudest who are in the right. Their shouting is just a cover-up for their lack of solid arguments.

My Incorrect Conclusions Regarding PC

Political correctness, as it exists today, is a tool intended to promote a more inclusive and understanding society. While its intentions are noble, like any tool, its effects depend entirely on its application.

Balancing respect for the experiences and feelings of others with factual accuracy and open dialogue is the real challenge here. By fostering an environment of education, understanding, and open dialogue, we can navigate the terrain of political correctness without ignoring reality or failing to respect the actual truth.

In the information age, I would say that critical thinking has become our most valuable asset. Embracing political correctness responsibly means understanding its implications, both the positive and the negative ones, and approaching each situation with empathy, knowledge, and openness.

You have to make your own mind up, essentially. Even when it feels difficult. Especially when it feels difficult, even.

PLAYING WITH NUMBERS

Have you considered the fact that, statistically, it would be correct to say that the average person has one ovary and one testicle?

In an era saturated with data, statistics have become a compelling tool for validating beliefs, selling products and services, and influencing public opinion in various directions. I think we need to address this matter some more.

Benjamin Disraeli, one of Churchill's predecessors as UK prime minister, is said to be the source of this oft-quoted phrase:

"There are three kinds of lies: lies, damned lies, and statistics."

You've probably heard it used before, perhaps mainly in jest. But this cautionary phrase does highlight the potential that statistical data has to both inform and deceive. The appeal of statistics is connected to their supposed objectivity. Numbers, unlike emotions and personal testimonies, promise to present an unbiased truth. However, as history has shown us, these truths can be easily manipulated to serve specific purposes. This also applies to practically any area you can imagine.

But are things really that bad? In the right hands, numbers can be invaluable. In the wrong hands, however, they can be weaponized and used to promote all manner of scams.

Here are some classic examples in which figures and statistics have been used to mislead:

Four out of five dentists recommend this toothpaste. (Who are these dentists, and what was the actual question they were asked?)

Our product is 50 percent more effective. (Than what? A product that does nothing at all?)

Studies show that 47.6 percent blah blah . . . (Which studies? How were they carried out? Were they funded by neutral parties?)

Crime has dropped by 10 percent. (Is this because crimes are no longer being reported, or because criminal activity has actually decreased?)

Nine out of ten people favor our brand. (What was the sample here? Did you survey ten of your own employees?)

Sales have increased by 200 percent! (Oh, so you sold three units this year, but only one last year?)

Our service has a 90 percent satisfaction rate with users. (Ten people used the service, and only one of them expressed skepticism.)

The average income of our employees is €100,000. (But the median income is €30,000, and the multimillion-euro salaries of management distort the average.)

Now, some comedy: Eighty percent of the time, it works every time. (This line comes from the film *Anchorman*, and it illustrates the idiocy of referring to statistics without providing any context whatsoever.)

When you come across statements like these, always remember to ask this important question: What is it they're *not* telling us?

Just for fun, I could add that this summer I have reduced my working hours in the garden by more than 80 percent. (What could be the explanation for this? Mainly the fact that it has been raining most every day all summer, and I've simply not been able to spend time outdoors. I've also delegated lawn-mowing duty to the neighbor's kid.)

Statistics require us to pay a specific kind of attention. When we see a percentage, an average, or a graph of any kind, we tend to accept the information we're given without too much thought. Why is this? Because numbers have such an immutable air about them. They represent certainty in an increasingly uncertain world. Moreover, as individuals, we tend to always be looking for patterns that can help us understand the world around us, and statistics serve this need by offering us quantified patterns. Numbers concretize the abstract and make the subjective suddenly objective.

In the right hands, numbers can be invaluable. In the wrong hands, however, they can be weaponized to serve all manner of lies.

Human Vision—Graphs and Charts

I'm sure you've heard this expression: *A picture is worth a thousand words.* In this context, perhaps we should ask: Why a *thousand* words, specifically? How did someone determine that it's a *thousand* words? That's a suspicious degree of precision. Would 950 words actually have been enough? Or maybe even 500? Why not 5,000, for that matter? How was this study actually designed, who selected the sample, what was their agenda, and what kinds of words are we talking about, anyway?

Anyway.

In a time when data reigns supreme, the old adage that *seeing is believing* has never been more relevant. Graphs, charts, and infographics have become common methods for serving up large amounts of data in a digestible format. However, images can just as easily be used to deceive as to inform and educate. Let's take a deeper dive into the art of lying with graphs and learn why a picture actually can be worth a thousand words, but also why it can be worth a thousand misconceptions.

Human beings are visual creatures. We process images sixty thousand times faster than text. This means that when we're shown a graph, our brains will instinctively lock on to certain visual cues before we've had any time to reflect on the data behind them. This instinct can be a blessing in some situations, but it can also make us easily misled when the images we're shown have been manipulated.

Perhaps the most common fraud you'll encounter is manipulation of the y-axis. Instead of starting at zero, graphs will often start at a higher value to exaggerate the differences.

Let's take a look at one of the more horrific examples.

What Does This Graph Actually Show?

The 1996 case of the pharmaceutical giant Purdue Pharma and their highly addictive drug OxyContin is still having repercussions for tens of thousands of people worldwide because of the way they used (or misused) statistics in their marketing.

When Purdue Pharma launched their new product Oxy-Contin, they presented the drug as a safe, nonaddictive opioid that offered highly effective pain relief. Doctors were skeptical because they had experience of the dangers of using addictive opioids to treat chronic pain. The severity of the addiction it could cause was even comparable to that of heroin addiction.

When you look at the image below, you will realize that it's actually very difficult to interpret. However, it still makes an impression. And, as we all know, first impressions are the most important thing.

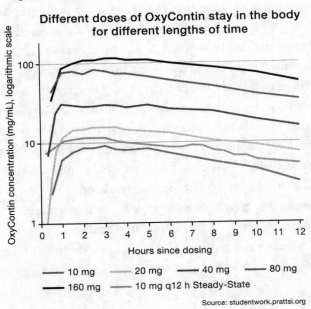

However, Purdue Pharma used a very specific graph to suggest to doctors that this drug wasn't addictive. The different lines indicate the effects of different drugs on patients. Along the vertical y-axis, we can see the dosage, that is, how many milligrams of the drug a patient receives. As you can see, the difference between the highest and lowest dose isn't that great, although there is some difference.

Along the horizontal x-axis, we can see how long (in hours) the drug remains in the body. The aim here was to show that adding more of the active ingredient to tablets would be risk-free and do no harm to patients.

The problem, though, was that the graph depicted below was constructed with a logarithmic scale along the y-axis instead of a linear scale, which means that the suggested outcome it presented was very different from the real one. The scale starts at 10, but quickly reaches 100.

If the y-axis had been linear, the graph would have looked like the following graph instead.

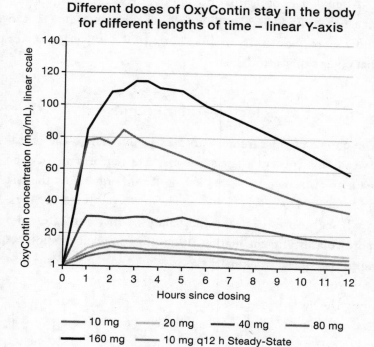

Different doses of OxyContin stay in the body for different lengths of time – linear Y-axis

Legend: 10 mg, 20 mg, 40 mg, 80 mg, 160 mg, 10 mg q12 h Steady-State

Source: studentwork.prattsi.org

This graph is fully accurate, but even it is somewhat difficult to interpret. It gives a very different impression from the first one. In this one, it's obvious that there is actually a significant difference between the lowest dose and the highest dose. The difference between these results is cause for concern for anybody who really knows what to look for. What happened as a result? A large number of patients received such high doses of the drug that they developed addictions more or less immediately. They basically became drug addicts because nobody (outside of Purdue Pharma) realized how addictive the drug really was. Pharmacists were turned into drug dealers.

After a series of deaths and lengthy investigations, Purdue Pharma was fined $600 million for this offense. If you want to know more about this, there is both a TV and Netflix series that covers this scandal.

Selective Time Frames

The choice of time frames can drastically change the narrative a graph presents. The stock market's performance can be made to appear to be skyrocketing if you only show the last six months. However, if you zoom out to the last five years, you'll see a series of peaks and valleys, which indicates a lot more volatility in the market. What do you want to show? A rapid rise in the stock market?

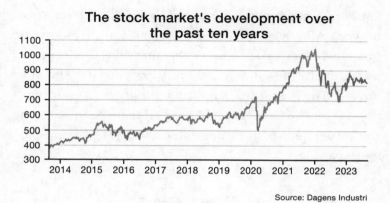

The stock market's development over the past ten years

Source: Dagens Industri

Or would you prefer to suggest that it has been steadily dropping for quite a long time?

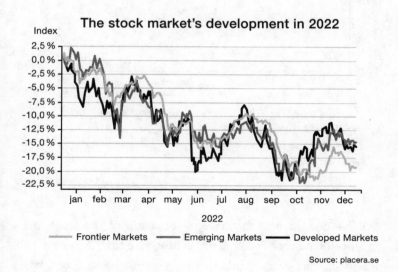

The stock market's development in 2022

Frontier Markets — Emerging Markets — Developed Markets

Source: placera.se

Some people are out to give others a proper scare. Perhaps they want to let people know that the stock market isn't a good match for people who don't have strong nerves? All the graphs below are individually accurate, but when you present them together like this they will undoubtedly discourage people from entering the stock market. The graph shows nothing but drops in value, leaving out all the rises in between, and more than anything, the incomplete picture presented will just give people a stomachache.

Market crashes

Source: Nordnet

What would be a fairer representation of the stock market's performance? Perhaps something like this. After all, this goes back ten years, and it can probably be said to give a decent picture of reality. There is an overall upward trend, but the market certainly isn't always going up.

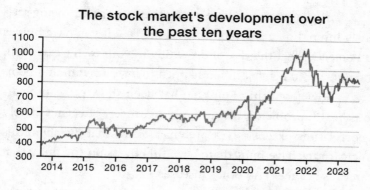

The stock market's development over the past ten years

Source: Dagens Industri

A funny thing that some people use statistics for is to conflate causality and correlation. These concepts are used in statistical research to describe the relationship between two or more variables.

Correlation measures the strength and direction of a linear relationship between two variables. It doesn't suggest that one variable causes the other, it just indicates that they tend to move together in some way.

Let's say that the statistics show that there is a correlation between ice cream sales and the number of drownings that occur. As ice cream sales increase, the number of drownings also tends to increase. This should hardly be taken to mean that buying more ice cream will cause more people to drown. It probably just means that people tend to both go swimming more and eat more ice cream . . . in the summertime. But there is no direct relationship between the two.

Causality means the existence of an actual causal relationship between two variables. If A causes B, changes in A will bring changes in B.

A fairly harmless example here is that your risk of being seriously injured by a sharp object will increase if you have knives at home. Or, that the risk of drowning in your own garden will increase by 40 percent if you happen to have a swimming pool.

Or, how about this: Smoking has been shown to cause various health problems, including lung cancer. This isn't merely a correlation; extensive research has shown that the chemicals in cigarettes have immediate harmful effects on the body that can cause cancer and other diseases.

As usual, you have to be extremely picky about what you believe here. Some correlations can often raise some eyebrows, and some correlations aren't even genuine correlations. They just appear to be. However, because graphs and charts seem to represent some kind of objective truth, some people seek to abuse the trust people place in graphical representations of data to present pictures that differ from reality.

Below, we can see data from the Uniform Crime Reports at the FBI. The accuracy of this data has been subject to lots of criticism, but we can set that aside for the moment. Now, I want us to use their data to demonstrate how graphs can be manipulated. Here is a bar chart that presents their data on the number of murders in the US in a way that makes it look as though the murder rates have increased alarmingly.

But take a closer look at the y-axis. It doesn't start at zero at all, but at 16,340 murders in a year. Now take a look at the following graph, which shows *the exact same data*.

In this graph, the y-axis ranges from 0 to 18,000 murders a year. Based on this graph, you might even have a hard time telling which year had more murders unless you zoomed in on the chart or studied it closely. Now, it's certainly terrible that more than sixteen thousand people were murdered in

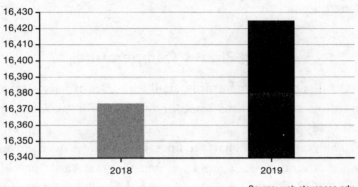

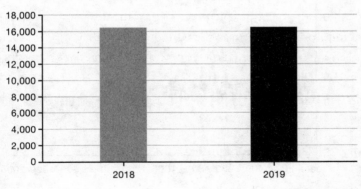

each of those years. But nonetheless, it seems absurd to claim that there was a large increase in murders if we look at the graph that took 0 as its lowest point.

And remember, all these graphs are accurate. What makes these different images interesting is the immediate reactions they trigger in us. We often subconsciously look for images in the world that will confirm what we already believe about something or other.

Taking Pirates' Temperatures

Let's talk about temperatures, shall we? That usually attracts attention and produces some invigorating discussions. Are you ready?

The graph below charts temperature changes over the last two thousand years. There is, of course, great variation over time. Then at the start of the Industrial Revolution, temperatures begin to change more rapidly.

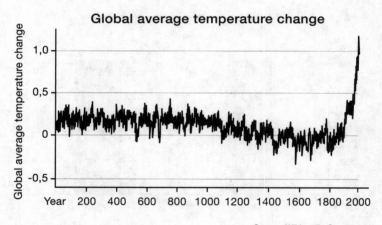

Source: Wikimedia Commons

If I've understood this correctly, this graph is absolutely correct. Please note the source if you'd like to investigate this further. However, there are entirely different approaches one could take. Just look at the graph below. Here, it looks like the temperature has never done anything but rise, rise, rise. The steeper you want to make the rise, the more you can fine-tune the y-axis. You could draw it up in hundredths of a degree if you wanted to make things look really dramatic. In this case, they settled for tenths of a degree. (If you look back to the earlier graph, it showed half degrees, which will also give a different impression.)

Global average temperature 1860–2020

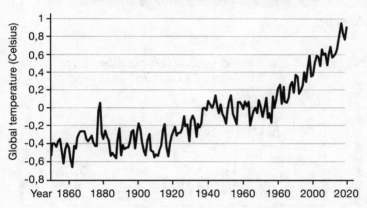

Source: berkeleyearth.org/2019-temperatures/

But what if, instead of using shorter time axes, you used longer ones? And what if you also accounted for something else: temperature anomalies. Then the results might look like this.

Temperature variations

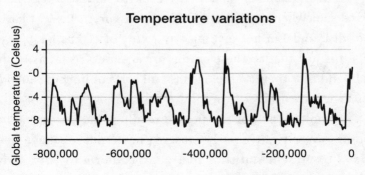

Source: earthobservatory.nasa.gov

Here, the ranges used are expressed as whole degrees. Nevertheless, the changes still look big. What would they look like if we used tenths of a degree? This, right here, is my whole point. As a layman, you never have a clue what you're actually looking at, but you still feel *something* when you look at this material.

Why not, as some prefer to do, go back really far in time instead?

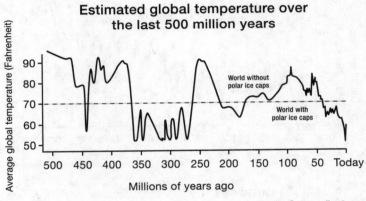

Estimated global temperature over the last 500 million years

Source: climate.gov

Would human beings have been able to survive if they had lived somewhere near the middle of that curve? Look, I have no idea, and I'm not making any kinds of claims here. My point is just that all these graphs are accurate, as far as I can tell, and that they can be used for all sorts of purposes. And that they *are* used.

A whole bunch of the people reading this are probably boiling over right now because of how rudely I have decided to present statistics that don't conform to your own personal opinions on these issues. To all of you, I just want to say this:

I'm not making any claims. I'm not smart enough to understand how we ought to interpret all this data. Discussing temperature changes tends to bring people's political opinion out within a fraction of a second. Soon, loud voices will enter the discussion from all sides explaining what they think is happening to our climate. That's not something I engage in.

All I can say is that all these graphs come from so-called official sources, and that I realize that all these graphs would probably need to be accompanied by a lot of explanations before we can interpret them correctly. But we still look at them with our eyes, and once we have formed opinions based on the things we've seen, those opinions can be hard to change. Whether you're a skeptic or a believer is actually irrelevant. The reason why there is a debate going on out there at all is because statistics can be used in many different ways, and that's the point I'm getting at. If this had been easy, the conversation would have ended a long time ago.

People can twist and turn reality around to their heart's content and underline almost any view they like. *Don't kill the messenger.*

Nonsensical Relationships

In fact, when I think about it, I wonder if the reason why global temperatures are rising isn't actually the lack of pirates on this planet. I can prove it, too: Just look at this:

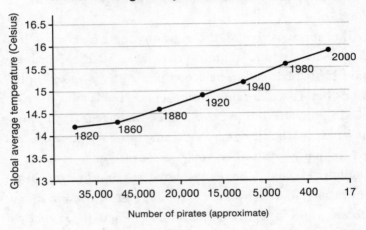

Global average temperature vs. number of pirates

Source: spaghettimonster.org

You see, there is a clear correlation between the decrease in pirates and the increase in temperature. If only we had more pirates! Now, it can certainly be fun to find strange correlations like this, and they can, of course, be used to confuse the public. For instance, we could insist that banning ice cream would be a great antimurder measure, because ice cream sales obviously drive murder rates. It's a tragic state of affairs.

Number of ice creams sold vs. number of murders

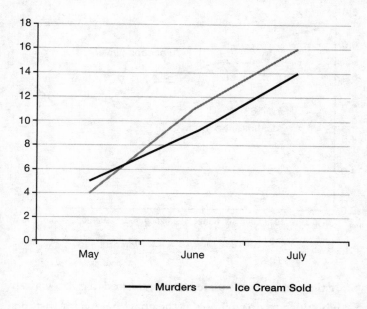

Source: Buzzfeed News

Or how about this one: Justin Bieber's birth had the effect of lowering cholesterol levels in the population, but only until the creation of Facebook canceled out the effect. What, you don't believe me? Look at the chart below for yourself! There's no need to look for this one online as it's obviously not a serious attempt at finding a correlation, even though the input data could be real for all I know.

Population cholesterol levels

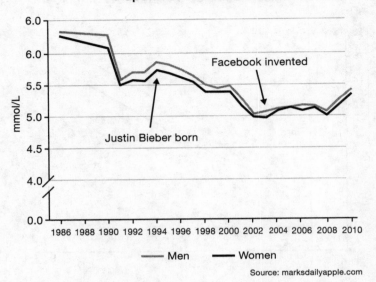

Source: marksdailyapple.com

Statistics can be manipulated and presented in crazy ways by those who wish to do so. Look at the chart below, for instance. In this example from Microsoft, its attempt at a conceptual design led the company to visualize the data in a particularly misleading way.

Welcome to Microsoft Edge: Faster than both Chrome and Firefox—according to Google's benchmark

Source: venngage.com

Even if Microsoft Edge actually is faster than both Google Chrome and Mozilla Firefox, it's not by any particularly impressive margin. It's nowhere near being close to 25 percent faster than Chrome or 50 percent faster than Firefox, which is the impression you might get from seeing the image. They could have used a bar chart instead. But I suppose they didn't feel that it looked equally impressive.

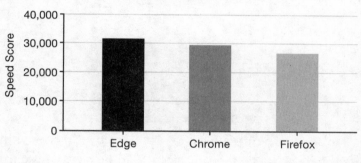

Browser speed test

Source: venngage.com

Afterword

As I've mentioned, even the drier or more factual parts of the information we have at our disposal can be questioned. In general, the world would be an easier place to live in if facts could be facts and it was less easy to distort them.

But things are the way they are.

As I have mentioned elsewhere in this book: Nobody is going to reward me for being naive. I have to root around for the truth myself, especially regarding subjects that are close to my heart. Taking a closer look at things that might seem to be facts at first glance has sometimes brought me to reconsider things I held to be true. Sometimes you have to pay more attention to the sender than the actual message.

I don't know if the good old days were actually any better, but I do think things were easier then.

Take care of yourself, and stay vigilant, always.

References

2. WHAT IS TRUTH?

Aronson, Elliot, Robert P. Abelson (Red.). *Theories of Cognitive Consistency: A Sourcebook.* Rand McNally, 1968.

Dunbar, Robin, I. M. "The Social Brain Hypothesis." *Evolutionary Anthropology: Issues, News, and Reviews.* 6, no. 5 (1998).

Janzon, Eva. "Gallup Confirms: Swedish Journalists Lean Left," *Världen Idag.* 28 July 2020. https://www.varldenidag.se/nyheter/gallup-bekraftar-svenska-journalister-star -till-vanster/reptgB!EB7Ci25AFJnUE0Zv9No9eQ/. Accessed 8 January 2024.

Moe, Hallvard. "Perceptions of Journalistic Bias: Party Preferences, Media Trust and Attitudes Towards Immigration." 2017.

Nietzsche, Friedrich. (1887). *Till moralens genealogi.* Björck & Börjesson, 2019.

Wakefield, Andrew J. "MMR Vaccination and Autism." *The Lancet.* 354, no. 9182 (1999). https://doi.org/10.1016/S0140–6736(05)75696–8.

5. THE CONSEQUENCES OF LYING

Dutton, Kevin. "Would You Vote for a Psychopath?" *Scientific American.* 1 September 2016. https://www.scientificamerican.com/article/would-you-vote-for-a-psychopath. Accessed 15 January 2024.

Loftus, Elizabeth F., John C. Palmer. "Reconstruction of Auto-mobile Destruction: An Example of the Interaction between Language and Memory." *Journal of Verbal Learning and Verbal Behavior.* 13, no. 5 (1974). https:// doi.org/10.1016 /S0022–5371(74)80011–3.

Mazzoni, Giuliana, Alan Scoboria, and Lucy Harvey. "Nonbelieved memories." *Psychological Science*. 21, no. 9 (2010). https://doi. org/10.1177/0956797610379865.

Mehrabian, Albert. *Nonverbal Communication*. Aldine-Atherton, 1972.

Rousseau, Jean-Jacques. *The Social Contract*. Natur & Kultur, 2009. Originally published 1762.

Sullivan, Bill. "The Truth About Lying and What It Does to the Body." *Psychology Today*. 5 January 2020. https://www.psychologytoday.com/us/blog/pleased-meet-me/202001/the-truth-about-lying-and-what-it-does-the-body. Accessed 8 January 2024.

8. HOW PSYCHOPATHS AND NARCISSISTS LIE

Boddy, Clive R. "Insights Into the Bernie Madoff Financial Market Scandal Which Identify New Opportunities for Business Market Researchers." *International Journal of Market Research*. 66, no. 1 (2023). https://doi.org/10.1177/14707853231173260.

9. EXPOSING LIARS

Blanchard, Matt, and Barry A. Farber. "Lying in Psychotherapy: Why and What Clients Don't Tell Their Therapist About Therapy and Their Relationship." *Counselling Psychology Quarterly*. 29, no. 1 (2016). https://doi.org/10.108 0/09515070.2015.1085365.

Counselling Psychology Quarterly, vol. 29, no. 1, 2016.

Erikson, Erik H. *Child and Society*. Natur & Kultur, 1950.

Lee, S. W. S., and N. Schwarz. "Dirty Hands and Dirty Mouths: Embodiment of the Moral-Purity Metaphor Is Specific to the Motor Modality Involved in Moral Transgression." *Psychological Science*. 21, no. 10 (2010).

Sturgeon, J. A., et al. Den psykosociala kontexten av smärta och depression. *Depression och ångest*. 33, no. 11(2016): 921–929.

Bok, Sissela. *Att ljuga: moraliska val i offentligt och enskilt liv*. Rabén & Sjögren, 1979.

Vacharkulksemsuk, Tanya, and Barbara L. Fredrickson. "Strangers in Sync: Achieving Embodied Rapport Through Shared Movements." *Journal of Experimental Social Psychology*. 48, no. 1(2012): 399–402.

APPENDIX

Graph on page 330, Different doses of OxyContin stay in the body for different lengths of time, was taken from https://studentwork.prattsi.org/infovis/labs/a-history-of-dangerouslymisleading-data-visualization, in January 2024.

Graph on page 331, Different doses of OxyContin stay in the body for different lengths of time—linear Y axis, was taken from https://studentwork.prattsi.org/infovis/labs/a-history-of-dangerously-misleading-data-visualization, in January 2024.

Graph on page 333 (top), The stock market's development over the last ten years, was taken from di.se/bors, in August 2023.

Graph on page 333 (bottom), The stock market's development in 2022, was taken from https://www.placera.se/placera/redaktionellt/2023/01/25/riskaptiten-tillbaka-med-fullkraft.html, in January 2024.

Graph on page 334, Market crashes, was taken from https://www.nordnet.se/blogg/bear-market, in Janaury 2024.

Graph on page 335, The stock market's development over the past ten years, was taken from di.se/bors, in August 2023.

Graphs on pages 337, Murders in the United States, were taken from https://web.stevenson.edu/mbranson/m4tp/version1/fake-newsmisleading-graphs.html i januari 2024 och datan från https://ucr.fbi.gov/crime-in-the-u.s.

Graph on page 338, Global average temperature change, was taken from https://commons.wikimedia.org/wiki/File:2000%2B_year_global_temperature_including_Medieval_Warm_Period_and_Little_Ice_Age_-_Ed_Hawkins, in January 2024. From a graphic by Ed Hawkins. Data from PAGES2k (and HadCrut 4.6 from 2001–).

Graph on page 339 (top), Global average temperature 1860–2020, was taken from https://berkeleyearth.org/2019-temperatures, in January 2024.

Graph on page 339 (bottom), Temperature variations, was taken from https://earthobservatory.nasa.gov/features/GlobalWarming/page3.php, in January 2024.

Graph on page 340, Estimated global temperature over the last 500 million years, was taken from https://www.climate.gov/news-features/climate-qa/whats-hottest-earths-ever-been, in January 2024.

Graph on page 342, Global average temperature vs. number of pirates, was taken from https://www.spaghettimonster.org/pages/about/open-letter, in January 2024.

Graph on page 343, Number of ice creams sold vs. number of murders, was taken from https://www.buzzfeednews.com/article/kjh2110/the-10-most-bizarre-correlations, in January 2024.

Graph on page 344 (top), Population cholesterol levels, was taken from https://www.marksdailyapple.com, in August 2023.

Graph on page 344 (bottom), Welcome to Microsoft Edge: Faster than both Chrome and Firefox, was taken from https://venngage.com/blog/misleading-graphs, in January 2024.

Graph on page 345, Browser speed test, was taken from https://venngage.com/blog/misleading-graphs, in January 2024.

Index

evolution, 156–57
exposing liars, 90, 249–66
 body language and, 252–53
 how it's done, 251–55
 lie detectors in, 260–62
 professional expertise in, 250–51
 psychologists and, 251, 256–60
extroversion, 20–27, 259
eye contact, 81, 184, 185, 187, 253

Facebook, 343–44
 Cambridge Analytica and, 162–64
facial expressions, 187
false amplification, 132–33
Farber, Barry, 256
Faust (Goethe), 32–33
filter bubbles, 308–11
flat Earth, 37–41, 117, 118
Foundation for Humanity, 247

Galileo Galilei, 38
gaslighting, 231
Gates, Bill, 41, 312
God, 31, 37–38
Goebbels, Joseph, 15, 187
Goethe, Johann Wolfgang von,
 32–33
good cop/bad cop approach,
 252
graphs and charts, 53, 328–45
Greens, 20–27
 list of characteristics of, 24–25
 lying by, 208–11
 lying's impact on, 159
 lying to, 219–22
 silence and, 60, 61
guilt, 234
Gulf of Tonkin incident, 153–55

habitual lying, 121–22
Hare, Robert, 245
Hayut, Shimon, 197–99
High-Value Detainee Interrogation Group
 (HIG), 251–52
historical facts, 36
Hitler, Adolf, 15, 36
Holocaust, 36

honesty, 2–3, 5–6, 14, 17, 18, 20, 74, 91,
 143, 171, 195, 268, 296, 302
 personal growth and, 43–44
 political correctness and, 324–25
 truth, tact, and complexity of, 67–70
 see also truth
Howard, Robert E., 117–18
Hubbard, L. Ron, 40–41

ice cream, 335, 342–43
Inferno (Dante), 32
influence versus manipulation, 205–6
integrity, 113–15, 147, 302
internet, 91, 129, 136
 browsers, 344–45
 see also social media
interrogators, 250–51
introversion, 20–27, 259
intuition, 274, 275
Iraq, 91

Joan, Pope, 280–82
job recruitment, 193–95
Johnson, Lyndon B., 154, 155
Jones, Paula, 226, 227
judges, 250

Kant, Immanuel, 45, 93, 127
Kennedy, John F., 228
King, Stephen, 200
Knives Out, 146

Lancet, 54
Landis, Floyd, 174
Law of Jante, 19
lawyers, 250
Lenin, Vladimir, 181
Leviev, Simon, 197–99
Lewinsky, Monica, 225–28
Lewis, C. S., 30
liars, 1–6
 confronting, *see* confronting a liar
 exposing, *see* exposing liars
liars, infamous
 Anderson, Anna, 75–78
 Armstrong, Lance, 173–75
 Calloway, Caroline, 137–41, 143

About the Author

Thomas Erikson is a Swedish behavioral expert, active lecturer, and best-selling author. For more than twenty years he has been traveling all over Europe delivering lectures and seminars to executives and managers at a wide range of companies including IKEA, Coca-Cola, Microsoft, and Volvo.

Surrounded by Idiots has been a Swedish runaway bestseller since it was first published in 2014. It has sold over three million copies worldwide and been translated into forty-nine languages.

Read the entire
Surrounded By Series
By Thomas Erikson

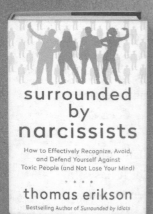

surrounded
by
narcissists

How to Effectively Recognize, Avoid,
and Defend Yourself Against
Toxic People (and Not Lose Your Mind)

thomas erikson

Bestselling Author of *Surrounded by Idiots*

Turning Obstacles
into Success
(When Everything Goes to Hell)

surrounded
by
setbacks

thomas erikson

From the 2-million copy bestselling
author of *Surrounded by Idiots*

surrounded
by
bad bosses
(and lazy employees)

How to Stop Struggling,
Start Succeeding,
and Deal with Idiots at Wo

thomas
erikson

Bestselling Author of
Surrounded by Idiots

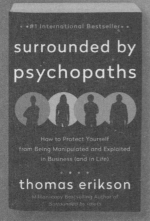

• #1 International Bestseller •

surrounded by
psychopaths

How to Protect Yourself
from Being Manipulated and Exploited
in Business (and in Life)

thomas erikson

Million-copy Bestselling Author of
Surrounded by Idiots

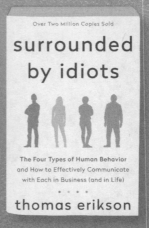

Over Two Million Copies Sold

surrounded
by idiots

The Four Types of Human Behavior
and How to Effectively Communicate
with Each in Business (and in Life)

thomas erikson

How to Slay the
Time, Joy, and Soul Suckers
in Your Life

surrounded by
energy
vampires

thomas erikson

Bestselling Author of *Surrounded by Idiots*

ST. MARTIN'S
ESSENTIALS